Gala Riv.
Galashiels
Galamouth
Caldsheels
Briggend
Dernick
Mellroß
Heeldoun
Heeldoun hills
Danieltoun
Newtoun
Old Melroß
Drygrange
Rippetth
Coldunknowes Castel
Wood of Coldunknowes
Sorlers field
The Mill
Erssiltoun
Carolsyde
Haggs
Mosshousess
Coumsly
Hillslopp
Calshill
Wesshouses
Ouisbyre
Gatounsyde
Boudoun
Boudoun K.
Morpople
Whytmurchat
Whytmure
O. Prestoun
N. Preestoun
Kyppylaw
Lessiddinn
Maxtoun
Maxtoun K.
Tweed Riv.
Littildernn
Rutherford
Stockstouther
Newtoun
Trowis
Barns
Old Rosburg
Castell of Rosburgh
Cailso
Carrhoome
Ylistoun
Corylaw
Lessiddinn B.
Murrislaw
Langnewtoun Comon
Langnewtoun K.
Wodehead
Fernitoun
Ormistoun
Pleuland
Newhall
Maisondieu
Spittelbanck
Grymslo
Sanlaes
Freres
O. Anerumm
N. Anerumm
Pamchelhill
O. Nisbett
N. Nisbett
Spittell
Chestars
Barnhills
Grange
Pendickill
Mintotoun
Newtoun
Langtoun
Timpendein
Roucastell
Iedd-brugh
Houstoun
Crelingdenn
Walls
Hundelie
Fernyhirst Castel
Mill
Abbotroull
Abbotroull Kirck
Bunchester law
Antroope
Blackchester
Knoks B.
Knoklawes
Stunleyfoord
Langburne
Grindoun b.
Blackbra
Bondlashed
Greenghawe
Hyndhoope
Eddisleuch
Chesterhouse
Dennbrae
Gaitshaw
Grubethous
Woodside
Clistoun
Sprowstoun K.
Haddenn
Proffuonn
Thanklesß
Whytburn
Botland B.
Catelench
Blackchester B.
Scala Miliarium
1
2
3
4
Auct. Tim. Pont.
Io: Blaeu Excudit

This is number two hundred and sixteen in the
second numbered series of the
Miegunyah Volumes
made possible by the
Miegunyah Fund
established by bequests
under the wills of
Sir Russell and Lady Grimwade.

'Miegunyah' was Russell Grimwade's home
from 1911 to 1955
and Mab Grimwade's home
from 1911 to 1973.

My GRAND FATHER'S clock

My GRAND FATHER'S clock

Four centuries of a British–Australian family

GRAEME DAVISON

THE MIEGUNYAH PRESS

THE MIEGUNYAH PRESS
An imprint of Melbourne University Publishing Limited
Level 1, 715 Swanston Street, Carlton, Victoria 3053, Australia
mup-contact@unimelb.edu.au
www.mup.com.au

First published 2023

All Davison family photos unless otherwise stated are in the Davison family collection.

Cover design by Pfisterer + Freeman
Typeset in 11.5/15.5pt Adobe Caslon Pro by Cannon Typesetting
Printed in China by 1010 Printing Asia Limited

NATIONAL LIBRARY OF AUSTRALIA

A catalogue record for this book is available from the National Library of Australia

9780522879582 (hardback)
9780522879599 (ebook)

For Jim, Lucy and Miriam
and their children

Contents

The Generations of the Clock xiii

Introduction 1

1 Listen, Our Ancestors! 9

2 Before the Clock 21

3 The Peasant in the Town 51

4 The Sad Sound of the Factory Bell 73

5 The Workshop of the World 97

6 Towards Australia 109

7 Voyage and Landfall 127

8 The Years between 147

9 A Tale of Two Houses 169

10 Revving up 191

11 Taking off 215

12 Towards England 239

Acknowledgements 260

Notes 263

Index 295

My grandfather's clock was too large for the shelf,
So it stood ninety years on the floor;
It was taller by half than the old man himself,
Though it weighed not a pennyweight more.
It was bought on the morn of the day that he was born,
And was always his treasure and pride;
But it stopped short—never to go again—
When the old man died.

Ninety years without slumbering
(Tick tock, tick tock),
His life seconds numbering
(Tick tock, tick tock),
It stopped short—never to go again—
When the old man died.

Henry Clay Work (1876)

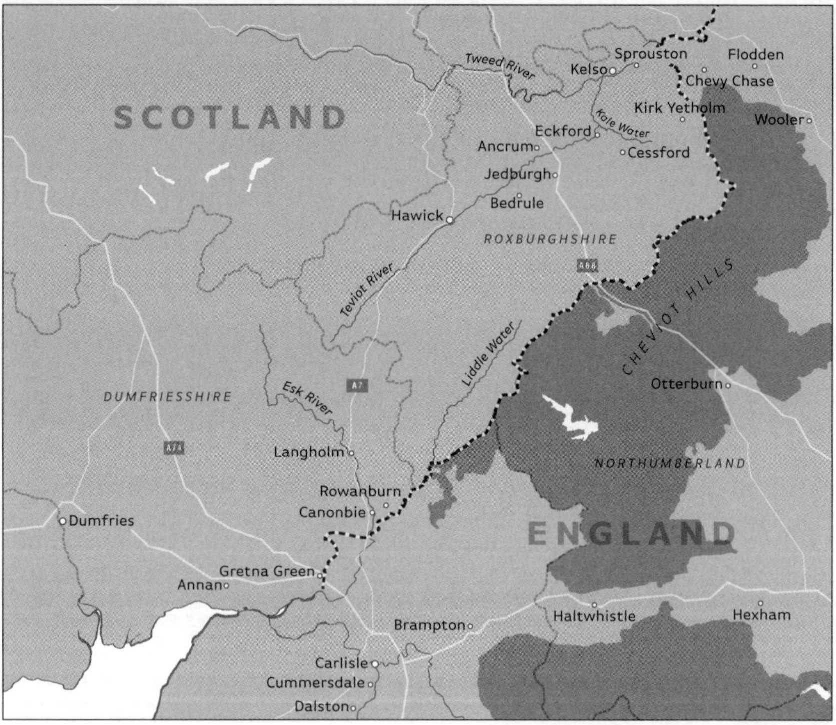

Carlisle and the Scottish Borders—ancestral home of the Davisons.
Map by Guy Holt.

THE GENERATIONS OF THE CLOCK

John Davidson (born c.1745, died Annan 1817)
Breeches-maker, Annan, Scotland
m. Mary Allan

|

William Allan Davidson (born Annan 1782, died Cummersdale 1858)
Block printer, Cummersdale, Co. Cumberland
m. Mary Dixon

|

Richard Allan Davidson/Davison (born Carlisle 1807, died Carlisle 1874)
Bootmaker, Caldewgate
m. Elizabeth Downie

|

Thomas Davison (born Carlisle 1838, died Birmingham 1930)
Tinplate worker, Carlisle, Manchester and Birmingham
m. Mary Shepherd

|

John Potter Davison (born Birmingham 1869, died Essendon 1934)
Ironmonger and painter, Birmingham and Melbourne
m. Ada Cardall

|

George Henry Davison (born Birmingham 1911, died Melbourne 1998)
Plumber, Essendon, Victoria
m. May Hewett

|

Graeme John Davison (born Melbourne 1940–)
Historian, Melbourne
m. Barbara Grant

Introduction

EVERY FAMILY HAS its myths. They are the stories, true or false, about who we are and where we come from. They are fictions, not because they are necessarily untrue, but because they are fashioned or made up. Every family sifts its past, deciding which bits to keep and which to cull or let go. Photograph albums, eulogies, obituaries, genealogies, anecdotes, letters, diaries and heirlooms are products of this winnowing.

When we are children, our family seems so much a part of us that we cannot imagine a life outside it. Its story is ours. As adulthood approaches, we begin to question its myths as we encounter those of others. When we marry, some of our partner's family story becomes ours too. As we become parents, we may take a new, perhaps more forgiving interest in the experiences of our parents and grandparents. Towards the end of life, we review our family's story in the light of what life has taught us. At each stage we learn a little more, and peer a little further into the mystery of our becoming. Being at that stage myself, I like to think that the seventh and last of the classical 'ages of man' is the highest, a vantage point that offers the clearest and wisest view of our past; but that may be just another myth.

This book recounts an expedition into the past of my father's family. When I published *Lost Relations*, a history of my mother's family, some readers asked why I wrote so little about my father. As I grew up, he discouraged interest in his family's past, not because it was scandalous—although, as I later learned, there were buried sorrows unknown to me and perhaps to him—but because it was, at least in his eyes, so recent and undistinguished. Only towards the end of his life did he begin to change his mind. He joined his local historical society and wrote a brief account of his life. Even then he seemed quite uninterested in his English origins. He made only one trip back to the land of his birth, to visit his daughter who had married and settled there.

For a long while I took my cue from him and spared little thought for the Davisons' history. Only recently did I also change my mind. After my mother died, I inherited a 200-year-old grandfather clock willed to my father by his aunt Elizabeth Ann Davison. Clocks and watches have always fascinated me. I love their precision, their delicate self-regulation and their astonishing craftsmanship. My book *The Unforgiving Minute*, a history of time-telling in Australia, was a product of that interest. The clock also stirred my longstanding interest in material culture. I have devoted many years to the study of Australia's historic buildings, landscapes and museums. I am attracted to the histories hidden in commonplace objects, like cars, houses, furniture—and clocks. Modern ideas of heritage, I believe, are an extension of the sense of personal identity derived from our connection with ancestral objects or heirlooms. The clock now installed in a corner of my living room demanded to be read both as history and heritage, for its meanings in history and for me.

For a historian, a clock is not like any other object. Time is the very stuff of history. The great French historian Fernand Braudel likens it to the soil that sticks to the gardener's spade. Many of the social theorists and historians who shaped my vision of history were preoccupied by the mystery of time and change. So in investigating my great-aunt's clock and the times it measured, I was also inspired to think more deeply about the nature of time in both its personal and historical dimensions.

When we begin a family history, we usually go looking for versions of ourselves, only to encounter strangers, inhabitants of that foreign country, the past, where they do things differently. The path between our ancestors' time and ours may turn out to have more twists and turns than we anticipate. People who we thought we knew well appear in a different light when we uncover more of the circumstances that made them. Family traditions we assumed to be ancient turn out to be quite recent, while others we thought recent are found to have deeper roots. So it is with this story: it is full of roads not taken, strokes of luck and lost opportunities, as well as surprising continuities.

Like most family histories, it is a search for personal identity. In telling it, I inevitably reflect on what my discoveries mean for me. Identity, the philosopher Charles Taylor suggests, is an essentially 'dialogical concept': we define who we are in conversation with our significant others, and against the background of the times and places in which our forebears lived. When we get around to researching and writing it, some of our most significant others, such as parents and grandparents, have often passed on: so the conversation may be a one-sided one, with those who may have known the answers to our questions but can no longer answer us. While they were alive, we did not think to ask them; only when they died did we realise the gap they left in our memory. Elements of their story may survive in the memories of their children, so in researching and writing this book I have drawn on conversations with my sister Helen Hobbs and my Davison cousins, especially Tom Davison, Joan Welsh, Helen Spring and Bev Brooks, and childhood friends Roy Dunn and Jim Coomes.

The account we now give of our forebears' lives, based on historical sources and memories, is inevitably conjectural, and different from the one our forebears may have given if they were still here to testify. Different, but neither better nor worse, I would say, for while the story we reconstruct from genealogical sources and public records is less immediate and intimate than one made from personal memory, it is also less subject to its slips and distortions. So, it is that paradox—a tale told as though to our parents and for their sake, but in the knowledge that they are no longer here to correct us.

The Davisons were a family of no great distinction and I have had to reconstruct its history from the slender archive of family letters, diaries and photographs still in family hands, together with the traces its members left in the massive and ever-expanding digital archive of parish registers, censuses, newspapers and institutional archives. This book could not have been written even a decade ago, so rapid has been the growth of searchable online databases. It is as much a history of my forebears' times as of their individual lives. It aims to put flesh on the bare bones of genealogy and to link the intimate history of the family with the larger history of neighbourhoods, cities, nations and empires. I offer it as a small contribution to the burgeoning conversation between family and academic historians. Just as family history needs the insights of general history, so, I believe, the story of an individual family may illuminate and unsettle the grand narratives of national history, giving large events like the Great War or the Industrial Revolution a human face. By narrowing the focus to just one family, we may enlarge our understanding of how dimensions of history usually considered separately fitted together, and of how the fortunes of each generation influenced its successors'. Every family, happy or not, is different, and I make no claim to the Davisons' typicality; yet their passage from country to city, from the Old World to the New, and through the huge transformations of the postwar era, may illuminate the experiences of other families.

Like any history, this one is selective, most obviously in following only one path—the male line—through the Davisons' past. In more recent times, where the sources allowed, I have attempted to write more about the lives of the women who married my male forebears, but the reality is that, for much of human history, the sources are as patriarchal as the society that created them. Often, it seemed, a woman had no sooner arrived on the stage than she was ushered off. There is an irony here for, as my great-aunt's bequest illustrates, women, especially single women, are often the great keepers of family memory, although the memories they keep are often not of their own lives.

History is usually written forwards, as the historian relates how each event impacts upon the next. Genealogy and family history, however, are often written backwards, as the researcher traces a pedigree, generation before generation, until the trail of evidence grows faint, the lineages ramify uncontrollably or the researcher's curiosity is exhausted. Combining history and family history, as I do in this book, therefore involves an oscillation between two modes of inquiry: one, a tracing back to find my 'lost relations'; the other, a looking forward to consider how their actions and decisions affected their descendants, including me. One should not distinguish too sharply between these ways of thinking. Every kind of history contains elements of both.

The Davisons were a different sort of family from my mother's family, the Hewetts, the subject of *Lost Relations*. There were common threads to be sure, especially the Methodism that brought my parents together, but in following their story I have been led into questions and themes not considered previously. I have attempted to push the story further back, into the 'deep time' where conventional genealogy loses its footing, and further forward into my own early years. Family history is a search for one's roots, a journey back to a time and place where we think some original version of ourselves lies waiting to be discovered. Thanks to the wonders of digitisation and the World Wide Web, millions can now make that journey. Our restless, mobile, urban society longs to 'return' to a more organic or tribal past. Many features of contemporary culture, from DNA genealogy and 'roots tourism' to television dramas like *Outlander*, attest to its popularity.

The idea that we can return to the land of our ancestors is, of course, another myth, one that flourished in the country from which my Davison ancestors came, the borderland between England and Scotland. Through the writings of Walter Scott it lived strongly in the minds of colonial Australians. The border ballads were a template for their attempts to conserve an Australian folk literature. The poet

Banjo Paterson, a descendant of Scottish immigrants, published the collection *Old Bush Songs*, emulating Walter Scott's *Minstrelsy of the Scottish Border*. In the second chapter of this book, I 'return' to that country, searching not just for my own remote ancestors but also for an understanding of the impulse that draws us to such places.

As an Australian of British immigrant descent, I ponder these questions aware of their resonance with the life and culture of the First Peoples of the land in which I live. For Aboriginal Australians, 'going back to country' is not another kind of roots tourism. The places to which they return are still alive with ancient songs and stories. They maintain a connection with ancestral lands that have been seized but never surrendered. Many younger Australians now feel more affinity with their stories than they do with the stories of their European forebears. Yet there are similarities too, for such have been the disruptive effects of colonisation that many Indigenous people draw on the evidence and skills of genealogy and family history.

Surely a mature Australia has room for both journeys. In pondering the living connection of Indigenous people with their land and ancestry, we gain a deeper understanding of what was lost, as well as gained, in our immigrant forebears' long march out of their homelands and in their attempts to sink roots into new soil. And in recognising the enduring importance of ancestry in our own lives, we may begin to measure how profound were the injuries our colonial forebears inflicted on the ancestral keepers of the land.

In the final chapters, I have extended my narrative into the postwar years and my own childhood and youth. These are not instalments of autobiography so much as social history based on personal memory. Autobiography is about the author's self-making and includes the external world only as background. But I want to bring the background to the fore, and view myself as a product, as well as a witness, of my times. We are now far enough away to recognise the years between 1940 and 1970 as one of the most transformative periods in the history of the planet. They are almost precisely the period between my birth and becoming a father. In those years families like mine, which for generations had remained just a step above the poverty line, suddenly achieved the benefits of full employment, house and car ownership and secure retirement. They saw their children enter higher education, travel abroad and enjoy superannuated professional employment. Born in 1940, I was just ahead of the big wave we call the baby boom—I caught it as it crested. I was aware, even then, of being borne along by forces beyond my knowledge and control, and of doors opening even before I knocked.

The long postwar boom was an optimistic time when it seemed that our material progress would be more widely shared. We view it now through a darker lens, as the prelude to problems we had yet to know or name, such as globalisation, resource depletion, species extinction, climate change and rising social inequality. 'Be careful what you wish for' the saying goes. In retrospect we might wish we could have seen further or exercised more care for our planet. But it took some time for the consequences of our choices to become apparent. In the meantime, many millions of people were lifted from poverty into a better standard of living. In writing about my family's history, I have tried to portray their life as they experienced it, with all their limitations of knowledge and insight. I have avoided nostalgia on the one hand, and hand-wringing regret on the other. 'You can't turn back the clock' goes another saying. True, but history is the next best thing, for in reimagining the past and putting ourselves in the shoes of our forebears, we take a step towards a deeper understanding of ourselves and the world we will leave to our descendants.

CHAPTER 1

Listen, Our Ancestors!

IN 1968 MY ninety-year-old great-aunt Elizabeth Davison died. She had never married or worked in a regular job, so she had little of great value to bequeath. She left her most precious possession, a grandfather clock, to my father, instructing him to pass it on to me when he died. I was in my late twenties, busy with my own life, and although I knew about her bequest, it meant little to me at the time. I didn't even bother to travel down to Melbourne for her funeral, a bleak little gathering to mark the end of an unfulfilled life. Only after my mother's death, when the clock at last arrived in my house, did I examine it more closely. By then, age and approaching mortality had made me more receptive to the claims of ancestry. Why, I now wondered, had the old lady valued the clock so highly and taken such trouble to ensure it stayed in the family?

As a boy I was not very close to Aunty Cissie, as we called her. None of us were, really. A fierce, eccentric old spinster, she lived alone in a tiny flat behind my grandparents' old house in Washington Street, Essendon. In memory's eye I see her enthroned in a wingback chair with a large framed photograph of her father, a bearded patriarch, gazing down from the wall behind her. From her cramped kitchen–living room, with its utilitarian gas ring, meat safe and tin canisters of Horlicks's malted milk powder, I can see into the adjoining bedroom. It is crammed with relics of her life back in England: framed prints and photographs, crockery and tin plate, an iron bedstead, an oak sideboard and a grandfather clock. Hoarding is said to be a psychic reaction to loss, but I knew nothing then of the trail of deaths and disappointments that had left her stranded so far from home.

Elizabeth Davison was the last of the family to migrate to Australia. Her brother John, my grandfather, and his wife Ada had left England in 1912 with their four children. My father George, the youngest, was just over a year old. He remembered nothing of the England his parents always called Home. 'I'm Australian,' he would say if we reminded him of his English birth, firmly closing the door on the world his parents had left behind.

Yet the Davisons were much closer to their homeland than my father acknowledged. Migration is a young people's game—a middle-aged migrant may bring their body but half their mind remains behind. Like an old tune playing somewhere in the background, the tones and accents of English provincial life permeated the Davisons' lives in Australia. Old sayings, songs, recipes, loyalties and bigotries resurfaced far from their origins. Old crafts and skills, along with the tools for practising them, passed quietly from generation to generation. When my father taught me how to paint a wall—mixing the oil paint, cutting in around the window frames, and meticulously cleaning the brushes after we finished—he was passing on skills he learned from his own father, a painter by trade. John Potter Davison, my grandfather, died in 1934, well before I was born, and my grandmother followed in 1948 when I was only seven; the only surviving witness to their English youth was John's younger sister Elizabeth. Her flat Midland vowels and brusque commands echoed the Birmingham in which they had all grown up.

The Hewetts, my mother's family, were Southerners: Hampshire farmers, Cornish miners and London servants. The Davisons were

Northerners: tradesmen, factory workers and shopkeepers from the Scottish Borders, the garrison city of Carlisle and the industrial Midlands. The Hewetts were bigger, physically, than the diminutive Davisons. Their horizons seemed wider, their mood lighter, and their ambitions larger and worldlier. The Davisons were modest, practical, plain-speaking folk, their manner abraded by the grit of their industrial origins. There was something uptight as well as upright about them; an effect, I suppose, of the hard school in which they had grown up. In Melbourne, my Hewett aunts married white-collar men and moved across the city to what my mother, with a mixture of longing and disapproval, called 'the other side'. The Davisons stayed on in Essendon or moved further up the Broadmeadows line and deeper into the working-class northern suburbs. In *Lost Relations*, I paid tribute to the influence of my maternal grandfather, the printer, autodidact and Methodist local preacher Vic Hewett, a hero to both my parents. Without realising it, I underestimated the quieter influence of the Davisons and especially of my father, a gentle, wise, unselfish man.

When John and Ada migrated, Cissie remained in Birmingham to keep house for her widowed father, my great-grandfather Thomas. Hers was the fate of innumerable women in an age when few of their sex achieved economic independence outside the family, or even much respect within it. The preferred destiny for women like Cissie was marriage but whether she had the opportunity to wed, or wanted it, I do not know. She was already in her mid-thirties when that destroyer of maidens' hopes, the Great War, broke out. Remembering the fierce old woman she became, I thought, uncharitably, that she probably scared men off. Yet old photographs depict an attractive, even beautiful and vivacious young woman.

Was she, as the only surviving daughter, a hostage to family duty? Or was she a willing servant of a father she adored? Perhaps her feelings were so mixed, and her choices so limited, that even she did not know. When her father died, aged ninety-one, in 1930, she was past fifty, too late for marriage or a fresh start. Three and a half years later, in the midst of the Great Depression, she voyaged alone to join her brother and his family in Melbourne. Her situation may look sad to us, although judging by her own account of the voyage, she was a happy, sociable passenger. 'I wore my white silk frock and had a real good time,' she wrote after an evening of dancing.

Two months after she arrived in Melbourne, however, she suffered another blow when her brother also died. His years in Australia had not been prosperous and his health had been failing for some time. When he was unable to find employment in his trade as an ironmonger, he worked as a coach painter and later as a house painter. On his sixtieth birthday, already afflicted by the bad ticker that killed him, an old life insurance policy matured. He put the £100 as a deposit on the timber cottage in Washington Street. When he died four years later, his sons, Frank and my father George, were left to keep up the mortgage payments.

Twenty years had passed since Cissie worked alongside John and Ada in the family hardware business on Moseley Road. She had crossed the world to be with her brother, hoping to rejoin that happy household. But now he was dead and his grown-up children were making their own ways in life. Unwilling to be a burden, Cissie departed for a while to work as a live-in nurse at an old people's home in the Dandenongs but later returned to share the house with Ada. While John was alive they had got on well enough, but below the surface there were old grievances. Cissie blamed Ada for making John a Methodist and persuading him to migrate. When they clashed, Ada sought occasional respite with her daughter Grace, now married to a banker in Victoria's Western District.

When Ada died, George and Frank inherited the house. Dad then bought out Frank, making a small flat for his aunt and renting the rest of the house to tenants who undertook to share the bathroom and laundry and take a friendly interest in the old lady. In her eighties, Cissie became crankier. She fell out with her neighbours, the kindly Bingham sisters, and with most of her nieces and nephews. When my mother greeted her in the street, she stalked past as though she did not know her. I realise now that she was probably suffering dementia, but we had neither a name nor sympathy for it in those days. My father, with his unfailing patience, continued to visit his aunt, sometimes taking one of us in the hope, perhaps, that a child's presence would cheer her.

When at last she died in her ninety-first year, Cissie had only two bequests: a framed photographic portrait of her father Thomas, and his grandfather clock. The portrait presented by his friends and admirers on his retirement she willed to my uncle Frank, and is now owned by my cousin Tom. The clock she left to my father. While the clock was precious to Cissie, it is no priceless antique. A similar clock by the same maker was recently advertised in a European auction catalogue for less than a thousand dollars. Readers of other heirloom histories, like Edmund de Waal's *The Hare with Amber Eyes* and Tim Bonyhady's *Good Living Street*, may pity the Davisons, who had nothing like their exquisite wood and ivory carvings or Klimt portraits on their hard-living streets.

In traditional societies, precious heirlooms conferred social status but in modern ones, the historian David Lowenthal says, their value is mainly sentimental. One should not say 'merely' sentimental, however. A lawyer who has administered many deceased estates notes that families who happily agree about the division of large assets, like real estate or stocks and shares, can come to blows over heirlooms of comparatively little monetary value. 'People can get intensely sentimental over stuff,' she observes. When Jacob stole his brother Esau's birthright, he got more than his father Isaac's property; he also won his blessing. So too with heirlooms: deserved or not, they confer the favour of the dead on the living.

Somewhere along the line—perhaps in the hold of the ship, or even before Cissie left England—her father's clock lost its original case. The one advertised in a Danish auction catalogue has an elaborately carved mahogany case. My uncle Alan Porter, a watchmaker by trade—also an amateur cabinet-maker, birdwatcher, violinist, home movie-maker and fisherman—had previously made his wife, my aunt Phyllis, a grandfather clock as a wedding present. He came to Cissie's rescue by making a new case for her homeless timepiece from Australian hardwood. Connoisseurs would be appalled but I rather like the symbolism: a sturdy British heart in a plain Australian body.

I had always supposed that Cissie's clock was the same as the one presented to Thomas, along with the portrait, on his retirement in Birmingham around the turn of the twentieth century. But closer inspection revealed it to be much older. Its maker's name and address, 'R. Hodgson Annan', are engraved on the attractive brass dial. Annan, a small port town in Dumfriesshire, is just thirty kilometres across the Scottish border from Thomas Davison's birthplace, Carlisle. Robert Hodgson conducted his business in Annan from the 1780s until 1820 when he handed it over to his son John. Later clocks bear John's name, so Cissie's clock must be at least 200 years old, and thus four decades older than Thomas and almost a century older than his portrait.

For more than 200 years, between the seventeenth and early twentieth centuries, grandfather clocks, or long case clocks as they were originally known, were the most accurate way of keeping household time. In 1656 the Dutch scientist Christiaan Huygens utilised Galileo's discovery of the periodic oscillations of a pendulum to regulate the escapement of a mechanical clock. While a clock's time might previously have varied from true solar time by as much as fifteen minutes in a 24-hour cycle, the pendulum clock reduced the variation to as little as ten or fifteen seconds. The length of the pendulum required to regulate the clock—about one metre—determined the height of the case in which the clock was housed. The opening and closing of the escapement produced its characteristic rocking sound.

Like a dog that must be walked every day, Cissie's thirty-hour clock disciplines its owner. I must remember to wind it every morning by pulling the 'endless chain' to raise the five-kilogram weight that powers its movement. I may then leave it to tick quietly and obediently through the following day and night. Its pulse, slower than my own heartbeat, has a mesmeric effect, creating a reassuring aural backdrop to the activities of my day. Every hour, however, it suddenly springs to life. To the growling of gears, it strikes the number of the hour in a brisk metallic voice easily audible throughout the house. Then, having reminded me of its presence, it resumes its steady gait.

The surest guide to the age and character of a clock, as to a human's, is its face. The brass dial of Cissie's clock, with Roman numerals marking the hours, Arabic the five-minute intervals, and indentations to mark each minute, typifies the more precise notation on clocks of the late eighteenth century. Its distinctive hands and spandrels also belong stylistically to that period. According to the historian David Landes, the radically improved accuracy of the pendulum clock and its rapid spread across Europe revolutionised everyday life: 'The availability of reliable, accurate timekeepers, working day and night, on cloudy days and clear, led people to order their lives more and more by mean time rather than the sun.' A common measured time, he suggests, was the foundation of 'the modern world'. Whenever they got their grandfather clock, my family were joining a very large project indeed.

But when, exactly, did they acquire it? Had Thomas purchased it second- or third-hand on a trip home to the Borders? Or could it have been in the family for longer? By a remarkable stroke of luck I can answer those questions. In 1801 Richard Forrest, Annan's schoolmaster, was appointed to collect the household returns for the first British national census. Forrest walked through the town from house to house, listing the members of each household by name and occupation. These returns were supposed to be destroyed as soon as the statistics had been tabulated and sent off to the government in London. But Forrest held on to his and they are preserved in the local library, where I found them on a visit to Annan in 2018. They show that in 1801 Thomas Davison's great-grandfather John Davidson—my own four-times great-grandfather—was living with his family on the northern side of Annan's High Street, just around the corner from Robert Hodgson's clock-maker's shop.

This surely was when the grandfather clock in my living room came into our family. When I hand it on to my son Jim it will have passed through seven generations. For an ordinary family like the Davisons it was a significant purchase. The average price for a long case clock in the late eighteenth century was £3 to £5, or between five and ten weeks' pay for a skilled tradesman. Robert Hodgson's clock, according to a horologist who repaired it, was a 'good middle-class clock', not as expensive as the beautiful works of other local clockmakers I saw in the Annan Museum nor as cheap as the 'simple, cheap, pull-wind grandfather clocks' that sold for around £2 10s. In today's money, it was a much more expensive purchase than a home computer; more like a luxurious home theatre or a small second-hand car.

Confirmation of the clock's long connection with my family came more than a century later. In 1929 my uncle Frank Davison, a keen Scouter, became the first Davison to return to England when he took part in the Third World Jamboree at Upton near Liverpool. Afterwards, he visited his relatives in Birmingham, relishing home-cooked meals and soft beds after his spell under canvas, visiting local beauty spots, and pursuing his interest in the reform of delinquent boys. (He even interviewed Lady Cadbury, the queen of organised charity in Birmingham.) One afternoon towards the end of his stay, he visited his grandfather Thomas, then in his ninety-first year. They were looking at photographs and chatting about the Davisons' family history when suddenly the grandfather clock struck. The old man raised his finger. 'Listen,' he exclaimed, 'our ancestors!'

This scene—a diminutive old man nearing death and the striking of an ancient clock—reminds me of another clock, the one in the old popular song:

> My grandfather's clock was too large for the shelf,
> So it stood ninety years on the floor;
> It was taller by half than the old man himself,
> Though it weighed not a pennyweight more.
> It was bought on the morn of the day that he was born,
> And was always his treasure and pride;
> But it stopped short—never to go again—
> When the old man died.

Written by Henry Clay Work and published in the United States in 1876, the song became a worldwide hit. Its popularity was the reason why long case clocks became known as grandfather clocks, according to the *Oxford English Dictionary*. Fifty years later, it was still being sung around the piano by my Davison aunts and uncles.

In humanising the old man's clock, the song drew on a popular tradition. A long case clock was about as tall as a man, its face level with his. It had moving hands and a ticking mechanism that was a passable simulacrum of the human heart. It was the nearest thing our forebears knew to the human qualities we now attribute to robots and computers. In Cumberland, Thomas's home county, it was customary to stop household clocks when a person died and restart them only after the funeral. When Albert the Prince Consort died in 1861, the inconsolable Queen Victoria ordered that the clocks in his bedchamber should continue to be wound each day, as though their ticking might keep her beloved husband alive. In Richard Strauss's opera *Der Rosenkavalier*, the Marschallin, an ageing princess, walks the house at night stopping the clocks. By holding time still, she imagines that she can slow the decay of her fragile beauty. Whether the clock was stopped to signify the finality of death or rewound to stave it off, its ticking was a potent symbol of the human life force.

When Thomas invited Frank to listen for 'our ancestors', he implied that his clock could speak for the souls of his departed kin. Antique objects appeal to us because they bear visible evidence of the passage of time and the handling of previous owners. In his poem 'Old Furniture', Thomas Hardy ponders the ancestral history of such 'relics of householdry':

> I see the hands of the generations
> That owned each shiny familiar thing
> In play on its knobs and indentations,
> And with its ancient fashioning
> Still dallying:

When his eye lights on a clock, Hardy imagines the hands of its previous owners setting the time.

> On the clock's dull dial a foggy finger,
> Moving to set the minutes right
> With tentative touches that lift and linger
> In the wont of a moth on a summer night,
> Creeps to my sight.

Now, when I wind my great-grandfather's clock, I think of the foggy fingers of Thomas and the shadowy generations—'our ancestors'—who wound it before me. I visualise the households in which the clock stood and imagine the routines that it measured. I know that my ancestors cannot really speak through an inanimate object, but touching its surface and repeating the actions of its owners stimulates my historical imagination. Who were the ancestors who owned and used my great-grandfather's clock when it was new? How did it order their lives and times?

In an age before automobiles, computers and robots, clocks were the most wonderful machines to enter the homes of ordinary people. They were not only useful but also beautiful, not just status symbols but tools in their self-making. In *The Unforgiving Minute*, I wrote that 'the clock on the wall or in the waistcoat pocket is but the metronome for a soul already singing the music of modernity'. I was aware, when I wrote that passage, of being a child of that revolution in time-consciousness myself. But I knew little then of how it had shaped the lives of previous owners of my great-grandfather's clock. In reconstructing its history I am peering into that dark space where heredity and nurture, memory and history combine to make us who we are.

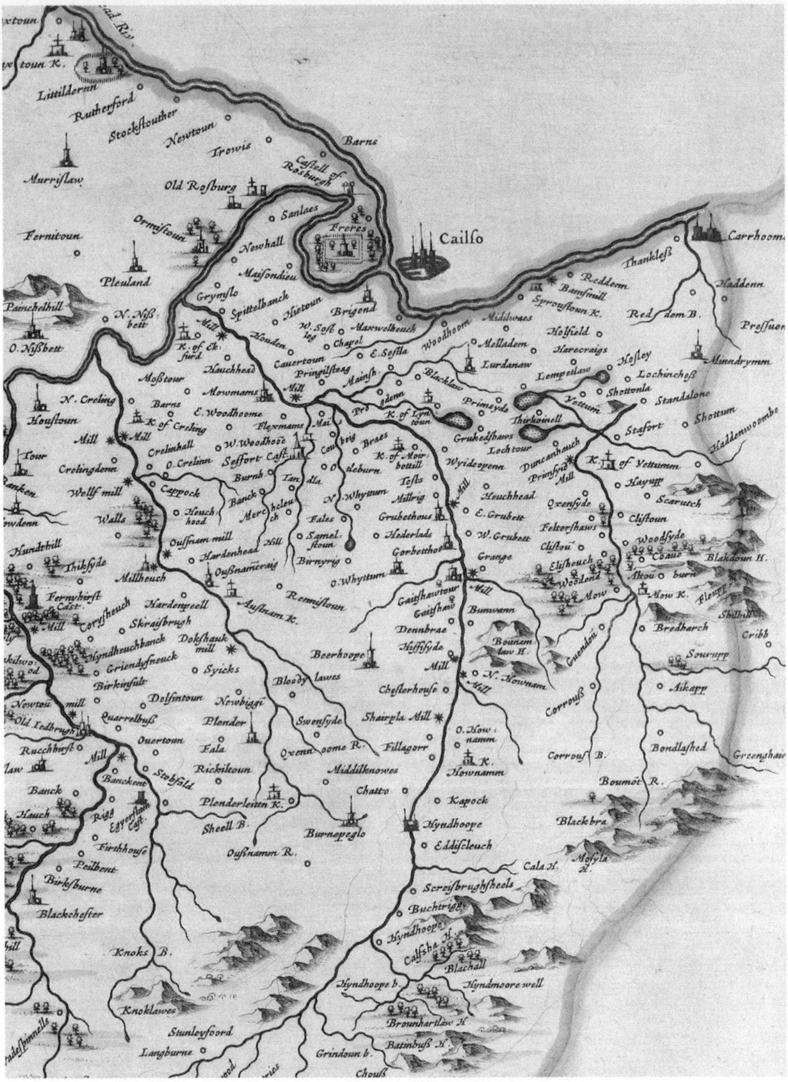

Detail from Joan Blaeu's *Teviotia Vulgo Tivedale*, Amsterdam, 1654. Based on a sixteenth-century survey by Englishman Timothy Pont, this beautiful map shows the Davisons' ancestral homeland in East Teviotdale in exquisite detail. Courtesy National Library of Scotland.

CHAPTER 2

Before the Clock

When my great-grandfather Thomas Davison heard his clock strike and urged my uncle Frank to listen for our ancestors, I wonder whose voice he was listening for? How far back along our family tree did his own memories take him?

Memory, after all, is a treacherous path into the past. Only a little of all that we have known lodges in our long-term memory. Only fragments of what we remember are passed on to the next generation. By then, inevitably, they are refracted through more recent experience. So the traces of memory that reach descendants may not bear much resemblance to what their ancestors actually did, said or thought.

Yet memories can have a surprisingly long life. In preliterate societies, knowledge of some important matters, such as kinship rules and property ownership, was transmitted with remarkable accuracy over many generations. When memory is the only record and speech is the only conduit, people seem to retain details that, despite the crutches of writing, print and digital memory, we can simply forget. They cultivate the art of recollection. In the Scottish Borders, for example, fathers ensured sons remembered the trees and stones that marked the boundaries of their land by literally beating the knowledge into them. Historians of pre-colonial Africa and early colonial Australia have learned to trust the evidence contained in the oral traditions of indigenous peoples. In more recent times, too, historians have vouched for the accurate memory of unlettered people. The historian Geoffrey Blainey contended that people with little education, like the old-timer he interviewed for his history of a mining community in Tasmania, were 'more likely than a professor to retain an accurate memory of events they had actually experienced'. As an absent-minded elderly professor, I'm inclined to believe him. Thomas Davison was the first of his family to enjoy formal education but he grew up in an oral culture where 'listening to' one's ancestors and holding onto their memories was taught and esteemed.

Ancestral memories are more likely to survive when the generations are long and grandparents can talk to their grandchildren. Thomas's great-grandfather John, a breeches-maker, was dead well before Thomas was born in 1838, but his grandfather William, a block printer, lived in the same town until Thomas was twenty. His father Richard, a Carlisle shoemaker, was still alive in the 1870s when Thomas, now in Birmingham, was a married man with children of his own. So stories of the family's times in Annan could well have passed from father to son—or from mother to son—until ninety-year-old Thomas relayed them to his Australian grandson Frank.

The Ancestral Past

Thomas's use of that word 'ancestors' intrigued me. It hints at a deeper past than words like 'family' or 'forebears'. It evokes the twilight zone beyond the paper trail of census and birth records where genealogy dissolves into folklore and the family tree becomes entangled with the buried roots of the clan and tribe. In Scotland, the written record of births, marriages and deaths in parish registers is less complete than in England: of approximately 900 Scottish parishes with baptismal registers in 1800, only about two-thirds have records dating from the 1760s and less than one-third from 1700. So while I can trace Thomas's ancestors back to his great-grandfather's generation with relative ease, my attempts to reach back beyond 1750 through traditional records run into difficulty.

To enter that deeper past, I need to take a risk. Instead of following the paper trail, I must leap the centuries into a time when the name Davison had a more tribal significance. If I could locate the Davisons' tribal homeland, the ancient root from which they sprang, perhaps I could then follow them forward in time, connecting their deep past with the family whose documented genealogy petered out in Annan sometime in the mid-eighteenth century.

Two centuries before the birth of John Davidson and a hundred kilometres east of Annan, the Davisons were a distinct clan with their own ancestral homeland. Davidson and Davison were not local names in Dumfriesshire, where William Davidson was born, whereas the names were approximately fifteen times more common in the adjoining county of Roxburghshire. If John the breeches-maker was a descendant of that clan—a plausible contention—what history, I wondered, could account for the family's fortunes over the generations that separated his world from theirs?

When Frank recorded his grandfather's injunction to listen for 'our ancestors' in his travel diary, he unfortunately added no further details. Some years later, however, I recall him telling me that our Davison ancestors were 'cattle thieves from the Scottish Border'. Was this a memory of his conversation with Thomas or something Frank had discovered, or imagined, himself? The 'cattle thieves', I realised, were reivers, the notorious brigands whose blood feuds convulsed the Borders during the fifteenth and sixteenth centuries. As an undergraduate English student, I knew the reivers as the creators of a great folk literature, the anonymous 'riding ballads' collected by their most famous descendant, the novelist Sir Walter Scott, in his *Minstrelsy of the Scottish Border* (1802 and later editions). Professor Ian Maxwell, descended from a famous Border family, inspired generations of Melbourne University students with his stirring recitations of

'Lord Randal' and 'The Douglas Tragedy'. We thrilled to these elemental tales of tragic love, reckless courage and bloody revenge. They seemed to spring from a time far from our own cosseted age. It was exciting to think that their heroes—desperate and daring men on horseback like Kinmont Willie, Hughie the Graeme and Jock o' the Side—could be my ancestors.

So I was disappointed when my cousin Tom said he had no recollection of his father Frank ever mentioning ancestral 'cattle thieves'. I began to wonder if his memory was playing tricks—or mine. But then Tom asked his sister Rosemary. Oh yes, she insisted, her father was always talking about his ancestors, the Border cattle thieves. How could I explain this discrepancy? Memories, psychologists tell us, are not like cards that can simply be drawn from a filing cabinet or downloaded from the hard drive of our minds. A memory 'is not a PDF we open and reread on a computer, or a camera filled with high-definition images', two experts observe. 'Memory is more like live theatre, where there are constantly new productions of the same pieces.' When we hear a story, it needs to lodge in our minds and become a part of our own story. When we lift a memory into consciousness and retell it, we write a new scene in the production. If Rosemary and I remembered (or imagined) what Tom forgot (or never knew), perhaps it was because it filled a gap (or didn't) in stories we had each begun to imagine.

Mention of the Border reivers, however, prompted Tom to produce something more tangible, an old book entitled *Tales of the Borders* by John Mackay Wilson. John Davison received it as a Sunday school prize in Birmingham in 1894 and left it to Frank, who later passed it on to Tom. The frontispiece, depicting a crofter's cottage built into the ruins of pele tower, evoked the aftermath of the heroic days of border warfare. But Wilson's moralistic tales of farming and artisan families seemed to offer little to bridge the gap between the family of legend and the family of history.

That gap is one that many moderns yearn to fill. Our mobile, globalised, urban world longs for a primordial past. 'We yearn for our

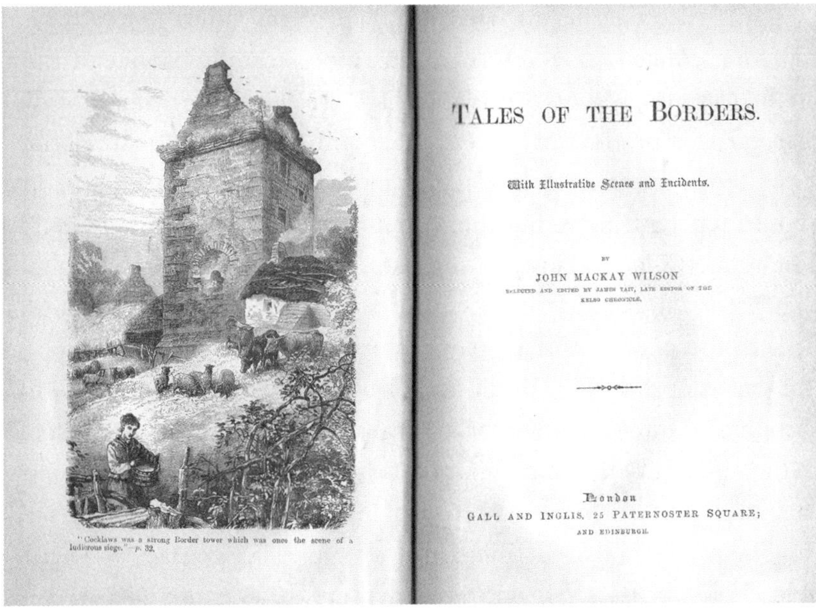

John Mackay Wilson's popular *Tales of the Borders* (1835) celebrated the virtuous farming communities that grew up after the pacification of the Borders. Courtesy Tom Davison.

origins; we yearn for an innocent terrain,' writes the novelist Hilary Mantel. This yearning may take many forms. In modern Australia, New Age pilgrims may follow the example of their Indigenous countrymen by going 'Back to Country' in sacred places like Uluru. Or they may send a sample of their saliva to Ancestry.com in the hope of discovering their Celtic, Saxon or Viking ancestry. When we set out on the family history trail we imagine returning to an ancestral homeland where we find a more primitive, unspoiled version of ourselves. Perhaps that's why the idea that my forebears were descended from wild frontiersmen appealed to me. It made me wonder who we Davisons were before towns and factories, clocks and calendars, Methodism and migration turned us into the quiet, respectable folk I knew. If we were able to lift the overburden of modern civilisation to reveal our buried roots, what truer—maybe wilder and stranger—people would appear?

I was surrendering to what one half of my mind knew to be a romantic conceit. The 'return' to our roots, the philosopher Ernest Gellner argues, is a response to a distinctively modern sense of displacement, a product of our estrangement from traditional religions as well as ancient homelands. 'We must switch from asking people about their faith to asking them about their grandparents,' he quips. The romantic nationalist, he suggests, may not care too much about the historical accuracy of ancestral memories. Like Scott's border ballads, these memories are part history, part invention. Their appeal does not depend on their truth. Yet while modern discontents may account for our yearnings for an ancestral past, they do not dispose of the possibility that some part of us is indeed a relic of things below the horizon of history. I am a historian, a product of that distinctively modern movement, the critical study of the past. Accuracy and verifiable evidence matter to me even if they don't matter to everyone. So in looking for my ancestors, I bring my scepticism as well as my romanticism along for the ride.

Into the Borders

In October 2018 my wife Barbara and I drove east from Carlisle across Solway Firth and along the A7 highway into Scotland. We were joining the thousands of other 'roots tourists', as the industry calls them, who visit Scotland each year. Relatively few international tourists actually visit the Borders. The majority head north into the Highlands in search of tartans, bagpipes, castles, rugged mountains, misty glens, wild salmon and malt whisky. These are symbols of traditional Scotland, although the traditions, as historians have shown, are actually quite recent—products of romantic nineteenth-century nationalism and twentieth-century tourism rather than innocent survivors of the remote Scottish past.

Literary men like the ballad-collector Sir Walter Scott—a man of the Borders rather than the Highlands—fashioned our image of Scotland as a nation rooted in wild landscapes, clan loyalty and a deep

Celtic past. Scott was also the creator of the most popular version of Border history, the legend of the Border reivers. In the preface to his poem 'The Lay of the Last Minstrel' (1805), he described the Borderers as 'living in a state partly pastoral and partly warlike … combining habits of constant depredation with the influence of a rude spirit of chivalry'. They were 'engaged in scenes highly susceptible to poetical ornament'. Scott's genius for 'poetical ornament' helped to transform the reivers from murderous brigands into chivalrous national heroes.

In the Borders, images of the reiver are never far from sight or mind. Leaving Carlisle, the statue of a steel-helmeted reiver, pike in hand, guards busy Kingstown Road. Just across the border, a larger-than-life effigy of the legendary Lang Sandy Armstrong overlooks

Lang Sandy Armstrong, the most notorious of the reiver chiefs, guards the main street in Rowanburn, a few miles from Gilnockie Tower where the Armstrongs took refuge from English troops and rival surnames.

the main street of Rowanburn. At Langholm, the highway leaves the Esk and, a few miles further on, joins the headwaters of the Teviot and descends eastwards towards the heart of Davison country in Teviotdale. In Hawick's main street, another reiver brandishes a captured English flag in celebration of the Scots' victory over marauding English troops at nearby Hornshole in 1514.

Near Jedburgh we paused to view a roadside map depicting the home territories of Border families, a larger version of those I had already consulted in local guidebooks and museums. The maps agree on the territorial origins of the most prominent families, such as the Armstrongs, Grahams, Elliots, Scotts, Kers and Douglases, but disagree on the whereabouts of lesser tribes like my own. Sometimes the Davisons appear as neighbours of my wife Barbara's Rutherford forebears, just north of Jedburgh, while on other maps they are placed further south near the English border. On some, alas, they do not appear at all.

Nearing our destination, I was seized by an attack of nostalgia for a homeland I had yet to see. I paused at a souvenir shop outside the Reiver Café to purchase a Davidson tartan scarf and a slim booklet, *Davidson: The Origins of the Clan Davidson and Their Place in History*. The Davidsons, the author notes, are a sept of the Clan Chattan, descended from the Highland chieftain David Dhu, fourth son of Muirdich. Their ancestral homeland, he writes, is actually in the Highlands, near Kingussie on the edge of the Cairngorms, almost four hours' drive from the Davidson haunts in the Borders. Was I on the wrong track? Are the Highland Davidsons and Border Davisons branches of the one family? Nobody seemed to know.

Some of the uncertainty, I later discovered, derives from the name itself, which was used by the sons of men named David, as well as by male descendants of those already calling themselves Davidson. Early Scottish tax records from around 1400 refer to a 'William filius [son of] David, baillie [magistrate] of Peebles' and to a 'William Davidson, baillie of Peebles', evidently the same person. In the Borders, surnames like Davidson (or its variant spellings Davison,

Daveson, Davyson, Davisoune) had a tribal character similar to the Highland clans or Sicilian Mafia. My own forebears used the names 'Davison' and 'Davidson' almost interchangeably until the mid-nineteenth century, when they settled on 'Davison'. When I quote from primary sources I will use the original spelling, but in speaking more generally of my own line I will use the name 'Davison'.

In the Borders, people speak of 'surnames' rather than 'clans', a usage that dates from the late fifteenth century. Men of the same surname dwelt, farmed, rode, fought, thieved and sometimes murdered together. They were blood relatives by birth and sometimes through bloody feud. The English Warden Sir Robert Carey observed in 1590:

> If the country rise upon them when they are stealing in England, and either kill one by chance, or take him 'with the bloody hand', delivering him to the officer for execution, 'if they be but foote lownes [footsoldiers] and men of no esteame amongst them', it may pass unrevenged; but if he is of a surname, 'as a Davyson, a Younge, a Burne, a Pringle or Hall or any that they make accompt of', then he who killed or took him is sure himself, and all his friends (especially those of his name) is like, 'dearly to buy yt', for they will have his life or 2 or 3 of his nearest kinsmen, in revenge of their friends so killed or taken stealing here.

Surnames implied geography as well as kinship. So a Davison seldom appeared in sixteenth-century sources without mention of the place from which he came: Robert Daveson of Primside, John Davidson of Dennerlaw, Thomas of Samieston, Hob Davysoun of Fowermurden, or Henry of Morebattle. Many of these hamlets and farms have now disappeared but can be found on early maps of the region, like *Teviotia Vulgo Tividale* (1654), based on a remarkable late sixteenth-century survey of Scotland by the Englishman Timothy Pont.

Most of the Davison strongholds lay within about ten kilometres of each other in picturesque undulating country between the Teviot

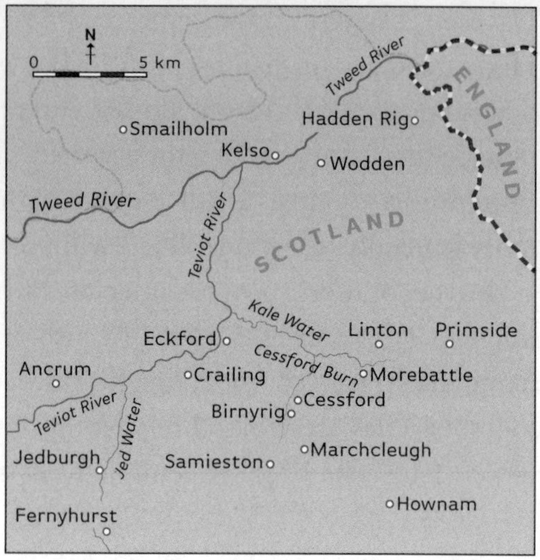

East Teviotdale. The hamlets, villages and castles associated with the Davison surname clustered within a few miles of each other close to the Cheviot Hills and the towns of Kelso, Jedburgh and Sprouston. Map by Guy Holt.

and the eastern flank of the Cheviot Hills. The most notorious Davison reivers came from just four hamlets: Birnyrig, Marchcleugh, Samieston and Wodden, situated on well-watered farming land along Cessford Burn near Cessford Castle, seat of the powerful Ker family. Others lived on higher grazing land near the English border at Fowermurden, Frogden and Primside, or on the upper reaches of Kale Water at Morebattle, Linton and Hownam. The Davison lands lay directly in the path of invading English armies and were bounded by the historic battlefields of Flodden (1513), Chevy Chase (1436), Hadden Rig (1542), Ancrum Moor (1545) and Reidswire (1575). To the south, the bald, rounded Cheviot Hills, rising to a thousand feet, presented a formidable barrier to English invaders, although not to the Borderers themselves. Three ancient passages, one a Roman road, connected East Teviotdale with the English settlements in upper Tynedale and Redesdale. There were Davisons on both sides of the border, then and now.

In East Teviotdale the Davison surname was often coupled—as in Carey's mind—with other local families such as the Pringles, Rutherfords, Robsons and Halls. A recent study of the Border gentry categorises the Davidsons of Fowermurden, Wodden and Marchcleugh as 'bonnet lairds', smallholders on fifty or 100 acres which they worked themselves rather than letting out to tenants. Surprisingly, the Davisons are seldom mentioned in general histories of the Border reivers, yet they often headed English wardens' lists of local troublemakers. Far from being recent migrants from the Highlands, they were 'ancient indwellers', or old inhabitants of the district, with connections stretching back to medieval times.

Most bearers of the Davison surname were not landowners themselves but 'kindly tenants' of the biggest local landowners. The term 'kindly tenant' was a relic of feudalism, a form of hereditary tenure that required the tenant to give manrent or military service to his lord. In Teviotdale, a contemporary observed, 'the most part of the Heritours of the Countrey gave out all their Lands to their Tenants for Military attendance upon Rentals and reserved only some few manses [houses with allotments] for their own sustenance, which were laboured by their Tenants besides their Service'. For much of the sixteenth century the most powerful local lairds, the Kers of Cessford and their cousins at Fernyhurst near Jedburgh, were locked in a bitter family feud. Dwelling close to both, beholden in different ways to each, and vulnerable to attack by invading English forces, the Davisons lived precarious lives. It is not surprising that they gained a reputation for treachery and violence.

Little remains in records or ruins to reconstruct their way of life. The impressive stone or pele towers constructed by the Kers as refuges from invading armies or rival surnames, and visible still at Smailholm and Morebattle, were large enough to accommodate several households from the same surname or clan. The bastles (bastilles) or fortified farmhouses, suitable for one or two farming households and their animals, and which survive in Tynedale and Redesdale, seem to have been rare in Teviotdale. In any case, only the richest and most powerful families could afford these substantial stone structures. English observers were contemptuous of the 'miserable' cottages and cabins inhabited by most of the Borderers.

In 1551 the Welsh traveller Andrew Borde remarked that 'the people of the borders toward England … lyveth in much povertie and penury, having no houses but such as a man may buylde wythin iii or iiii hours: he and his wyfe and his horse standeth all in one rome'. Their houses were 'not to be compared to many a dog kennel in England', another Englishman declared. The Davisons probably belonged to the doghouse rather than the bastle or the castle. Their timber and thatch houses were more akin to the frontier settlements of colonial America, where households of extended kin huddled together in such abodes for shared labour and mutual protection, than to the brick and stone farmhouses that appear on early nineteenth-century maps. Exposed to the constant threat of invasion and destruction, they invested only as much labour and material in their housing as its vulnerability justified.

Nature's Time

Much of what we know about the Border Davisons comes from a hostile source, the reports by English wardens on lawlessness along the frontier. As we will see, their bad reputation was not altogether undeserved; yet the wardens may have painted them blacker than they were, for there was much about their lives that these sources cannot capture. In the intervals between their brushes with authority, the Davisons lived the more mundane life of farmers: growing corn and tending sheep, rearing children, and struggling to stay alive in a harsh climate and turbulent times. Reiving, the activity that made them notorious, is best understood against the backdrop of their everyday lives.

Life on the Borders was shaped by the agricultural cycle of ploughing, sowing and reaping, and the seasonal migration of livestock from the river valleys to the Cheviot Hills, a practice known as transhumance. Nature provided the farmer with most of the time signals he required. Scanning the evening skies, observing a sudden

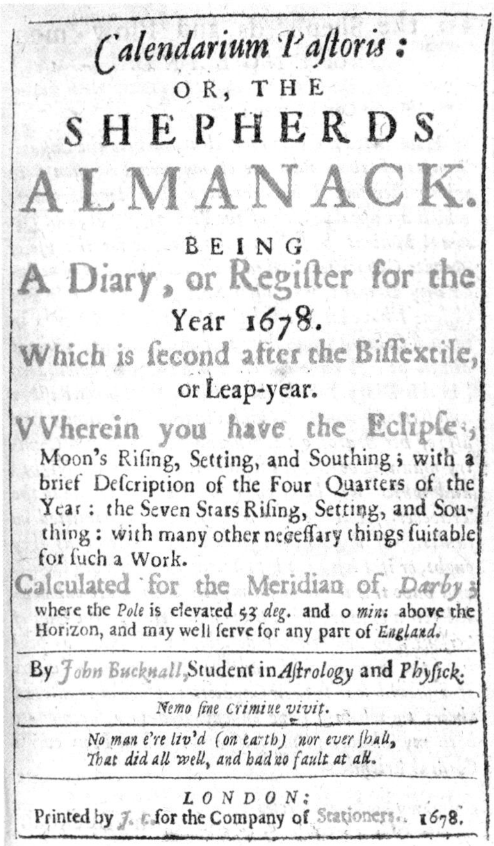

Calendarium Paſtoris:
OR, THE
SHEPHERDS
ALMANACK.
BEING
A Diary, or Regiſter for the
Year 1678.
Which is ſecond after the Biſſextile,
or Leap-year.
VVherein you have the Eclipſes,
Moon's Riſing, Setting, and Southing; with a brief Deſcription of the Four Quarters of the Year: the Seven Stars Riſing, Setting, and Southing: with many other neceſſary things ſuitable for ſuch a Work.
Calculated for the Meridian of *Darby*;
where the *Pole* is elevated 53 *deg.* and 0 *min:* above the Horizon, and may well ſerve for any part of *England*.

By *John Bucknall*, Student in *Aſtrology* and *Phyſick*.

Nemo ſine Crimine vivit.

No man e're liv'd (on earth) nor ever ſhall,
That did all well, and had no fault at all.

LONDON:
Printed by *J. C.* for the Company of Stationers. 1678.

The Shepherd's Almanack, 1678. Almanacs offered the farmer guidance on everything from the best times to plant crops and shear sheep to the dates of local markets and the festivals of the Christian year. Courtesy John Emmerson Collection, State Library Victoria.

shift in the wind, listening for the call of a bird or the frightened cry of sheep and cattle, he read nature's clock and pondered his next move in the perennial battle with the elements. In his mind, the seasons of winter, spring, summer and autumn synchronised with other cycles: the orbits of the sun, moon and stars, the fluctuating humours of the human body, and the fasts and festivals of the Christian year. The Borderers' sense of time and space was a blend of ancient and modern, pagan and Christian influences. They endowed hills, trees, stones and springs with magical or sacred significance: the Holy Well at Caverton, the Lady Well at Linton, Prior's Meadow and Priest's

Crown were local landmarks whose enchanted names survived the Reformation. Similarly, when they told the time, they attended as much to the omens and portents of the horoscope as to the embryonic sciences of meteorology, medicine and horticulture.

Contemporary almanacs enable us to reconstruct the rhythms of their collective life in some detail. Through the early months of the year, when snow covered the ground, the farmer was largely confined to the immediate surrounds of the house together with his stock animals. Only in spring did he begin sowing, shearing, crutching and preparing his sheep and cattle for summer pastures. In May the tempo of farm life in the Borders increased, 'usher[ing] in the pleasant summer and reviving the husbandman's heart'. If the farmer had not already sown his barley, this was the time to do it, 'else look for a late harvest, and little profit'. Lambs were weaned and male ones castrated, and by the end of the month shearing was underway. Along the Teviot and its brimming tributaries, stands of birch, rowan and alder burst into leaf. Shepherds mustered their sheep and drove them along narrow upward paths into the well-grassed pastures of the Cheviot Hills. Through the warm summer months they kept watch, sleeping in rough huts or sheilings, while down in the valley the husbandman—or tenant farmer—got in his harvest.

The first of August, the Feast of St Peter in Chains, was the traditional harvest festival. Lammas, or 'loaf-mass', named for the custom of presenting a loaf made from harvest grain to the local church or landlord, occurred halfway between the summer solstice and the autumn equinox. The farmer's livestock had now returned from their upland pastures and grazed in the fields near the farmhouse, while the farmer filled his barn with hay and corn.

Lammas was the traditional season for reiving:

> It fell about the Lammas tide,
> When the muir-men win their hay,
> The doughty Earl of Douglas rode
> Into England, to catch a prey.

So begins 'The Battle of Otterbourne', one of the most famous border ballads. Riding over the hills, often in darkness, the reivers fell upon unsuspecting households, seized whatever property they could carry, drive or ride, beat up or murdered their 'prey', and retreated before resistance could be raised.

Reiving, however, was not confined to Lammastide. Some of the Davisons' most daring raids occurred in winter and mid-summer, and in broad daylight rather than under cover of darkness. In June 1590 the English Warden Sir John Forster listed 130 Scottish raids that occurred between 1587 and 1590, including sixteen in which the Davisons were involved, and dated over a hundred of them. About half the raids occurred during the traditional reiving season, between August and early October, but there were smaller spikes of activity in mid-winter and in early summer, before the harvest claimed everyone's attention and energy. Part-sport and part-blood feud, reiving was also inspired by the exigencies of the agricultural year. 'The object was always plunder, often with wanton destruction thrown in,' writes George MacDonald Fraser, the leading historian of the subject; but smallholders like the Davisons may have stolen partly to survive.

The Doings of the Davisons

To an Australian, the reivers have a familiar look. We have our own rural bandits celebrated as folk heroes—the bushrangers. Wild colonial boys like Jack Donohoe and Ned Kelly are distant cousins of Kinmont Willie and Jock o' the Side. Normally I would regard Kelly as a murderous thug but I am obliged to admit that my Scottish ancestors were men of a similar stamp.

One afternoon Barbara and I made a trip from Jedburgh, where we were staying in a stone cottage beside the river, to Abbotsford, the astonishing baronial house built by Sir Walter Scott from the proceeds of his phenomenal literary career. There, on the shelves of the beautiful Gothic library overlooking the Tweed Valley, still stocked with Scott's own collection, I was surprised to spot a copy of TE Wells's *Michael Howe: The Last and Worst of the Bushrangers of Van Diemen's Land*, published in Hobart in 1818. I realised that the novelist who had collected the riding ballads of the reivers from their last singers was a contemporary, even possibly an admirer, of our own frontier outlaws.

Two centuries and half a world apart, the reiver and the bushranger were both products of rural societies under stress. Scotland, notes the historian Jenny Wormald, was 'a country where kings were weak and kindreds strong, and feuds raged endlessly and bloodily'. Like the Mafia, the 'surnames' or clans thrived in the power vacuum created by the inability of central governments, be it Rome, London, Edinburgh or Hobart, to impose their rule on wild frontiers. Blood feuds were endemic in the Borders but bloodiest when local rivalries became implicated in the intensifying struggle between the two kingdoms.

Many of the Davisons' crimes were petty, local and opportunistic but, from time to time, they joined their neighbours in more daring schemes of plunder. In August 1532, for example, a raiding party of 400 'Rotherfordes, Carrs, Davysons, Pryyngelles, Trumbilles, Hunters, Robsons, Waughes, and Wais' crossed the Cheviot Hills at night under a full moon—the most propitious time for raids—and attacked the village of Haltwistle more than fifty miles away. The English Warden, the Earl of Northumberland, was alarmed by the Scots' ability to mobilise a sizeable force, cross the frontier with impunity, and strike an English village far from home in broad daylight. The East Teviotdale surnames, led by the Davisons, Pringles, Youngs and Halls, could reputedly muster a force as large as 3000 men. In December 1541 the Warden of the East March, Sir William Eure, submitted a list of Englishmen recently slain by Scots. Three of the ten listed murders—all of farmers struck down while labouring in their fields close to the border—were attributed to Davisons.

Over the following decade, as Henry VIII strove to subdue the northern kingdom, conflict along the border intensified. On 24 August 1542 an English army led by Robert Bowes, Deputy

Warden of the East March, assembled close to the border, in sight of the 10 000 strong army of James V of Scotland. The English had already made several raids across the border and the Scots knew from their spies that they planned to burn and sack the towns of Jedburgh and Kelso. When Bowes crossed the border at Hadden Rig, the Scottish commander, the Earl of Huntly, committed 2000 of his best troops to the battle, quickly putting the enemy to flight. Bowes was hunted down and captured by John Davysoune of Dennerlaw and George Davison of Frogden. Thomas Forster, son of a prominent Northumberland family and Bowes's lieutenant, was captured by another Davison, Stephen Davysoun, and his brother-in-law, the Laird of Craisthorne. These Davisons were all locals—the battlefield was just a mile or two from their homes. 'Five Stone Field' on George's property at Frogden was named after a circle of five upright stones that once stood there, known as 'The Tryst' and the local rendezvous point for raiders setting off over the border.

After the battle, Stephen Davysoun handed Forster over to the English in the expectation of a ransom, but it was not forthcoming. An English raiding party later burned down his house, set fire to his corn and stole all his cattle. After a few nights' pause, Stephen and his companions were riding back into England bent on revenge when they met some of Lord Lisle's men coming in the other direction. The night was dark and windy and the parties came upon each other unawares. A clash ensued. In the confusion most of the Scots escaped, but Stephen, his nephew and their companion Wat Young were captured. The English were elated. Their prize captive, Stephen Davysoun, Lisle explained, 'has done more harm to the King's subjects than any Scot in Scotland'.

George Davison, who had captured the enemy commander, was also eager to extract a reward. In January 1543 English spies reported that he was openly boasting on the High Street of Edinburgh that

> in case he and his company could not get their prisoners delivered (to the English), they would take as much upon the cawcye (which

> in the Scottish tongue signifieth the highway) as should recompense them, and would become English men, and whosoever they met withal, they should rather send him into England or they remained unrecompensed.

By so brazenly auctioning his loyalty, and threatening to become a highwayman, George may have encouraged the English to believe that other Borderers could be brought over to their side. In June 1543 he negotiated a £40 sterling ransom, together with a secret payment of a further 20 merks (equivalent to an English pound) on the understanding that 'neither his landlord, nor booty fellows, nor partners should know or have any portion of the said twenty marks'.

Henry VIII and the English wardens had become alarmed by how freely 'the Davisons and other of the Tevidales' were continuing to wreak havoc on the border. Ker of Cessford, on whose surety they had been released from English imprisonment, appeared simply 'to smile and wink' at their continued depredations. In July 1543, the King instructed his emissary in the north, the Duke of Suffolk, to alert his Scottish allies, the Earl of Angus and his brother Sir George Douglas, to 'the doings of their retainers the Davisons'.

Patriots or Traitors?

With the death of the Scottish King James V in December 1542, Henry VIII intensified his campaign against the northern kingdom. He proposed the betrothal of his son and heir, five-year-old Edward, the future Edward VI, to James's heiress, the newly born Mary Queen of Scots. To force the reluctant Scots to accept the marriage proposal, he increased military pressure along the border, a policy of harassment that became known as 'the rough wooing'. Henry's advisers hatched a plan to subvert the northern kingdom by securing the collaboration of selected Borderers, beginning with 'all the chief men of the surnames of the Davisons, Pringles, Taits, Youngs, Turnbulls, Robsons, Rutherfords and Halls in East and West Tevydale'.

The English objective was to divide the lesser surnames from their overlords. Mixed motives—fear of further English raids, hopes of English soldiers' pay, prospective profits from the provisioning of English troops and sympathy with English Protestantism—weakened the Borderers' resistance to Henry's overtures. The Davisons were among the first to sign the secret 'covenant' with the English. The Kers held out for a time but eventually joined the 'assured Scots', as the collaborators were known. By swearing loyalty to the English king, they were agreeing to fight on England's side, or to become, as their accusers would later say, 'false Scots' or 'Scottish Englishmen'.

Their loyalty was soon put to the test. On 27 February 1545, at Ancrum Moor near Jedburgh, the English army under the command of Sir Bryan Layton, comprising Spanish and German mercenaries, English Borderers and 700 'assured Scots', engaged the Scottish army, under the command of the earls of Angus and Arran, who had now deserted the English cause. The smaller Scottish force included a contingent of loyal Borderers under the Kers' rival, Sir Walter Scott of Buccleuch.

Hiding most of their forces behind a hill, the Scots lured the enemy into a vulnerable position before launching an attack. The low winter sun was setting behind them, dazzling the English forces. Smoke from the Scots' arquebuses and pistols blew in their enemy's faces. The Scots' pikemen, wielding weapons longer and more deadly than the English spears, pressed home their advantage. The English tried to rally but at the critical moment the assured Scots tore off their red crosses and turned on their English allies. In the ensuing slaughter, about 800 English troops, including their commander and Warden of the Middle Marches Ralph Eure, were killed and 1000 taken prisoner. It was not the most bloody or decisive battle of the time, but it brought Henry's rough wooing to an abrupt end.

The chief cause of their defeat, according to one of Henry's principal advisers, the Earl of Shrewsbury, was 'the treason of the assured Scots of Tyvydale who did kill and take mo Englisshe men that day, then did any of the enemyes'. The volte-face of the assured

Scots has remained a contentious issue ever since. In his *Tales of a Grandfather* (1828–30), Walter Scott compared the valour of his courageous and patriotic kinsman and namesake with the 'renegades' who changed their colours only to 'make amends for their desertion of the Scottish cause'. Other historians excuse the turncoats, arguing that on a wild frontier, beyond the reach of Edinburgh and London, their 'crimes [if crimes they were] were due rather to the peculiarity of their circumstances than to their own inherently evil dispositions'. I share the historians' quandary. Should I admire my Davison forebears' cunning, condemn their treachery or excuse their actions as a forced choice in adverse circumstances? Was Scottish patriotism as unaffordable as it was anachronistic?

Consequences

Whatever their motives, the collaborators paid heavily for their actions. In September 1545, the Earl of Hertford, Lieutenant General of the North, directed 16 000 English troops to 'burn, raze and cast down' the towns, villages, abbeys and farms of Teviotdale. In less than a fortnight the English army destroyed over 230 of these communities and homesteads, about one-third of them in East Teviotdale, including the Davison strongholds of Wodden, Hownam, Primside, Whitton, Marchcleugh, Samieston, Cessford, Frogden, Morebattle, Howden and Fowermurden. The timing of the campaign was deliberate: by striking when barns were full and winter was approaching, Hertford aimed to maximise his enemy's suffering.

The scars inflicted by Henry VIII's army are still visible in the Borders. A nineteenth-century antiquarian noted that Eckford, the parish where several of the Davisons' farms clustered, had been 'the scene of frequent rapine and devastation in former times'. The massive ruins of Cessford Castle, the truncated watchtowers at Whitton, Eckford, Linton and Morebattle, and the skeletal arches of Jedburgh, Kelso and Dryburgh abbeys are relics of a holocaust that incinerated countless more ephemeral dwellings.

Cessford Castle, seat of the powerful Ker family, looked towards the Cheviot Hills and the English Border. It was among the Scottish strongholds razed by Henry VIII's army in 1545. Geograph photo by Jim Barton.

The Kers, who had been among the last to join the assured Scots, were the first to be rehabilitated. Enthusiastic collaborators like the Davisons were slower to be forgiven, especially if they had profited from their treason. John Davisoun of Samieston was remitted for his treason at Ancrum Moor only in 1551, along with other crimes including theft and rape. George Davison, the captor of Sir Robert Bowes, together with his sons George and Andrew, his brother Robert, and his kinsman John Davison of Linton, were ordered to forfeit all their goods and be 'put to the horn'—publicly denounced as rebels—'for their treasonable sitting under assurance of our old enemies of England, intercommuning, assistance, taking of plain part, and furnishing of them with victuals, etc'.

Three years later, George Davison was among three notorious Teviot surnames selected by the Regent Mary of Guise to be held as pledges for the good behaviour of their followers. The hostage-taker had become a hostage himself. He became a guest of the Queen's 'trusty friend' John Wemyss on his estate ninety miles away in Fife, but barely a month into his enforced holiday he absconded. His guarantor, Walter Ker of Cessford, was ordered to forfeit a surety of 1000 merks (about £76 English). The episode is revealing for confirming George's representative status among the Davisons, his continued defiance, and his ultimate reliance on the protection of his landlord—and secret abettor?—Walter Ker of Cessford.

After his escape, George was absent from the historical record for a time. His next appearance, almost a decade later, was apparently his last and most puzzling. In 1563, at Marchcleugh, in obscure circumstances, he was murdered by his kinsmen Robert and William Davidson. After the crime, the killers were banished, and their story surfaced only two years later when they appeared before the Privy Council of Scotland pleading for their pardon and return. To promote the 'quietness of the country', the authorities wanted the families to settle their differences. George's family, represented by Robert Davison of Samieston and William Davison of Fowermurden, were at first unwilling to be appeased, but eventually they relented and allowed the assassins to return. Why was George murdered? It appears that the Davisons had got caught up in the feud between rival branches of the Ker family who, at that moment, were also on opposite sides of the religious divide that had opened up with the arrival of the Scottish Reformation.

When English observers listed the Border surnames, they put the Davisons in the Cessford camp. Most of them lived on Ker lands close to Cessford Castle or near the English border. George and his family were men of the wild frontier, among the most daring and incorrigible reivers. The Marchcleugh Davisons, however, lived about five miles away on better land nearer the Teviot. They were landowners in their own right: in the mid-seventeenth century they had a modest estate and subsisted as gentlemen. The family's head, Robert Davidson of Marchcleugh, even became a member of the Scottish Parliament. Like their neighbours, the Davisons of Birnyrig, who had committed 'diverse odious crimes and offices in the company of Thomas Ker of Fernyhurst', the Marchcleugh Davisons may have been less beholden to the Cessford Kers and closer to the Fernyhursts. There may also have been a religious dimension to the feud, for while the Cessfords were early and eager converts to the Reformation, the Fernyhursts remained, for the moment, Catholic. They also seem to have been less active reivers than the Fowermurdens. These differences of status, territory and allegiance may help to explain their feud.

Whatever his killers' motives, I regretted George's violent end. George Davison was my father's namesake, although so unlike him that it is hard to think of him as an ancestor. I wondered if my great-grandfather Thomas, who urged Uncle Frank to 'listen' for our ancestors, would have identified with a murderer like Stephen Davysoun or a violent outlaw like George of Frogden. We may admire their daring and entrepreneurial streak, but what of the killers who cut down English farmers in their fields, or the turncoats who volunteered to fight on England's side only to desert their allies in the midst of battle? Of the qualities Walter Scott found in the Borderers—'constant depredation' and 'a rude spirit of chivalry'—George seemed to display more of the first than the second. He had lived by the sword and it was fitting that he died by the sword.

Pacification and Reform

From the 1560s, as military pressure from the south relaxed, the history of the Borders entered a new phase. The revolution of 1558–60, which delivered Scotland to the Protestant cause, was the first in a series of changes—the dissolution of the religious houses, the confiscation of church property, the triumph of the landed magnates, and the godly rule of the kirk and minister—that would gradually transform the culture and power structure of the region.

In the countryside, reform progressed only as fast as the most powerful lairds allowed. In 1559 John Knox declared that 'Jesus Christ is begunne to be preached on the south borders', yet fifty years later many parts of East Teviotdale still lacked regular ministers. James I and VI issued a series of proclamations against feuding, attempting to make the greater lairds responsible for the misdeeds of their followers. Reiving parties became smaller, the raids less frequent, and the settling of accounts between English and Scottish wardens more codified.

The accession of James I and VI ushered in a new period of peace in the region. For centuries the Borders had been recognised as a distinctive region with its own subculture and laws. James's objective, however, was to 'extinguishe as well the name as substance of the bordouris, I meane the difference between thaime and other pairts of the kingdome'. The greater Scottish lairds, long a thorn in Tudor England's side, were ennobled and given royal pensions. Under the Stuarts, Britain became a great kleptocracy, as the King's most powerful friends helped themselves to the land and treasure liberated by the dissolution of the religious houses. The Kers and Scotts of Roxburghshire boosted their already massive estates by calling in or buying up the leases of their poorer tenants, consolidating their holdings and turning them over to the production of wool and mutton for the booming consumer markets of Northumberland and Yorkshire.

The feudal relationship between lord and tenant slowly assumed a more contractual character. 'So long as the Borders remained a troubled area, the large estates would have been tolerant of a numerous tenantry,' observes the historian Tom Devine. But a more peaceful countryside meant that there was less of the landlord's dirty work for kindly tenants to do. They became lairds with little property or rent-paying tenants of a new kind. Some, like the Davisons at Samieston, hung on for several generations before eventually surrendering their lands to the Earl of Roxburgh. Others became cottars on smallholdings—that is, farm labourers occupying a cottage in return for their labour as ploughmen, smiths, shepherds or herdsman—or landless farm labourers. Many more were driven from the land. In 1622 John Davidsoune of Birnyrig, a notorious nest of reivers, was banished from Scotland.

The 1663 land tax rolls starkly reveal the disparities in wealth and power between the three tiers of Border society: the magnates, like the Kers and Scotts, with rents valued in the tens of thousands of pounds a year; a second rung of gentry, such as the Rutherfords, Pringles and Turnbulls, with estates valued in the high hundreds; and a third tier of smallholders like William Davidson at Primside, Robert at Marchcleugh, Robert at Samieston, Andrew at Hoselaw and Robert at Hownam, all with holdings around £200 a year. Of the 269 Davidson households in the Roxburghshire hearth tax returns in 1694, only a few were living on the surname's traditional lands. The rest were tenants or cottars. Davisons living on the land were now outnumbered by those living and working as tradesmen and shopkeepers in nearby towns like Sprouston, Kelso and Yetholm. The parish registers confirm a similar pattern: of 960 Davidson children born in Roxburgh before 1800, about half were in the nearby towns of Kelso, Jedburgh, Sprouston, Yetholm and Hawick, with the rest scattered across the county but clustering in their old haunts: the parishes of Eckford, Hownam, Linton and Morebattle.

A New Sense of Time and Space

As they left the land and dispersed, the Davisons and their neighbours lost the tribal and territorial character of the old surnames. While networks of extended kin continued to shape their lives, they no longer relied on their brothers, uncles and cousins to defend them from English invaders and rival surnames. These changes in the Davisons' economic and domestic lives cannot really be disentangled from the effects of the most profound contemporary change in Scotland's cultural and political life, the Reformation. After centuries of Catholicism, Scotland embraced what its followers regarded as the purest, most thoroughly biblical model of reform. John Knox's *Book of Discipline* became the template for a godly life, to be preached by the parish minister, taught by the parish schoolmaster and enforced by the kirk session and presbytery.

Knox was determined to purge Scotland of all vestiges of pagan and popish superstition. Almost half the festivals of the old church year, especially those honouring the Virgin, were abolished.

Lammas Day, the traditional end of harvest—and in the Borders, the beginning of reiving—was replaced by a new Day of Thanksgiving for the accession of James VI. 'The Kirk within this Kingdome is now purged of all superstitious Observation of Days,' the Scottish Parliament announced in 1640. Bonfires, pilgrimages, dancing, carol singing and plays were among the traditions forbidden by the new regime. In 1610, George Davidson of Hoselaw—possibly a descendant of his notorious namesake—was hauled before the Presbytery of Kelso to be fined and admonished for playing the part of Little John in the forbidden Christmas revels 'The Abbot of Unreason'. Known elsewhere as 'The Lord of Misrule', this midwinter festival cheered a gloomy time of the year, but because of its association with drinking, gambling, dancing, masquerades, magic and subversive attacks on local authority, it was an abomination to the reformers. George Davidson had evidently put himself on the wrong side of the local thought police. Yet the old feast days and customs disappeared only slowly from the countryside. Almanacs continued to list Candlemas, Lady's Day and Lammas Day as occasions for local fairs long after they had disappeared from the church calendar.

The spirit of religious reform was a wildfire: once lit, it was hard to extinguish. In 1636 King Charles I attempted to draw the Scottish church back towards the liturgy and polity of the Church of England. The Scots reacted strongly and two years later, amidst dramatic scenes at Greyfriars Church in Edinburgh, nobles and people signed a National Covenant declaring their opposition to any change not approved by a free Scottish assembly and parliament. Some reformers did not stop there. The Covenanters, determined to follow the full radical implications of the Protestant revolt, challenged the rule of bishops and the right of the landed classes to appoint their ministers. Over 300 clergy refused to accept episcopal rule and lost their livings.

Pursued by the foot soldiers of a frightened establishment, the movement went underground. The expelled ministers began preaching to their followers in conventicles, secret assemblies held in private homes or in the open air. The authorities insisted that the great

Expelled from the established Church of Scotland, the Covenanters drew their followers to clandestine services in private homes or in the hills along the Border. Courtesy JA Wylie, *The History of Protestantism*, 1878.

landlords and 'life-renters' promise to 'keep no conventicles'. In 1670 Robert Davidson of Hownam reluctantly signed the band (pledge) but was later charged with persistently flouting it. Robert Davidson at Marchcleugh was fined 500 merks for attending conventicles and a further 200 merks for being absent from services of the established church, but he pleaded his need to look after his sick wife and got off. Passive resistance rather than open revolt seemed to be their style.

East Teviotdale was a notorious 'rendezvous of rebellion'. The Covenanters found eager supporters in the hamlets along Kale Water and among the hills and moors towards the English border. At Hownam, the popular Covenanter preacher John Blackader drew an enthusiastic following among the district's smallholders, cottars and shepherds.

> His eloquent and powerful discourses in the fields and fortresses of Teviotdale were blessed, not only for the refreshment of the

> persecuted Presbyterians, who flocked from all quarters to hear him, but for the conversion of many of the inhabitants of these neglected districts, who, living in ignorance of the gospel, had hitherto been addicted to rapine and every species of outrage.

While persuading the reivers to turn from their murderous ways, the gatherings reinforced their age-old spirit of resistance. They had become more virtuous but not more compliant. In rejecting the local establishment of lord and kirk, the new dispensation voiced the discontent of the lesser surnames, like the Davisons, who had been pushed to the margins of Border society.

Becoming a Davison

As I travelled the Borders I realised that something was happening to me: I was becoming a Davison by identifying with the story I was piecing together about them. I was making my ancestors' country mine, at least for as long as I was in it. The further I travelled, the more I became immersed in the story. As a critical historian, I knew that I was surrendering to a romantic myth. I wanted to experience, as much as I could, that sense of connection to an ancestral home and a tribal past that we moderns yearn for. But I was under no illusions. The Borders are a beautiful place, full of memories, but they are not really my homeland. What's oldest in my lineage is not what's closest to my heart.

I had gone to the Borders looking for ancestors who were wilder and more primitive than the respectable, modest folk I knew. And, sure enough, I found them. But then I discovered something else: a story of how those wild ancestors moved closer to the folk I knew. The Davisons, even in their reiving days, had been men of the middling sort, smallholders and tenants adapting themselves as well as they could to the struggle for survival on the margins of a violent society. When their society became more peaceful and devout, they adapted to that too, while remaining socially on the margins.

Some of those habits, I would find, stayed with them. At last, as life on the land became precarious, they moved to the towns, beginning the long journey that led, a century later, to Australia.

Recently I looked again at my grandfather's copy of John Mackay Wilson's *Tales of the Border*. When Tom first passed it on, I set it aside, finding nothing in its sentimental stories of virtuous farmers and ambitious journeymen to equal the bravado of the Border reivers. Yet in its day, Wilson's *Tales* rivalled Walter Scott's novels in popular appeal. Wilson was the son of a workingman, a Methodist and an admirer of the Covenanters. His picture of 'the peasant life of the Borders' resonated with those, like himself, who had been uprooted from the region and moved to the cities.

When my grandfather John Potter Davison read Wilson's *Tales*, he was a shop employee living amidst the foundries and factories of England's biggest industrial city, Birmingham. What details of his ancestors' lives in the Borders reached him from his father's recollections or other family sources I do not know. Perhaps, like most young people, he had little time for old folks' memories. Yet he held onto that book, and brought it with him to Australia, and passed it on to his own son Frank, who prized it, perhaps, as a link with the 'ancestors' whose memory was awakened by the striking of his grandfather's clock.

The pacification of the Borders and the decline of the small tenant farmers left a landscape of deserted villages and abandoned cottages. Geograph photo by Jim Barton.

CHAPTER 3

The Peasant in the Town

One of the darkest chapters of Scottish history is the tragedy of the Highland Clearances. During the late eighteenth century, thousands of starving crofters were evicted from their northern homelands by their landlords, sometimes at the point of a gun, and scattered to the ends of the earth. Their story lives still in history, poetry and song. But a hundred years earlier, a similar tragedy unfolded 150 miles to the south. The Lowland Clearances are not as renowned as their Highland counterparts but they proceeded just as remorselessly and with almost as much devastation. In the Borders their impact was visible long afterwards in the form of deserted villages and ruined homesteads.

In the 1790s, the statistician Sir John Sinclair invited ministers across Scotland to contribute short accounts of the history, economy, population and society of their parishes to his *Statistical Account of Scotland*. His inquiry is sometimes described as the first modern social survey. Many of Sinclair's informants were old residents with memories stretching back half a century or more. In Hownam, one of the Davison strongholds, the Rev. James Rutherford estimated that the local population had almost halved in the previous forty years. Many houses were left empty or ruined; at least thirty had been demolished in the previous ten or fifteen years. Some of the decline followed the opening of the border with England, which deprived locals of an old source of livelihood, smuggling, and exposed local farmers and enterprises to English competition. But this was not the main cause of the exodus:

> The great decrease of inhabitants, within the last 40 years, is evidently occasioned by the too general practice of letting the lands in great farms; but may be, in some measure, owing to the mode of agriculture almost universally adopted in the parish, (especially since sheep and wool brought so high a price), of converting the arable into pasture land. The lands, 50 or 100 years ago, were parcelled out into at least four times the present number of farms. As late as the year 1750, five tenants, with large families, occupied a farm now rented by one tenant. There were also, about these times, several small, but proud lairds in the parish. Their lands are now lost in the large farms, their names extinguished, and their mansions totally destroyed.

The situation in neighbouring rural parishes was similar. In Linton the number of farmers had declined over forty years from twenty-seven to twelve, in Makerston from sixteen to nil. Sixty or seventy years earlier in Oxnam, twenty-two tenants had worked the land with sixteen ploughs drawn by oxen and horses; by 1791 there were only three farmers with seven horse-drawn ploughs. Meanwhile the nearby towns of Kelso and Yetholm more than doubled their populations. 'This great increase may, in part, be accounted for from the destruction of many small villages in the neighbourhood, occupied by small farmers and mechanics,' the minister of Yetholm observed.

Those who remained in the border farms and hamlets lamented a landscape of ruination and loss. Their most eloquent voice, the 'peasant poet' Robert Davidson, was born in 1788 in Lempitlaw, close to the English border in the heart of the old Davison lands. When he was ten he became a cowherd in the Cheviot Hills. 'I had by that time a great inclination for reading,' he recalled. He satisfied his thirst for print by borrowing the penny histories and ballads he found on the shelves of hospitable farmers. At sixteen he was a ploughman and by his twenties a day labourer, an occupation he followed, with occasional periods on public relief, until his death in 1852.

Shyly, because he was fearful of the jibes of his workmates, he began writing poetry. He celebrated the deeds of national heroes like Robert the Bruce and William Wallace, and reflected on mythic landmarks, like the Witch's Cairn at Lempitlaw, and legends like the mysterious collapse of the belfry of Linton Kirk—without the regular ringing of its bell, according to locals, the village was a prey to evil spirits.

The Borders's most famous folk heroes, the reivers, were surprisingly absent from Davidson's poetry. As a poor but respectable workingman, he may have been repelled by their bloody crimes and horseback heroics. He was just a boy tending cattle in the Cheviot Hills in the 1790s when the young Walter Scott 'raided' Liddesdale in search of ballads for his *Minstrelsy of the Scottish Borders*. Scott was a gentleman who travelled by carriage and on horseback, stayed with well-connected friends, and ate duck and drank brandy on what was probably as much a summer holiday as a serious research expedition. He had recently read Gottfried Burger's popular ballad 'Lenore' and became, as he confessed, 'German mad'. Like the German Romantics, Scott was an uncommon man in love with the songs and folktales of the common people. 'A real old Scottish song,' he wrote, 'is a cairn gorm … a precious relic that bears the national character stamped on it.'

For Davidson 'the true border men' were not the reivers but their opponents, the Covenanters. As champions of the people's religious liberties, the Covenanters seemed to anticipate the political struggles of Davidson's own day. His most heartfelt poetry, however, was not heroic or political but elegiac. He lamented the passing of his ancestors, the pitiful sight of abandoned farms and ruined cottages, and the memory of the young men and women who had left the land for distant parts.

> The very thought is like to blind my e'e,
> To think what changes we have lived to see—
> A croft converted to a sheep walk wild,
> Where twenty separate happy harvests smiled;
> Their owners, free from servitude and strife,
> Found peace and plenty through the blink of life!
> But now these pleasing scenes have disappear'd,
> Around their former haunts no sounds are heard,
> Save when the bittern wheels wi' dreary moan,
> Or lonely lapwing screams in plaintive tones—
> Such is the devastation splendor makes,
> And mis'ry waits on every step she takes;
> The peasant's forced from his native shed,
> The much-loved walks where his forefathers stray'd—
> To endless wand'rings round he's restless toss'd,
> Till in his breast the love of country's lost;
> He flies for shelter to distant climes,
> Or crowded towns, to swell the tide of crimes.

Davidson wrote from hard experience: three of his own sons left the Borders for the 'distant climes' of the United States. They were among the many other Borderers who joined the great exodus of Scots to England, Ireland, North America, Australia and New Zealand.

What's in a Surname?

I began this story with a family legend—that my Davison ancestors were 'cattle thieves' from the Scottish Borders—and a hunch that I might find them in their tribal homeland. I made some progress in that quest. I confirmed the power and territorial significance of the

Davison surname, and their daring, as well as their treachery, in the border raids that made them notorious. I followed their declining fortunes as the pacification of the Borders and the rise of the greater lairds pushed them towards the margins of rural society. And I found evidence of the great cultural changes that came in the wake of the Scottish Reformation when many of the lesser lairds of East Teviotdale embraced the cause of the Covenanters. By the end of the eighteenth century, many of the Davisons had left their ancestral lands. I suspected that my own ancestor was among them. Could I close the circle and connect the reivers of East Teviotdale with my last known ancestor, John Davidson, the breeches-maker of Annan?

In a world of fluid identities, our surnames are a stubborn reminder of a time when personal identity was inherited not chosen. People do change their surnames, of course: a declining proportion of women when they marry, migrants sometimes to fit in, and others by deed poll or deception. But to a remarkable extent, people seem content to keep whatever surname they were born with, either proudly as markers of family or ethnic identity, or passively because they are too much trouble to change. Other than our genes, there are few markers of personal identity as stable over the generations as surnames. Of course they delineate only one path, the male line, obscuring the identities of all those women who lost their names, along with their property and power, when they married.

By the eighteenth century the surnames of the Scottish Borders had lost most of their original tribal character. Like the ballads, they were 'relics' of a time, almost past, when the extended family and its territory shaped much of people's lives. The scattering of the surnames is an indication of the gradual loosening of that tie. By mapping them, as one might map the migration of a tagged bird or animal, we may be able to discern the paths followed by their bearers to new lands in Scotland or abroad.

Before 1650 Davidson and Davison babies brought for baptism concentrated in two main Scottish homelands: in the Highlands near Aberdeen, and in Roxburgh, especially East Teviotdale. Within the

County of Roxburgh, three-quarters of the surname's baptisms were in just one parish, Kelso, where the abbey was a notable centre of religious life. Between 1650 and 1750, Davidson baptisms became more scattered and 'urbanised', with the largest concentrations in the towns of Sprouston (eighty-nine), Jedburgh (eighty-one), Kelso (seventy-five), Hawick (forty-four) and Ancrum (thirty-three), and the largest numbers of village baptisms in the old Davidson heartlands at Hownam (thirty-seven), Eckford (twenty-nine), Linton (seventeen) and Morebattle (ten). By the late seventeenth century, a handful of Davidson baptisms appeared in the adjoining county of Dumfries, and in the early eighteenth century there were almost sixty, scattered in what appear to be small family clusters in villages east, north and west of the principal towns, Dumfries and Annan.

With the unification of the two kingdoms under James I and VI, the restraints on the southward dispersion of the Davison surname lessened. Today, it is almost as common in Northumberland and Durham as it is in Teviotdale. The exodus followed paths well known to the reivers: around the eastern shoulder of the Cheviot Hills and along the coastal plain towards Berwick and Bamborough; westward down the valleys of the Teviot and Liddel towards Canonbie and Solway Firth; and southward along the passes through the Cheviot Hills into Tynedale and Redesdale. Davison and Davidson baptisms in the late sixteenth and early seventeenth centuries clustered near the border in the upper Tyne Valley in villages such as Rothbury, Eglingham, Bywell, Allendale and Hexham as well as in larger towns such as Berwick and Newcastle.

The Davisons, whose status had always been precarious, may have had more reason to migrate than other families. In the sixteenth century, when they became 'assured Scots'—collaborators with England's invading army—they seemed to have little regard for national loyalties. Even today many Borderers make light of the political divide.

On our drive along the A7 we stopped in Longtown, our last town on the English side, where a petrol attendant with a strong north-of-England accent filled our tank. Fifteen miles further on at Langholm, on the Scottish side, we chatted with an elderly gentleman in a tam-o'-shanter walking his dog, who spoke in a broad Scots accent. Coming from Australia where speech hardly changes over a thousand miles, the abruptness of the transition was striking. I tentatively broached the subject of English–Scots relations with the dog-walker. The division, he insisted, was of little importance, citing the border communities' strong vote against Scottish independence. Other recent writers agree, insisting that the linguistic division is superficial, a recent product of the English and Scottish schooling systems rather than primordial differences. I wondered if my Davison ancestors were just as careless of national divisions.

Could John Davidson, father of my great-great-great-grandfather William, have been among the Davidsons uprooted from East Teviotdale? On our journey from Carlisle we detoured into the picturesque village of Canonbie. Only twenty-two miles from Annan, it occupies a strategic position at the junction of the Esk and Liddle rivers in the heart of the once-disputed territory known as the Debatable Lands. We parked beside a grey stone kirk overlooking a walled graveyard. There I counted twenty-three Davidson headstones—another researcher says there are thirty. The Davison graves were fewer than those of the main local heritors, such as the Bells, Armstrongs, Grahams and Littles, but they outnumbered most other surnames. Could Canonbie, once a refuge for outlaws, have been a staging post for my ancestors migrating westwards from their ancestral lands? Perhaps, but most of the headstones were from the late eighteenth and early nineteenth centuries, too young to be ancestors of the family in Annan.

In search of more complete evidence, I scoured the parish registers of Dumfries and Roxburghshire. Since John and his wife Mary (born Mary Allan) had their five children between 1770 and 1782, he was probably born between 1735 and 1750. Only one John Davidson appeared in Dumfriesshire during these years and he lived and died in Eskdale Muir, not in Annan. In Roxburghshire, however, I found eight John Davidsons born in the right period, all in the old Davidson stamping grounds in Ancrum (two), Cavers (one) Ednam (one), Sprouston (one) and Yetholm (three).

Perhaps one of them was my ancestor. While I was pondering this question an unexpected email took me in a new direction. Years ago, intrigued by the genealogical potential of DNA testing, I sent off a sample of my saliva to the laboratories of Family Tree DNA in Texas. In reply I received details of my Y chromosome (male) DNA together with a list of other men with matching DNA and a map showing their geographical distribution. In the United Kingdom they clustered on the northern side of the Scottish Borders. Otherwise the results seemed inconclusive and I set them aside. Then Earlene Giglierano (née Davison) of Wisconsin emailed with the news that her brother Michael and I are a near genetic match. I consulted the Family Tree DNA company guide, which suggested that Michael and I have a one in three chance of sharing a common ancestor back four generations and an even chance of a common ancestor at the eighth generation.

A new path into the ancestral past had unexpectedly opened up. Perhaps genetics could go where genealogy could not. My cousin Tom had tested his DNA with another company, so we pooled our data and found twenty-five Davisons or Davidsons with DNA closely matching ours. Many of them had posted their family trees online. If a male in any of their lineages could be linked to John Davidson of Annan it increased the chance that they were related, if not directly then through a common ancestor.

When we reviewed the list, one individual stood out. Walter Davidson was born in 1718 in Ancrum, site of the famous battle where the assured Scots changed sides. In 1749 he became the father of a John Davidson, one of the eight I had identified as the possible father of my ancestor William Davidson of Annan. Described as a 'tyler', an old Scots spelling for tailor, he also seemed a possible father for a breeches-maker. His son John was of the right age to father the family I found in Annan.

Walter had also shown up in a genealogy posted by another match for my DNA, Jerome Davidson of Houston, Texas. I emailed Jerome who assured me that he had 'concrete evidence' of his descent from Walter of Ancrum. My excitement did not last long, however, for when I checked the parish registers they showed that Walter had died in Ancrum soon after the birth of John, rather than departing for America via Ireland, as Jerome supposed. When I pointed out this discrepancy, he replied, a little penitently: 'I picked the Walter Davidson born in 1718 in Ancrum as a putative ancestor out of a virtual sea of Walter Davidsons in the record in Great Britain in the early to mid-eighteenth century. In doing so, I was admittedly sowing a little mischief to stir the pot and see if anything would turn up.' Sure enough, the pot had stirred and Earlene and I had shown up! In an age of disruption and fake news, Jerome may represent the future of genealogical research. There's nothing new, of course, about creative genealogy—it's been going on for centuries—but with the revelation of Walter Davidson's mistaken identity, my confidence in DNA as a gateway to my family's deep past suddenly evaporated.

Another Frontier

My hopes of filling the gap were fading fast, but I cast my net a little wider and—fisherman's luck!—I made a catch. My ancestor John Davidson, I discovered, had married Mary Allan in 1770, not in Dumfries or Roxburghshire as I had expected, but almost fifty miles to the south in Morland, a village in the Eden Valley of Westmorland. The names matched exactly and the date, nine months before the baptism of the couple's first child in Annan, left little doubt of their identity. However, the discovery raised as many questions as it answered. If John was a descendant of the Teviotdale Davisons, how did he come to be so far from home? And if John and Mary were Westmorland folk, why did they move to Annan so soon after their wedding?

Mary's family, the Allans—sometimes spelt Allen or Allon—were husbandmen, with a lineage in Morland and nearby Bolton stretching back to the 1590s. The Davisons or Davidsons, however, appear to have been more recent arrivals. John, born in 1745, was possibly the only surviving son of another John Davison who married and fathered five other children in Crosby Ravenswood between 1733 and 1746. His probable grandfather, Mark Davison, had married in Temple Sowerby, another village in the Eden Valley, in 1705. Davison and Davidson were not local names. There is no trace of them in parish registers or tax records before 1700 and, apart from John's sister Elizabeth who married a local farmer, they had disappeared or died out by 1787 when the population was counted in a local 'census'. John was probably 'marrying up', for his family would use the name Allan as a second given name for the next three generations.

Motorists travelling north along the M6 motorway into Scotland or crossing the Pennines along the A66 from Durham pass within a

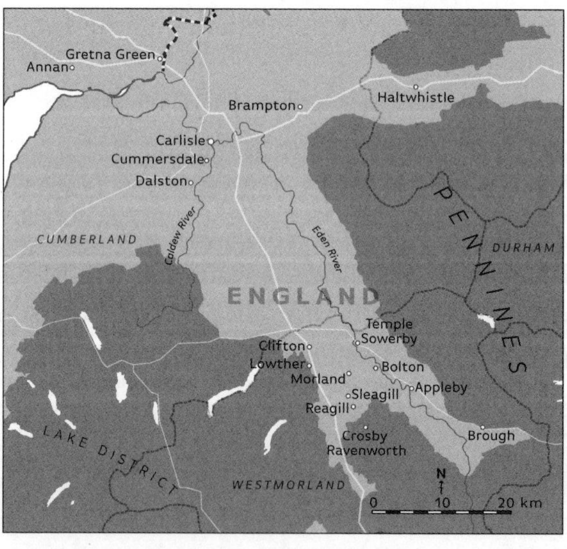

At the end of the drove roads connecting the Scottish Borders to English livestock markets, the villages of the lush Eden Valley were closer to Carlisle, Annan and the Scottish Borders than their physical distance suggests. Map by Guy Holt.

mile or two of the villages where John and Mary grew up and married. The A66 follows a similar route to an old Roman military road along the eastern bank of the River Eden, forming one side of a corridor of rich pastoral and arable land between the Lake District and the moors and fells of the Pennine Chain. The corridor had been well travelled since Roman times, and in Crosby Ravensworth John Davison was surrounded by reminders of the travellers' passage. At Reagill, on the village's northern outskirts, the tumuli, or burial mounds, of Saxon settlers were easily visible. From the high ground near Oddendale, where a stone circle marked an ancient site of druid worship, John could look down the valley, as military men had done since Roman times, to observe the approach of enemies from either the east or north. On the outskirts of the village he may have passed a memorial marking King's Well, the spring where King Charles II camped on his march south in 1651. A century later in 1745, the year of John's birth, at Clifton Moor, a few miles to the north of his birthplace, the Duke of Cumberland's redcoats confronted the retreating army of the Young Pretender, Bonnie Prince Charlie, in the last battle fought on English soil.

The Valley of Eden is an hour and a half's drive and several days' walk from the Scottish Borders. Yet its strategic location meant that incursions from the north were never far from people's minds. Since medieval times, tenant farmers had been required to render military service against the Scots, just as the Davisons in Teviotdale had been pledged to fight the English. Their sturdy houses were built like the Borderers' bastles for defence rather than ornament. Ancient battles against the Scots remained alive in popular memory, even in the school playground. 'The boys to this day have a play which they call *Scotch and English*; which is an exact picture in miniature of the RAID, that is the inroad by plundering parties,' a local antiquary observed.

Could a family from Teviotdale have migrated as far as this? The paths of migration are not always obvious from a casual reading of the map, and the Davisons, after all, may have taken several generations on the journey. Places apparently far apart as the crow flies were sometimes closely linked, particularly through the seasonal migration of livestock from the Highlands to summer pastures in northern England, where they were fattened for sale in local markets. In his classic book *The Drove Roads of Scotland*, ARB Haldane notes that the main barriers to movement were 'political and economic rather than physical'. Secure passage and grazing rights were more important than distance or terrain. From Teviotdale, the south-western route through the Cheviots provided 'a succession of easy passes … offering to the droves grass, water and quiet stances [stopping places]'.

During the late eighteenth century, the traffic of cattle across the border increased from about 30 000 head a year to over 80 000. The south-western routes increasingly came to dominate the trade, with some droves descending through Liddesdale and across Solway Firth, sometimes pausing in Dumfriesshire, while others crossed through Brampton and the eastern bank of the River Eden into the lush pastures near the market towns of Appleby and Brough. At the end of each September 10 000 head of Scottish cattle were sold in the Brough fair alone; some were driven further south but 'great quantities' were kept and wintered locally. For every fifty or sixty animals there was a drover to oversee the operation. After the summer most of the drovers returned to Scotland but some found new jobs and new loves in the valley and stayed on.

Were the Davisons among them? They do not appear in local hearth and window tax returns in the late seventeenth century but they bob up in parish records soon after the Act of Union in 1707, when the last official barriers to cross-border trade disappeared. The surnames of drovers employed on the nearby Musgrave estate were mostly Lowland Scots, including famous reiver names such as Bell, Armstrong, Graham and that of John's grandmother, Jackson. While there is no specific evidence that John Davidson's forebear was a drover (early parish registers seldom state occupations), it is a plausible possibility.

In 1787, after John and Mary had departed for Annan, a census commissioned by the local JPs revealed the order of local society.

John's village, Crosby Ravensworth, comprised some fifty-nine households and 295 individuals. The squire Thomas Gibson, the vicar of St Laurence's church Mr Reveley, and the schoolmaster George Redman were the main authority figures. Just over half the householders were 'yeomen' (eleven) or 'farmers' (twenty-two). About a quarter were tradesmen, including three tailors, a weaver, a carpenter, a blacksmith, a shoemaker and a shopkeeper, and, below them, two 'labourers' and two 'poor labourers'. Three 'widows', four 'spinsters', five 'poor men' and two 'poor women' made up the rest of the householder population. Bolton, Mary's village, had a similar occupational structure while Morland, where they married, had more tradesmen and fewer farmers.

In Annan, John Davidson would earn his living as a breeches-maker. He may have learned his trade from one of Crosby's three tailors or from the district's only breeches-maker, Caleb Mason of Bolton. Mason could have been a relative—John's mother was born Jane Mason. Even before the Industrial Revolution, clothes-making was a trade in transition. In earlier times farmers procured their

James Howe, *Cattle Droving*, 1780–1836, pen and brown ink on paper. Courtesy National Galleries of Scotland.

apparel from the raw materials they produced. 'These operations,' according to a contemporary observer,

> were performed by itinerant mechanics, consisting of wool-combers, dish-turners, rope-makers, and tailors, who travelled from village to village, or from house to house, in search of employment. All these wandering artists disappeared long ago, except the tailor, who still adheres to ancient customs, and may be seen working for daily wages in the farm houses of the country.

While tailors were itinerants, breeches-makers—a more specialised trade—were evidently more sedentary.

Were They Pushed?

Why did John and Mary leave their families in the Eden Valley and move fifty miles north across the border to Annan? Noting the abruptness of the move and the scant nine months between the wedding and the baptism of their first child, Jean, a prurient investigator might wonder whether Mary was already pregnant when they married and if they were fleeing the censure of their families and neighbours. Perhaps a sympathetic clergyman in Annan baptised their baby when she was already several weeks old? Or was she, like me, a honeymoon baby, born just nine months after the wedding? The question hardly matters to us, but if it mattered to contemporaries it could help to explain their move.

Some historians would dismiss the possibility. Rural communities, they say, took a relaxed attitude to sex outside marriage. Many ordinary couples lived together, happily or not, without a church wedding. Handfasting, the ancient ritual of joining or binding hands, was all the ceremony they needed. They married only when a child was on the way or even after it arrived. Modern de-facto couples may see themselves as reclaiming such a tradition.

Sadly there is more myth than truth in this idea. Squires and parsons as well as gossipy neighbours closely monitored the sexual behaviour of most village communities. Fornication, adultery, cohabitation and illegitimacy were offences against the good order of society and were strictly policed. In 1753, Lord Chancellor Hardwicke introduced An Act for the Better Preventing of Clandestine Marriage. Only marriages authorised by a licence or the publication of banns, conducted in church by a Church of England clergyman, and certified in a register signed by both parties, were legally binding. A couple who failed to comply or a clergyman who turned a blind eye was liable to heavy punishment. Rich families who wanted to ensure that property passed only to the children of legal unions instigated the new law. Moralists who worried that illegitimacy was on the increase also supported it. Rates of illegitimacy certainly increased during the late eighteenth century, partly, however, because the severe penalties for non-compliance under the marriage act forced expectant couples to marry, whether they wanted to or not. In Westmorland, compliance with the act was nearly universal: almost all the couples listed in local households at the 1787 census had been legally married. Because the new act did not apply in Scotland, an expectant couple could probably have eloped to Annan without marrying, or married hastily in nearby Gretna Green as other runaway English couples did. That John and Mary *did* marry before they left suggests that they wanted their families' approval and the public recognition that went with it.

In any case, they probably had other reasons to move. A village of two or three hundred people offered slimmer prospects for a young tradesman than Annan, a rapidly growing seaport almost ten times the size. Westmorland, described by Daniel Defoe as 'the wildest, most barren and frightful' county in England, had yet to shake off the vestiges of feudalism. Two-thirds of its farmers held their land under various forms of hereditary tenure. In John Davidson's parish, Crosby Ravensworth, their grip was so tight that even the notoriously avaricious local lord, Sir James Lowther, could not break it.

In 1769, the year before John and Mary married, Lowther introduced a parliamentary act to enclose the commons or 'unimproved' land, comprising several thousand acres, much of it on the moors and fells around the village. Since medieval times, the commons had been open to anyone in the parish for growing food, grazing animals or digging peat for fuel. But with the growth of the cross-border cattle trade, grazing land along the Eden Valley had become overstocked and degraded. Enclosing the commons, according to agricultural experts, was the only way to boost the supply and improve the quality of pasture. Lowther took the lead in seeking parliamentary approval but shared the spoils with the hereditary tenants. There were few protests. The main losers, apart from the drovers who lost free access to pasture, were local cottagers, tradespeople especially, who would no longer be able to dig peat, grow crops or keep livestock for their family's sustenance.

Similar acts to enclose the commons in the neighbouring parishes of Reagill, Bolton and Morland were passed around the same time. On their own, the passing of the enclosure acts may not have influenced John and Mary's decision to leave, for they were often not activated for many years. But they demonstrated how little room for ambition remained in a village where everything was owned by the local lord or controlled by a closed circle of hereditary tenants.

Or Were They Pulled?

The drove roads that connected the towns on either side of the Scottish border carried people and news as well as cattle. Although Annan was fifty miles away from the Eden Valley, a change of the economic weather in one place was soon known in the other. Perhaps that is how John heard about a new opportunity for garment-makers that had opened up in Scotland.

In 1745, the year of the battle at Clifton Moor, Bonnie Prince Charlie led his defeated troops northward along the Eden Valley towards Carlisle where, after a feeble attempt to hold the garrison town, he accepted a humiliating surrender. On 20 December, in driving rain, the Scots reached the border. Lifting their philibegs, or short kilts, the commander and his men waded through the icy waters of the Esk. Half the army headed north through Echelfechan towards Edinburgh while the Prince bore west towards Dumfries and Glasgow. He stayed the night at an inn on Annan's High Street, not far from John's later home. The 'fanatical Calvinists' of Dumfriesshire had little sympathy for the rebels and were glad to see them gone.

After the Jacobites' defeat, the English resolved to suppress all vestiges of Highlander culture, including kilts and bagpipes. Under a 1746 act of parliament, the wearing of 'the clothes commonly called *Highland Clothes* (that is to say) the Philibeg, or little Plaid, Kilt, Trowse, Shoulder Belts, or any part whatsoever of what peculiarly belongs to the Highland Garb' was outlawed throughout Scotland. Breeches replaced kilts not just because they were politically correct but also because they were practical and modern. 'It is vain to struggle against the spirit of the age,' *Blackwood's Magazine* declared in 1820. 'The Celt may struggle against it a little longer … but into breeches his thighs must go at last.' Ironically, it was romantic Borderers, led by writers like Walter Scott, who promoted Highland dress as a national costume. Scott was perfectly aware that breeches, not kilt or tartan, were the usual form of Lowland dress. 'The general proposition that the Lowlanders ever wore plaids is difficult to swallow,' he admitted. But nationalism seeks distinctiveness rather than authenticity and, as Scott and his followers realised, a tartan kilt stirred patriotic feelings in a way that a trouser could not. I will wear my Davidson scarf when the sentiment takes me, even though I know that its tribal origins are dubious, and that my own ancestor, John Davidson, made his living helping to drive the kilt out of fashion. After all, there was rather more money in workwear than in fancy dress. A 'common labourer' earning £17 a year in the 1790s was reckoned to spend about 5 shillings a year on new breeches and a jacket.

During the 1770s, John's family grew. A son, John, was born in 1773 followed by two daughters, Esther in 1778 and Mary in 1779.

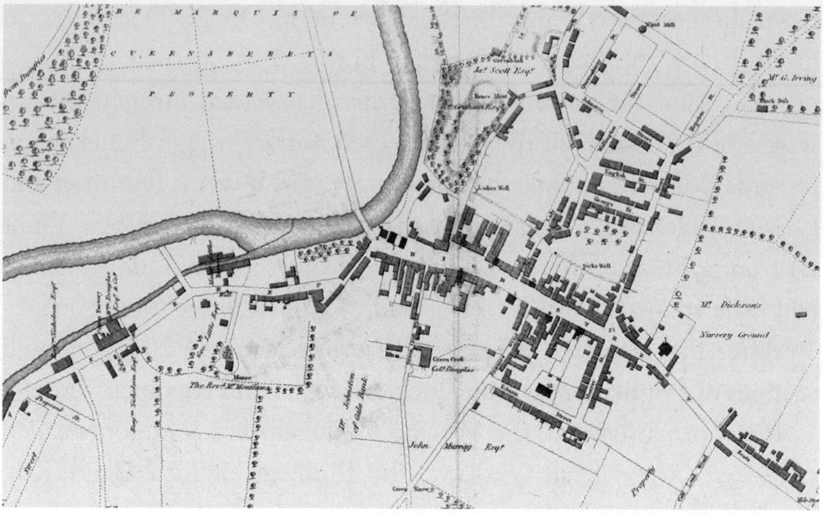

Detail, *Plan of Annan from an actual survey by John Wood*, Edinburgh, 1826. In 1801 breeches-maker John Davidson lived close to the High Street on the northern side of the town. On the town's western edge a cotton factory and brewery drew power from the Annan River. Courtesy National Library of Scotland.

His youngest child, William Allan Davidson, my ancestor, was born in 1782 when John was nearing forty. When they first arrived in Annan, John and Mary lived in Summergate, on the southern side, but later moved into the centre of the town where they occupied a house just around the corner from the clockmaker Robert Hodgson. John was probably a bespoke breeches-maker, cutting and sewing each garment to order, but by the end of the century they were all living on the brink of a revolution that would transform the town, and with it, the lives of my family.

In 1801 John was living in a house in the North Burgh of Annan on, or just off, its High Street, and close to the bridge across the Annan River. He shared the house with six other Davidsons: his eldest son, 28-year-old John; John's wife Janet and four-year-old son William; and his unmarried daughters, thirty-year-old Jean, 22-year-old Mary, and Hannah, age unknown but possibly born in the gap between the other two girls, and thus in her mid-twenties.

From the order in which the names appear, John senior, now probably in his early sixties, appears to have been a widower, although I cannot confirm the death of his wife Mary because the local church burial registers have not survived. Alternatively, the Mary who appears in the census is his wife, who would then have been about fifty-eight, and his daughter Mary had already departed the household.

Spanning three generations, with grandparents, adult siblings and a daughter-in-law, the Davidson household was closer to the 'traditional' pattern of rural families than the modern or 'nuclear' ones (dad, mum and the kids) beginning to appear in the towns and cities of the land. It was a workplace as well as a home. John junior may now have been the head of the household, and of the manufacturing business that was apparently being conducted on the premises, with his father now an assistant. In 1806 Hannah, described as a 'cotton spinner', would leave to marry Andrew Broach from Half Morton, a rural parish halfway between Annan and Canonbie. But the other daughters, so far as we know, did not marry.

A conspicuous absentee from the household was my great-great-great-grandfather William Allan Davidson. Where was he? With a wife, three sisters and an ageing father to provide for, his older brother, John junior, may have decided that it was time for William to find his own way in the world. A short distance away on the southern side of the High Street, a William Davidson was living, apparently as a boarder, with Robert Irving, a 'cottoneer', his wife and children. 'Cottoner' or 'cottoneer' was the old word for a person who formed a down or nap on a piece of cloth, but by this time it was also applied generally to workers in the cotton manufacturing industry. In 1785, a water-powered cotton mill, employing about 100 people, opened on a newly constructed millrace tapping water from the Annan River just below the town. Soon the mill was joined by a brewery and then by more mills. When the new century dawned, the old seaport had evolved a modest industrial base. Some of its old industries, like fishing and smuggling, were already in decline. However, for a young man like William Davidson, its opportunities were nothing compared with those in the industrial belt springing up around the old garrison city of Carlisle, thirty kilometres to the south. Sometime in the early years of the new century, he headed there.

A Penetrating Question

Many years ago, I was invited to give a guest lecture to a group of engineering students. The dean of the faculty had decided that their cultural horizons needed broadening and had engaged the art historian Patrick McCaughey to offer a course on 'The Art of the Industrial Revolution'. Patrick, a spellbinding lecturer, regaled them with images of the idyllic English countryside and dark satanic mills. My job was to fill in the economic and social background. I surveyed the transition from water to steam power, the growth of the factory system and the concentration of the industrial workforce in the overcrowded, unsanitary slums of the new industrial cities. At the end of the lecture a puzzled student tentatively raised his hand. 'Why,' he asked, 'did the peasants go to the city?'

A historian could quibble with the student's terminology—did England have a true peasantry?—but not with the point of his question. On the face of it, no rational ploughman or villager would exchange the fresh air of the farm and village for the smoke and squalor of the industrial city. Yet that is what millions of people, including my own forebears, did, and what millions are still doing in many parts of the 'developing world'. Their decision was probably more rational than my student realised, for village life was less romantic than the landscape painters made it look and factory work was usually better paid than agricultural labour. As the poet Robert Davidson noted, the 'peasant' was often 'forced from his native shed'.

Yet there is no denying the significance of the move. When William Davidson left Annan he began a journey that would take his descendants, step by step, from a small port town to an industrial village, to a factory suburb and finally to an industrial metropolis. Eventually, a century later, they would journey to the other side of the world. There was nothing planned about this long journey, anymore than there was about the one that had already brought them from their ancestral homeland in Teviotdale to a farming village in Westmorland. Each step was a one-off response to the map of opportunity at the time, but seen over the *longue durée* the moves fall into a pattern that suggests the operation of powerful unseen forces. We sometimes call these forces 'modernisation'. Modernity, a recent scholar suggests, is an aspiration to be 'up with the times'.

When my student asked why the peasants went to the city, he implied that they made the trip in one generation, knowing what they were relinquishing and what they were embracing. But, as the Davisons' story shows, the journey was usually a much longer one, extending sometimes over several generations and along circuitous as well as direct pathways. It was rare for a 'peasant' who had been reaping corn or tending sheep in the countryside one day to be spinning cotton or working a steam-powered loom the next. Rather than an industrial revolution, we should probably speak of an industrial evolution, for when we look at it in a wider perspective, and through the eyes of the people who lived through it, it seems more like a series of small adjustments than a leap from one way of life to another. At each step along the journey, they became a little more accustomed to the ideas and values that prepared them for the next. Many factors, invisible to us, probably influenced their outlook, including religious and political ones.

William Davidson's move from Annan to Carlisle culminated a journey that began in East Teviotdale a century or more before. Although we cannot read his thoughts, we know that he was already becoming attuned to the values that shaped everyday life in the industrial city. We know this not because of anything he said or wrote but because of something that his family owned. For it was probably then that the Davisons acquired from their neighbour, the clockmaker Robert Hodgson, one of his freestanding long case clocks. It was a significant purchase for it showed that my ancestors not only wanted to tell the time, they also wanted to be up with the times.

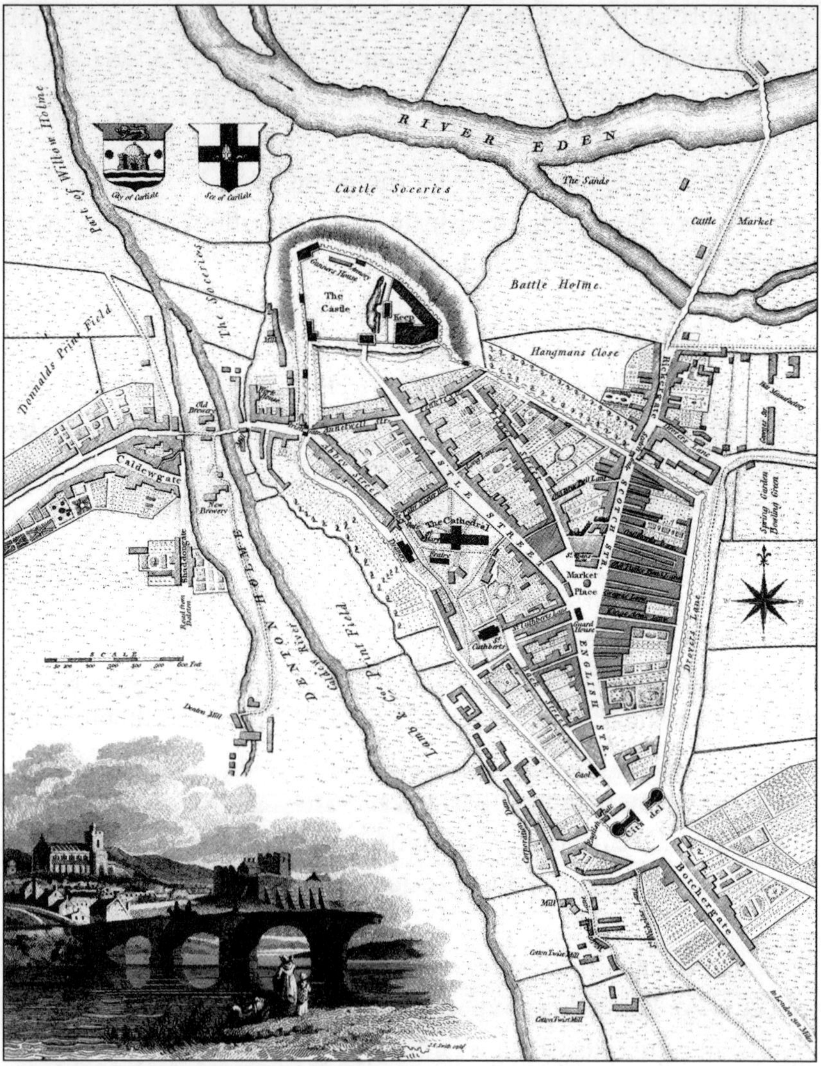

Carlisle, EW Brayley, 1805. Within its medieval walls, pre-industrial Carlisle clusters around the castle, cathedral and marketplace. Courtesy Cumbria Archives Centre, Carlisle.

CHAPTER 4

The Sad Sound of the Factory Bell

When William Davidson arrived in Carlisle it was still a garrison city. For 700 years it had been the last outpost of English rule, its medieval castle and cathedral rising above the ramparts of a strong protective wall. Periodically raiders and soldiers from the north challenged its defences. In 1596, Border reivers climbed ladders propped against the northern wall to snatch their kinsman William Armstrong from the gallows, an escapade celebrated in the famous ballad 'Kinmont Willie'. During the English Civil War, Scottish troops besieged and captured the stronghold in support of their allies, Cromwell's parliamentary forces. The last assault came in 1745 when Bonnie Prince Charlie's Jacobites seized the city, only to relinquish it a few weeks later without a fight. Each assault reinforced Carlisle's loyalty to the English throne. It was a Church and King town.

Gradually the old hostility between the English and the Scots subsided. After the 1707 Act of Union, most of the tolls on 'Outmen and Forroners' trading in the town were abolished, although low-level friction continued for much longer. 'It would be difficult for people nowadays to realise the bitterness of feeling that existed between English and Scotch boys,' an old-timer recalled as late as 1951. Some of the wildness of the Borders permeated Carlisle's plebeian subculture of heavy drinking, gambling and rough sports. In the winter months, when people retreated indoors, the tempo of town life slowed down, but in summer, the season of horseracing, otter hunting and wrestling, it speeded up again. In August, the 'cock-fighting fraternity' took over the streets to celebrate 'St Monday', a long weekend of intoxication and mischief after harvest.

Towards the end of the eighteenth century, the city leapt its walls and spread across the flood plain to the west. By 1780 one-third of its 7800 people were living there. Attracted by the waters of the Caldew River, the first factory—a calico printing works—was established in 1761, and by 1800 dozens of cotton mills, dyeing and bleaching works, flour mills and other industries lined its banks. As industry took off, it prompted an influx of migrants from across the Scottish border and the Irish Sea. Between 1800 and 1840 Carlisle more than tripled its population. William Davidson was part of that influx.

Around its long-established markets for cattle, horses, corn, pork and poultry, Carlisle still followed the old agricultural cycles of sowing, growing, reaping and droving. At the fashionable northern end of town, near the cathedral and castle, it listened for the peal of cathedral bells calling clergy, choristers and the faithful to worship, or for the bugles ordering the castle garrison to the parade ground. But beyond the walls it observed a new calendar and timetable. Each morning, almost drowning out the bells and bugles, a chorus of factory bells and whistles announced the beginning of the working day.

The townscape still bears witness to that transition. Stand in the historic centre of Carlisle, the old market square, and look towards its seventeenth-century town hall, now a tourist information office. Rising over the centre of the square, the point from which distances are measured, is the market cross, a tall ionic column erected by Mayor Joseph Reed in 1682 to replace the original medieval one. From here the city's three main streets lead towards its three historic gates: Scotch Street north through Rickardgate towards the Scottish border, English Street south through Botchergate towards England, and Castlegate Street west through Caldewgate, or the Irish gate, towards Solway Firth and the Irish Sea. Atop the market cross, a crouching lion gazes balefully towards the Scottish border while, just below him, a sundial measures the passage of the sun across the sky. Turn towards the town hall and a more modern timepiece comes into view. In 1800, just as Carlisle's industrial revolution took off, another mayor, John Richardson, installed a new mechanical turret clock in a handsome cupola on its roof.

In a famous essay, 'Time, Work Discipline and Industrial Capitalism', the historian Edward Thompson argued that the Industrial Revolution brought a radical transformation of people's 'inward notation of time'. Time proverbially was money and the industrialists were eager to teach their workers its value by inculcating habits of time-thrift. Public clocks, factory whistles, household clocks and, for those who could afford them, personal watches were their mechanical tutors. As the Industrial Revolution got underway in the late eighteenth century, there was a steep increase in the production of all kinds of timepieces throughout the kingdom. The number of clockmakers in Cumberland more than doubled from nearly thirty in 1740 to sixty in 1780. In 1798 the Carlisle clockmakers boasted that the local textile factories were 'entirely indebted for the state of perfection to which the machinery used therein is now brought to the clock and watch makers, great numbers of whom have, for several years past ... been employed in constructing as well as superintending such machinery'. John Richardson's turret clock and John Davidson's long case model were emblems of this revolution.

I read Edward Thompson's essay soon after it came out—around the time, incidentally, that Aunty Cissie died and left us the family clock. I was excited by his argument but it left me with questions. Did clocks change people's time-consciousness or were they tools for people who had already acquired a new sense of time? How much did the time revolution owe to technology, and how much to more elusive moral and religious forces? In Thompson's account, the change seemed to work mainly from the outside in, as workers were 'habituated' to the external discipline of the clock, the steam-powered machine, the factory timetable and their managers' rewards and punishments. The industrialists, he suggested, had to break their workers' attachment to older time regimes, like the 'natural' cycle of the seasons or the need for occasional release from the tedium of the working week, like 'St Monday'.

Yet the appearance of a clock in a household, a factory or a public square did not necessarily change the behaviour of those who saw or heard it. Industrial workers were not automatons, conditioned like Pavlov's dog to the sound of a ringing bell. Some workers acquired clocks of their own volition as instruments of self-management as well as status symbols. Clocks helped people take control of their time, as well as subjecting them to the temporal demands of others. In equating the Industrial Revolution with the large steam-powered mills of Leeds and Manchester, with their factory whistles, mechanised work rhythm, timetables and time-based pay, Thompson may have underestimated the persistence of other forms of employment based on handwork, 'task-orientation' and performance pay. And while the temporal demands of the industrial workplace had a powerful effect on the lives of everyone in its shadow, clocks surely ordered other aspects of people's lives, such as their domestic, educational, religious and leisure time. These were some of the thoughts buzzing in my mind as I pondered my family's new clock and William's arrival in the industrial city.

A Factory in the Fields

William Davidson appeared, very shortly after the turn of the century, aged in his early twenties, just as several new calico printing works were starting up, and he became a block printer, a trade he would follow for almost fifty years. In September 1805 in St Cuthbert's Church, aged twenty-three, he married 21-year-old Mary Dixon, a local girl whose shoemaking family had been in Carlisle since at least the mid-eighteenth century. On her wedding day Mary was six months' pregnant. Her first child, Ann, named after her mother, died just a few days after birth on 4 February 1806. Three other children followed: Richard, my own ancestor, baptised on Christmas Day 1807; Mary Anne in 1809; and Jane in 1812—all in St Mary's Church.

Thereafter the genealogical trail grows faint. In 1819 a William Davidson appeared at the Carlisle Assizes charged with a violent house robbery in the village of Wigton. From other evidence we know that his family may have lived there for a while. A pair of breeches was among the stolen articles. He was sentenced to death, a penalty later commuted to transportation. The possibility that my great-great-great-grandfather had arrived in Australia as another kind of assisted migrant more than a century before my father excited me for a time. Without an Anzac or a convict in my line, I thought he might boost my Australian credentials. I followed him all the way to New South Wales only to find, from his 1828 certificate of freedom, that the ruffian was too young to be my ancestor.

In the mid-1830s William and Mary resurfaced as inhabitants of High Cummersdale, an industrial village on a hill overlooking the Caldew River about two kilometres west of Carlisle. William was now working as a block printer for McAlpin, Stead & Co. (to be later known as Stead McAlpin) which had recently moved operations from Wigton, twelve miles further west. The McAlpins had migrated from Scotland in the aftermath of the 1746 Battle of Culloden and established a factory known as 'The Stampery' for the production of printed cotton in the late eighteenth century. In 1827 Thomas McAlpin married Mary Stead, the widow of a local collier, an alliance that furnished capital for the company's move to Cummersdale in 1835. According to company tradition, the entire workforce walked from Wigton to Cummersdale, pushing their possessions in hand-carts and wheelbarrows. Men born in Wigton continued to dominate the senior levels of the company's workforce well into the 1860s.

Cummersdale brought a sharp lift in the company's operations. The Caldew River was ideally suited to chemical manufacturing, such as dye works and textile printing. The location was also close to the factories and transport hub on Carlisle's western outskirts, and the facility could draw on a larger pool of labour. The company refitted its building—an old printing works abandoned when its proprietors went bankrupt in 1817—with the latest technology. At Cummersdale, traditional and modern techniques of textile printing happily coexisted. Block printers like William continued to produce limited quantities of fine printed fabric by a method that had hardly changed since the British learned it two centuries earlier from the Indian inventors of chintz and calico. Elsewhere in the complex, industrial workers applied a recently invented technique for printing fabric from designs engraved on a rotating metal cylinder. Powered by a waterwheel, the rotary press printed cloth much faster and more economically than the block printer, although the results did not compare with the handmade product. As the historian SD Chapman notes, 'cost cutting was not the only path to profitability; quality and social cachet could be no less effective'. So, far from being rendered technologically redundant, William Davidson remained a valued employee.

In 2018 I visited Cummersdale, where the Stead McAlpin works amazingly still survive. A retired employee and company archivist, Alan James, produced the early nineteenth-century wages books and demonstrated the techniques of block printing, which were still being practised at Cummersdale when he joined the company in the 1960s. The work called for exceptional 'dexterity and diligence' as the printer applied a wooden block carved with an intricate design and soaked with dye to lengths of calico. To achieve the desired effect, the worker had to apply several layers of colour, one print at a time. Printing a twenty-yard length of cloth might require hundreds of individual impressions and take the worker as much as a week. In winter, when the sun was low in the sky and the working days were short, he often had to work by candlelight. It was risky as well as skilful work, for if the printer made a mistake (colloquially known as a 'Daniel'), he could be fined and banished to the 'Convict Shop', as it was known. Two hundred years later, even modern computer-guided screen-printers are unable to equal the depth and subtle variations of colour achieved by a skilled block printer. Alan James showed me samples of the company's work, including fabric produced by appointment to the Queen to furnish the staterooms at Windsor Castle.

Crucially, William was paid, not by the hour, but by what he produced. The company's wages books show that his earnings fluctuated between nine and thirty shillings a week but averaged around twenty-five shillings, well above those of an agricultural labourer (fifteen shillings) or textile worker (as low as ten shillings a week) and sufficient to accumulate modest savings. He belonged to what people later called 'the aristocracy of labour'.

When William and Mary moved to Cummersdale, their older children—Richard, Mary Anne and Jane—had already left home, but in 1841 their household included two younger children, thirteen-year-old James and fourteen-year-old John, described by the census-taker as William and Mary's children. Their appearance was a surprise. Mary would have been forty-three when the youngest of the boys was born, a fourteen-year gap since the birth of Jane—a long hiatus in a woman's reproductive history. I unsuccessfully scoured the local birth registers for confirmation of their parenthood. Could William have been transported to Australia, after all, and returned to father a second family? The records seemed to belie it. Could Mary have suffered a long sequence of miscarriages before suddenly bearing two sons as she approached menopause? Such late pregnancies are unusual but not unknown. Could the first Mary even have died before William began a second family with a new wife, coincidentally named Mary? That seemed unlikely, since the census-taker put her in her mid-fifties in 1841.

Part of the answer to the conundrum lay back in Wigton where the family had lived before coming to Cummersdale in 1835. James, born there in December 1827, was the son, not of Mary and William, but of their unmarried nineteen-year-old daughter Mary Anne and an unknown father. John, the other boy, would later claim to have been born in Wigton but I have found no record of his birth or parents. He seems always to have been regarded as William and Mary's son and perhaps, despite Mary's relatively advanced age, he really was. He began working alongside his father as a calico printer in the 1840s and married twenty-year-old Harriet Hurst in 1853. Harriet was born in Manchester to a block cutter who also lived in the village and probably worked alongside William. John named his first-born son William Allan after his father and had four more children before dying aged only forty-five in 1871, leaving Harriet to bring up the youngest on a charwoman's pay. Some of their descendants lived on in the village working for Stead McAlpin well into the twentieth century.

Cummersdale was a relatively self-contained, semi-rural and patriarchal community. 'The situation is healthy and beautiful in the extreme [and] the labourers bear all the marks of robust industry,' a visitor remarked in 1836. The print works stood among open fields and farms and the workers enjoyed enough space to grow some of their own food—in 1846 William sent a 'very fine sample of new potatoes grown, unprotected, in the open air' to his local newspaper. In summer, they knocked off work for a few days to join their fellow workers hunting otters in the Caldew River.

The company's proprietors, the McAlpin family, lived in the village until the death of the last active hands-on manager in 1869. Many, if not most, village children grew up to work with their parents in the print works or at the nearby cotton mill. William's grandsons, William and John, were only eight years old when a doctor employed by the company certified their readiness to begin work. As head of the household, John assumed the role he learned from his father, teaching his sons the calico printing business and supervising their work. The family's earnings depended, as we have seen, on what they produced rather than on how many hours they worked. They were 'task-oriented' rather than 'time-driven', in Edward Thompson's terms. Yet, rather than abolishing the role of the manager, the effect of piece rates was to devolve it from the company to the head of the family. William and John were teachers and managers as well as fathers. Instead of listening each morning for the sound of the factory bell, the Davisons listened for the metallic ding of Robert Hodgson's long case clock and the voices of William and Mary summoning them downstairs to begin their working day.

Sometime in the early nineteenth century, perhaps after the death of his father John in 1817, William probably brought the clock from Annan to Carlisle. It would have been easier and safer to transport it by water across Solway Firth and up the new canal than by the bumpy overland route through Gretna Green. Quite apart from its utility in ordering his industrious household, it was also a symbol of his family's social status. A clock was 'the certain indication of prosperity and personal respectability on the part of the working man', the statistician GR Porter observed. It was also, and increasingly, a way of synchronising the family's activities with the timetables of the wider community.

In May 1843, William and his family would have witnessed the arrival of the first locomotive on the line from Carlisle to Wigton as it passed near Stead McAlpin's mill. Mr McAlpin fired a cannon salute and children from the nearby Dalston Sunday School sang a celebratory anthem:

> Sound the loud timbrel! Auspicious the day!
> Science Triumphant! Another railway!
> With grateful emotions admire the grand scheme,
> Of music and song let it be your high theme.
> Commerce be prospered, and Trade now revive!
> The poor with the rich be happy and thrive!

Cummersdale got its own station and locals could now travel to Carlisle or Wigton more speedily and punctually.

The locomotive, with its plume of smoke, hiss of steam and cheerful whistle, signalled that the era of water power and the factory village was drawing to an end. Industry was centralising in the towns where steam-powered mills, canals and railways drew thousands of workers into crowded streets and tenements. The railway and its timetable also brought a new consciousness of measured time, as outlying villages were linked telegraphically with the life of the towns. 'Space is killed by the railways and we are left with time alone,' the German poet Heinrich Heine wrote in the same year. The whole of England, another writer suggested, would eventually become like one great city.

Caldewgate

By 1843, William's oldest son Richard, a shoemaker, was living with his wife Elizabeth née Downie and their two sons, William and Thomas, in Church Street, Caldewgate, an industrial suburb just beyond the wall on Carlisle's western edge. Dominating the local skyline was the soaring chimney of Dixon Brothers cotton mill, the largest single enterprise in town. Dixon's factory hands lived in the newly built terrace houses that lined the long, straight streets off nearby Shaddongate. Although they may look small and grimly uniform to us, these single-family row houses, each with its own front door, were models of up-to-date working-class accommodation.

Richard and his family, however, were living in a jumble of older courts and alleys close to the canal and the river. They shared their dwelling, in a complex of apartments and small workrooms, with two other families: the stonemason Robert Nicholson, his wife and seven-year-old daughter, and a handloom weaver, Edward Berry, together with his widowed mother Jane and three children. Caldewgate had boomed during the first stage of the Industrial Revolution when advances in spinning technology outpaced those in weaving, providing plenty of well-paid employment for handloom weavers taking in work from the nearby spinning mills. In those days, an old-timer

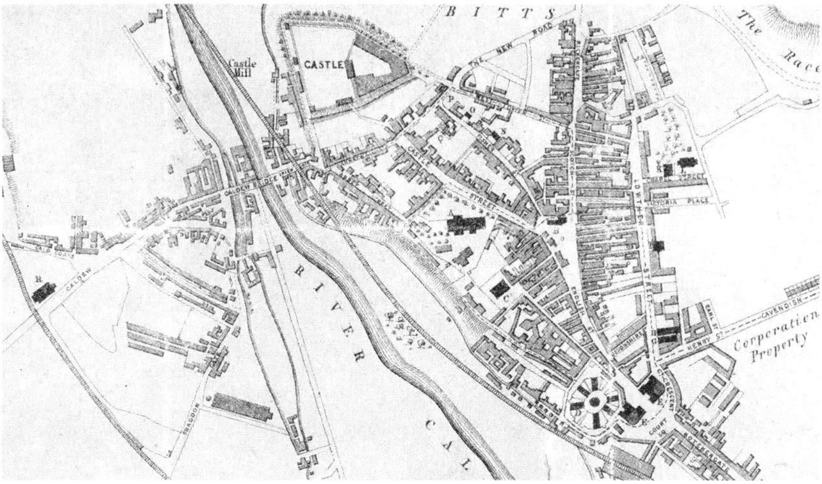

Detail from Asquiths' Board of Health *Map of Carlisle 1853* clearly shows the canal, railway line and long terraces of workers' dwellings in Caldewgate on the southwest side of the town. Richard Davison and his family lived amidst the courts and alleys close to the Caldew Bridge. Courtesy Cumbria Archives Centre, Carlisle.

recalled nostalgically, every weaver had a watch in his pocket and every house was 'well furnished with a clock in elegant mahogany or fancy face'.

But with the coming of the power loom in the 1820s, the weavers' trade began a long decline. They were among the first victims of what we now call 'technological redundancy' and 'deskilling'. Mechanisation did not entirely destroy their trade but it turned them into an impoverished and resentful proletariat. Some protested their plight by smashing the new machines, a movement known as Luddism, after its mythical leader Ned Ludd. By the mid-1830s, when a royal commissioner, Mr Muggeridge, visited the town, the weavers' spokesman, John Barr, claimed that they were working for up to ninety-six hours a week for piecework wages averaging just 9s 3d. The weavers' employer, George Dixon, doubted anyone could work such hours. But the weavers insisted: 'We invite you to come to our houses and see our wretched, unhappy homes.'

The few middle-class people who accepted the weavers' invitation were appalled by what they found. 'Many of the streets and smaller thoroughfares ... are imperfectly paved and swept,' reported Robert Rawlinson, a doctor who investigated the sanitary condition of Caldewgate in 1850. 'The lanes and the courts are in a most objectionable state, containing almost invariably pigsties, with open privies, dunghills, stagnant pools, the receptacles of every kind of filth.' Another local doctor, John Heysham, had compiled the first statistical tables of mortality in the country: they showed that Carlisle was among the deadliest cities in England, with a child mortality rate about fifty per cent higher than the national average. The whole city was unhealthy but Botchergate, a densely settled area in the old town, and Caldewgate, the industrial suburb on its western outskirts, were the worst hotbeds of killer diseases like dysentery and diarrhoea.

Remarkably, all of Richard and Elizabeth's children survived into adulthood. By 1851, the family had grown to seven, as nine-year-old Hannah, six-year-old John and four-year-old James joined fifteen-year-old William, now apprenticed to his father, and twelve-year-old Thomas, a 'scholar'. The census now described Elizabeth as a 'shoemaker wife' and the household was completed by a lodger—another shoemaker, 39-year-old James Blake—in what was almost certainly a family shoemaking business. Blake would later leave and be replaced by Richard's widowed uncle, William Dixon, another shoemaker. Most of their neighbours—thirty-two of the fifty-eight household heads in Byron Street—were weavers or other textile workers, often Scottish or Irish immigrants whose wives and children also worked as bobbin-winders or weavers. While the press and politicians agonised over the tragic plight of the weavers, the pay and working hours of other local handworkers, like shoemakers, tailors and saddlers, may have been little better. If families like the Davisons got by, it was by everyone in the family doing their bit.

In such a household, the line between home and work was quite hazy. The English had always valued domestic privacy more highly than other Europeans. Inspired by the evangelical revival and its sentimental cult of 'Home, Sweet Home', they pursued it with fervour. Houses in the Davisons' neighbourhood were designed for both business and domestic purposes, but 'dwelling rooms' were usually clearly divided from 'weaving shops' and workshops—sometimes vertically, with workshops below and dwellings above, or horizontally, with shops or workshops facing the street and dwellings behind.

Did families also try to separate work time from family time? Did Elizabeth perform all the domestic chores in addition to some shoemaking, or did Richard and the children share them? Did the older children, Thomas and Hannah, help to look after four-year-old James and six-year-old John while their mother worked? Did father and mother work day and evening shifts, as many parents in our 21st-century workforce are obliged to do? Did Thomas and John pitch in to help at busy times or, as 'scholars', were they exempted from shoemaking and household tasks? If Uncle William was a partner in the family business, did he draw a separate wage and pay board or did the family have some other method of dividing costs and earnings?

We cannot answer these questions except by reference to the experience of other, similar families. Middle-class households liked to order their days more precisely, with regular times for eating, working, walking and praying. Some respectable working-class families were beginning to follow their example. The daily struggle for survival may not have allowed the Davisons too much discretion in how they used their time. However, the appearance of a long case clock in such a household—if we assume for a moment that Richard inherited the family clock from William—may well have signified an intention on the part of the family to divide its days, as well as its living spaces, in a more deliberate way.

Had the Davisons made a bad bargain in exchanging the life of the village for the poverty and pestilence of the town? Many of their contemporaries thought so. In 1839, in the midst of a parliamentary debate on the factory acts, the member for Carlisle, local landowner Sir James Graham, lamented the change 'from "the breezy call of incense-breathing morn" to the sad sound of the factory bell—from the neat thatched cottage, the blooming garden, and the village green, to some damp cellar in the noisy alley of a crowded city'. Graham probably romanticised country life. Not every agricultural labourer enjoyed a thatched cottage, or if he did it may have been crowded and unsanitary. Graham's concern for the time-worn factory hand seemed hypocritical when it became known that he had sold off some of his own estate at Netherby to a factory owner and was apparently 'eager to encourage the music of the factory bell even within earshot of his own dormitory'. Yet, while knowing only a little of their lives, William Davidson, growing his potatoes and earning twenty-five shillings a week as a block printer at Cummersdale, looks to have enjoyed a better life than his son and grandchildren living amidst the poverty, overcrowding and disease of Caldewgate. Historians have endlessly debated whether the Industrial Revolution raised or lowered workers' living standards; my own family history, at least to the 1850s, seems to support the pessimists.

Through the early nineteenth century, Caldewgate simmered with political discontent. In 1819, in the wake of the infamous Peterloo Massacre in Manchester, the weavers carried their banner 'Liberty or Death' through the streets of the town. In 1830, during the political ferment leading to the passage of the Great Reform Act, they marched again into the market square and set fire to an effigy of the Duke of Wellington. At the height of the Chartist movement in 1839, a Female Radical Association based in Caldewgate vowed 'to follow our husbands, our fathers, our sons and our brothers into the battlefield, to cheer and comfort them in the hour of danger, bind up their wounds and instigate them to fresh deeds of valour'.

Richard cannot have been immune from the political excitement of his community. The radicals' reading room in John Street, the nerve centre of local political activity, was just around the corner from his home. His fellow shoemakers were often among the leaders of radical politics. As self-employed artisans, dealing directly with a largely working-class clientele, shoemakers were famously independent and outspoken. 'The solitude of their employment developing their internal resources' made them 'a stern, uncompromising and reflecting race', the journalist Henry Mayhew noted. The relatively sedentary nature of their work allowed time and opportunity for thinking, reading and political conversation, while their workshops were convenient meeting places for local activists. Compared with factory workers, their time was more their own, as shown by their reputed willingness to observe 'St Monday' and other holidays. I would be pleased if Richard had been among the radicals but there is no evidence that he was.

A New Direction

In the early 1850s politics in Carlisle changed direction. With the collapse of Chartism, working people turned away from revolution and towards schemes of moral reform, self-help, cooperation and emigration. 'You must either change your employment, or … direct your attention to emigration,' the Scottish MP Joseph Hume warned the weavers, noting the opportunities opened up in Australia by the discovery of gold. If they could not change their society, they could either change themselves or move to a place where their circumstances were better.

On New Year's Day 1851, the shoemaker Richard Davidson, until now a silent actor in this story, rose to speak 'two or three words' at a soirée held by the Carlisle Total Abstinence Society in the Assembly Room of the Carlisle Athenaeum. The local paper reported them and, thanks to the miracle of digitisation, I have found them amidst the millions of other words now captured in the British Library's newspaper archive. 'There was once a time,' Richard began self-referentially,

> when he thought he could not do without intoxicating drink. At that time he was a pest to society, but since he had signed the Temperance pledge he had become of some small use to society. He had been 24 years in one employment, and for 19 years of that

> time he had been in the habit of getting a pint of ale in one day, and sometimes two or three; but during the last five years he felt he could work with greater ease to himself without drink, and that he was a better workman, a better husband and father, and a better member of society. Since he had signed the pledge he had been trying to do what little good he could for society, and in forwarding their cause. Thank God, he had three sons sitting near him that evening, who, perhaps, if he had not joined the Temperance Society, would not have been present (Applause).

As surprising as the discovery of my great-great-grandfather's words was the familiarity of his message, which could almost have been spoken by my father and grandfather, both lifelong teetotallers. It seemed as though I had stumbled on the origins of a family tradition.

Richard had taken a radical stand, one that may have cut him off from the company of most of his workmates and neighbours. 'Drinking usages were woven into the very fabric of working class life,' the historian John Harrison observes. An apprentice signing his indentures treated the master to a drink, and again when he completed each stage in his training. 'Quarts of Beer and bottles of whisky were daily consumed on the premises', with employers generally turning a blind eye, according to one local observer. Weekend sprees often extended to Tuesday or Wednesday morning, while children were called upon to bring 'refreshers' during the rest of the week. In 1847 *Slater's Directory* listed about 150 taverns and public houses, thirty-two beer shops and thirteen wine merchants in Carlisle, about half a dozen of them within a few steps of Richard's house, including the Joiner's Arms, which still stands on Church Street. If he was not to frequent the public house, what company was still open to Richard and his family? Whether he was religious himself or not, he was thrown into the company of other abstainers, mostly chapel folk together with a number of secular radicals, and into the

The West End Temperance Hall, endowed by biscuit manufacturer JD Carr, and the nearby Joiners Arms pub competed for the allegiance of Caldewgate's working class.

round of temperance soirées, tea meetings and lectures that were their countercultural alternative to the dominant drinking culture.

In giving up alcohol, Richard was renouncing the commonest form of relief from the fatigue and stress of working-class life. Taking the pledge was often, although not always, associated with religious conversion. Richard thanked God that his sons would lead a better life for it, but his teetotalism had an essentially rational ethical basis: it would make him 'a better workman, a better husband and father, and a better member of society'. The 'strong-mindedness' required to keep the pledge would make him thriftier, more punctual, more diligent and industrious, and even, perhaps, more prosperous. Another temperance advocate rammed his message home by showing off his new black suit, raising his pocket watch into the air and asking rhetorically, 'Who wouldn't be a teetotaller?' In Carlisle, local employers, like the Quaker and biscuit manufacturer JD Carr, encouraged the movement by giving preference in employment to teetotallers and by sponsoring the construction of the nearby Caldewgate Temperance Hall.

I wonder what Richard meant when he said that, if he hadn't taken the pledge, his sons might not have been sitting with him that evening. I don't think he simply meant that they would not have come to the meeting; he was referring to the devastating effects of drink on family life. All around him in Caldewgate, there were reminders in the form of deserted wives and abandoned children. 'There,' he was saying, 'but for the grace of God and the pledge, go I.' But while taking the pledge may have benefited Richard and his family, it was not just an individualistic form of 'self-help'; he was also doing 'what little good he could for society'.

Of the three sons sitting with Richard that evening, the eldest, fifteen-year-old William, had already joined his father in the shoemaking business. But in 1846, when Richard signed the pledge, his second son Thomas, my great-grandfather, had recently been admitted as a probationer chorister at Carlisle Cathedral. Nine months later he became a full choirboy—one of just ten boys so chosen—a position that entitled him to a small stipend and an education in the Grammar School adjoining the cathedral. Were these two events—Richard's pledge and Thomas's admission to the cathedral choir—somehow connected? Was Thomas's education a reward for the father's pledge, or the pledge perhaps a condition for the son's admission to the choir? Or were both perhaps connected to the father's religious conversion? I do not know, but taken together, they produced the most significant change in the family's fortunes, at least until my grandfather's decision to emigrate.

Every morning now, as the other boys in Byron Street began work at the weaver's loom or trudged towards Dixon's Mill, Thomas climbed the hill from Caldewgate, mounted the stone staircase that pierces the city wall and entered the quiet precincts of the cathedral yard. Rather than answering the call of the factory bell, he listened for the striking of the cathedral clock. Manufactured by the Yorkshire clockmaker Henry Hindley and installed in 1760, this fine tower clock was connected by wires to the outer rim of the cathedral's largest and most sonorous bell. It was the master clock for all other clocks in the town, audible well beyond the precincts of the cathedral yard. In 1841, the dean ordered that it should be set to London, rather than local, time, a difference of twelve minutes and five seconds, in order to better regulate the running of trains and coaches.

After washing his hands and donning his surplice at the door, Thomas entered the Fratry where the cathedral's long-serving choirmaster, Henry Ford, administered the 'full and severe training' required of a chorister. As well as normal school lessons, the chorister's day included morning and evening services and rehearsals. Thomas would become familiar with the masters of English choral music—Purcell, Handel, Samuel Wesley, Gibbons and Boyce—and, on two occasions, participate in performances to honour the visiting monarch, Queen Victoria.

Thomas was a diligent student, winning certificates for his 'industry and good conduct' but no speech night prizes. The record of his

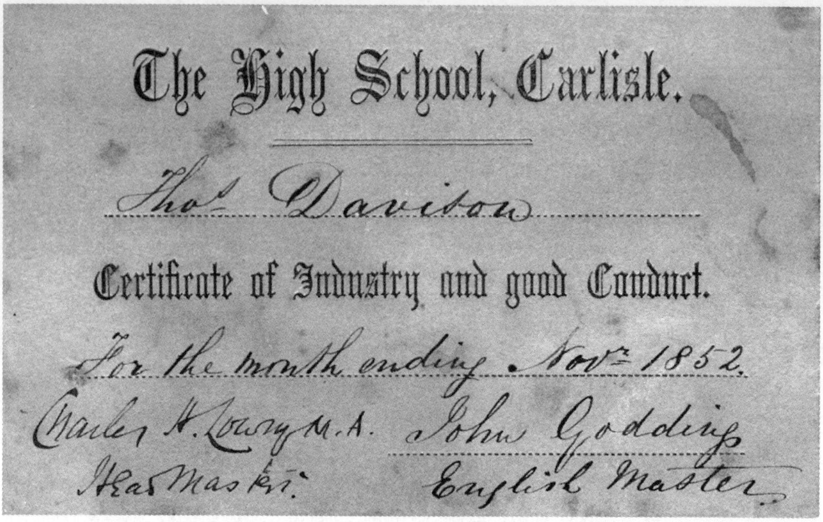

The High School, Carlisle.

Thos. Davison

Certificate of Industry and good Conduct.

For the month ending Novr 1852.

Charles H. Lowry M.A. John Godding

Head Master. English Master

In return for his service as a cathedral chorister, Thomas Davison became a diligent pupil at the Carlisle High School. Tom Davison Collection.

younger brother John, who also joined the choir in the mid-1850s, was spottier, judging by entries in the attendance roll:

> Davidson behaved very badly in choir as usual, not singing and inciting his neighbours to play.
> Davidson laughing during service.
> Davidson ½ hour late.
> Davidson slovenly.
> Davidson late and inattentive.
> Davidson's behavior is becoming intolerable.

In 1858 a precentor at the cathedral was dismissed for his unpunctuality, among other offences. He disputed the decision, citing the notorious unreliability of the cathedral clock.

On the day his voice broke, Thomas was obliged to leave the choir. The Dean of the Cathedral, Archibald Tait, a future archbishop of Canterbury, shook his hand, presented him with a cheque for two guineas, and urged him to be 'true and just in all his dealings'.

The dean's golden handshake lived long in Thomas's memory and entered family tradition: it was almost the only thing I knew about him until I began to write this book.

Tait, a young Scotsman of liberal outlook, had been educated at Balliol College, Oxford, where I would one day study myself. He was troubled by the social gulf between Carlisle's industrial elite and its poverty-stricken working class. In a public lecture, he reminded his middle-class audience that

> It was a very different thing to rise in time for the factory bell at five o'clock on a cold winter morning, to hasten to the factory there to spend the greater part of the day, [than] to live the quiet, easy life which the generality of those present were privileged to enjoy.

The rich also had their cares, he acknowledged, but they should not disdain the poor's lack of religion and refinement until they 'saved [them] from the misery and want in which they were now plunged'. Tait had modernised the Grammar School by introducing commercial subjects and he resisted attempts by the factory masters to make it more socially exclusive. He insisted, against the will of the headmaster, that choristers, previously taught separately from other pupils, were entitled to a full grammar school education. (In practice, it was modified for the choristers by substituting drawing lessons for Greek and Latin.) Education and emigration, Tait believed, were the great remedies for poverty. 'The more we could prevail upon [the weaving population] to put their children to school and to send them to work elsewhere, the more we could remove them from the dangers which now beset them,' he insisted. Thomas Davison and his descendants would take the lesson to heart.

Its impact was reinforced by the sad events that followed. In 1856 five of Tait's children, all daughters between the ages of two and ten, died from scarlet fever. The entire country, from the Queen down, was united in grief. Sympathisers collected donations for the beautiful memorial window that now lights the northern transept of the cathedral. Seventy years later, Thomas still treasured the memorial card the Davisons received from the bereaved family. Not long before he died, he renewed his link with the Taits by writing to Edith, the archbishop's last surviving daughter, now the widow of another English primate, Randal Davidson, enclosing the memorial card as a token of his undying gratitude to her father.

A week after Thomas finished school, Richard arranged for him to be apprenticed as a tinplate worker with his uncle, 'an old-established ironmonger'. Tinplate may seem a humble, even contemptible material to us. 'Tinny' and 'brummy' were synonyms for cheap and nasty—'brummy' coming from the nickname ('Brummagen') of the capital of the metal trades, Birmingham. Yet in Thomas's time tinplate had some of the glamour associated a century later with plastic. Light, cheap, impervious to rust, easily cut, folded, shaped and soldered, it was used for everything from canning food and roofing houses to making kettles, saucepans, baking tins and wheelbarrows. It gave working people utensils previously available only to those who could afford silver or copper. It could be printed and etched to remarkable decorative effect. The colourful tin boxes that packaged Carr's biscuits made the company famous nationally and internationally.

One apparent effect of Thomas's education was to standardise his family's name. In previous generations they, and those who named them in documents like parish registers and censuses, used the names Davidson and Davison almost randomly, presumably because they were unlettered. Only towards the end of his life did Richard seem to settle on Davison but Thomas used it consistently for the rest of his life. Davison was, and is, more common than Davidson south of the border, so its adoption was possibly also a subtle declaration of the family's English rather than Scottish identity.

With a grammar school education Thomas might perhaps have expected to enter some higher trade or profession, but in mid-Victorian Carlisle such opportunities required family connections more than education. In working with tinplate he was following in a family tradition of handwork. Like his great-grandfather the breeches-maker, his grandfather the textile printer and his father the shoemaker, he was taking materials that came to him in sheet form (cloth, leather, metal) and by his skill in measuring, cutting, shaping, joining and polishing, turning them into saleable articles. A boy needed to be good with his hands, and know a bit of arithmetic and solid geometry, to excel in these trades. An ability to read and write well might lift him to a supervisory job. But in the 1840s, the old skills of handwork were rapidly being made redundant by the advent of ingenious machines. Thomas had joined a modern, expanding industry, but would he rise with it or would it lure him in only to cast him off, like the handloom weavers of Caldewgate?

Thomas Davison and his family lived in Ladywood, an area of working-class row housing midway between the villas and spacious gardens of Edgbaston, lower left, and the factories wedged between the railways and Birmingham canal, right. Detail from Birmingham (West) Ordnance Survey 1887. Courtesy National Library of Scotland.

CHAPTER 5

The Workshop of the World

ONE OF THE great legends of English history is the story of Dick Whittington, the country boy who set off for London with his cat and rose to be its lord mayor. It celebrates the popular belief that a young man has to be prepared to move on to get on. As the Industrial Revolution gathered pace, thousands of young men were on the move, often gravitating, first, to the nearest large town, then to a provincial city, and later, perhaps, to London or the colonies. Trade unions, including the tinplate workers, pledged to assist travellers, or so-called 'tramping journeymen', with short-term accommodation and financial support while they looked for work, provided they agreed to move on if no work was available locally. As soon as he had completed his apprenticeship, Thomas Davison began to look beyond Carlisle. He moved first in 1861 to Manchester but in 1864, when the American Civil War interrupted supplies of cotton to the local textile industry, he moved again, this time to the mecca of the metal trades, Birmingham.

Carlisle and Manchester were among the 'shock cities' of the Industrial Revolution, convulsed by conflict between their wealthy mill owners and an impoverished proletariat of factory hands and weavers. Birmingham, however, with its mixed industrial base of small firms and skilled operatives, was a more complex and open society. 'The Workshop of the World' made everything from billycans to bicycles, from guns to electrical generators. It grew more steadily and for longer than the textile towns, offering more openings to talent and more pathways to advancement. Its culture, the historian GM Young observes, was 'more experimental, adventurous [and] diverse'. Relations between masters and men were closer and, usually if not always, more harmonious.

On 21 October 1864 Thomas began work at the Granville Street works of J. H. Hopkins and Sons. He had learned his trade in Carlisle the old-fashioned way, with compass, set square, mallet and soldering iron. But Hopkins's factory, located close to the industrial core of the city, near the railway and canal junctions, was a miracle of mechanisation, utilising steam machinery and pressure-plate presses for spinning, stamping and burnishing a wide range of hollow-ware. Thomas had joined one of the city's rising enterprises and over the following thirty-five years he rose with it, ascending from journeyman to foreman and eventually to manager.

A fortnight after his arrival, he joined the Birmingham Operative Tin-Plate Workers' Society. The society went back to 1812 in Birmingham but had only recently been revived after a period in the doldrums. Soon after Thomas arrived, the tinplate workers, along with the rest of the country, were swept up in the campaign for parliamentary reform. The 1832 Reform Act had left many skilled and respectable workingmen without a vote. Birmingham, led by its Liberal MP John Bright, demanded a reform of the borough franchise to include all householders. Being master of one's own house was their test of respectability and independence. Towards the end of 1866, as the campaign intensified, the society prepared to play a more active political role. It designed and purchased a new banner in anticipation of the 'monster' trades demonstration planned for the following Easter weekend. Its arms depicted a pair of workers dressed in leather aprons, bibs, paper caps and rolled shirtsleeves, one carrying a mallet and the other a pair of compasses, above the motto 'United to Support but Not Combined to Injure'. A 'splendid brass band' was engaged and four men were paid five shillings each to carry the banner. The Birmingham tinplate workers, unlike their brothers in Wolverhampton, apparently did not attend the first reform demonstration in August 1866, but by Easter 1867, with the fate of the reform bill in the balance, they were eager to join the struggle.

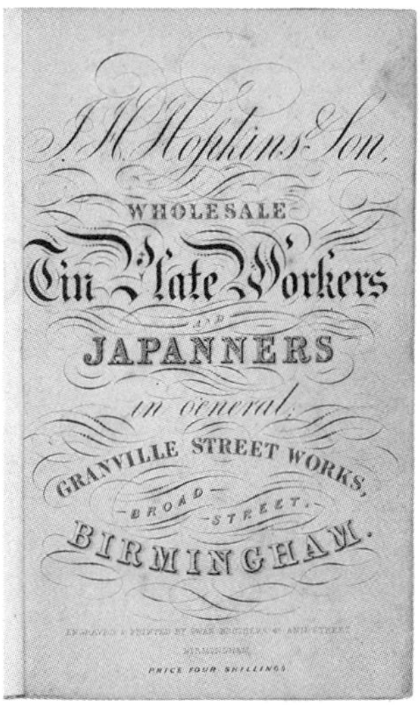

JH Hopkins and Son Catalogue illustrates the astonishing range of tinplate, both useful and decorative, produced by the firm during Thomas Davison's time as manager of its Granville Street works. Courtesy Te Papa/National Museum of New Zealand.

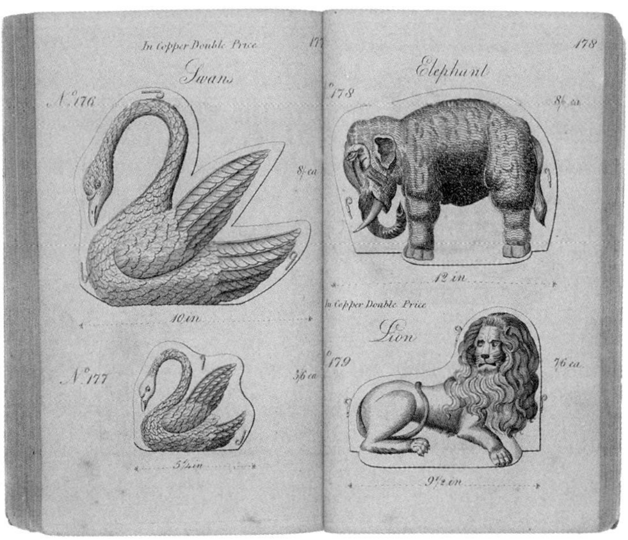

Birmingham's tradesmen assembled, in eight divisions, near the Bullring and marched in a north-westerly direction, skirting Ladywood, towards Brook Fields, an expanse of open country on the edge of town. The sight of the assembled trade societies, with their bands and banners, 'creep[ing] along among the living sea of human beings, like quaintly-decorated leviathans', was an impressive demonstration of the latent power of Birmingham's skilled working class. Thomas and his fellow tinplate workers marched in the Sixth Division, along with the button-makers, burnishers, brass cock founders, bedstead-makers, gunmakers, grinders, riveters, polishers and other representatives of the city's diverse metal trades. At Brook Fields, a crowd estimated at between 150 000 and 200 000—too large for a single speaker to address—formed around eight platforms mounted on wagons, where orators, including John Bright, Mayor George Dixon and the influential nonconformist clergyman RW Dale, voiced their first article of belief: 'The only true and permanent basis for a just and true representation of the people is registered residential manhood suffrage, protected by the ballot.'

The words 'registered residential' may have been as important to men like Thomas Davison as the words 'manhood suffrage', for when the Second Reform Act was passed four months later, the debate largely turned on how to enfranchise the stable and respectable working class without opening the door to the shiftless and disreputable. There was uncertainty about whether rents could be 'compounded' to include the poor rates paid on behalf of the tenant by the landlord: in Birmingham about two-thirds of tenants paid their rates in this way. And because many workingmen were obliged to move in search of work, or at the whim of their landlord, not everyone who qualified as a householder met the twelve months' residence qualification. In Birmingham it was said that the Liberal Caucus, which appointed overseers, ensured that applicants for registration were seldom refused. In England the size of an electorate roughly doubled as a result of the 1867 Act but in Birmingham it almost tripled. Even so, in Ladywood, Thomas's ward, less than half of all householders (4087 out of 8689) were enrolled and only three-quarters of enrolled voters (approximately 3000) actually voted in the 1868 general election, when John Bright and his running mate George Dixon outpolled the Conservatives more than four to one.

Thomas had played a small part in winning his fellow workingmen the right to vote, but I doubt that he voted himself in 1868. Around this time, aged thirty, he married Mary Shepherd, seven years his junior and the only daughter of railway labourer William Shepherd, from Scotby near Carlisle. I don't know exactly when or where they married, or set up house, for no record of it appears in either church or civil registration records. When Thomas left Carlisle, Mary was only fifteen and acting as housekeeper for her widowed father. She could easily have spent the rest of her life that way, as her own daughter, Cissie, was to do. But in 1868 William, her father, married Sarah Beatty, a fifty-year-old widow with two children, freeing—or perhaps even encouraging—Mary, now twenty-three, to leave home. Thomas appears to have waited until he had established himself in Birmingham and Mary had secured the blessing of her father before they married. By the time of the election in November 1868, however, it is unlikely that they had been married and living in their own house long enough—since November 1867—to get him on the roll, even if the local authorities were sympathetic.

If he had cast a vote, and we had been able to attend the polls, we could probably have discovered whom he voted for. The 1868 general election was the last held before the adoption in 1872 of the secret ballot, a reform long advocated by the Chartists and won in the Australian colonies more than twenty years earlier. After 1872 voters no longer had to declare their preference before their fellow electors, with the inevitable bribery and coercion that entailed, but could exercise their choice in the privacy of their own conscience. In 1868, however, so strong was local sentiment in Ladywood in favour of the Radicals that it would have been a brave man who publicly stood against them.

The Code of Respectability

Thomas had already begun to play a more active political role when he was elected, in 1868, aged thirty, as president of the Operative Tin-Plate Workers' Society. His grammar school education and astute management as steward of the union's finances may have brought him to the fore. In the early 1870s he led a campaign for an increase in the prices paid to workmen for piecework in the industry. Like his father and grandfather, Thomas was himself a pieceworker, paid by what he produced rather than by the hours he put in. Each worker, therefore, was a little factory, a form of production that combined elements of both individual enterprise and cooperation, and generated a distinctive form of unionism.

In October 1872 Thomas addressed a meeting of union and non-union workers in Birmingham's Temperance Hall. Leaning over the rail of the platform, he posed a rhetorical question:

> What was unity? This which we talk so much about, and to which so much importance is attached? … Unity is that feeling which draws the manhood of this country together as one man. The result of which is the strength and stability of the Empire. Unity is that happy feeling that we have in our homes, and brings about the possibilities of the family circle. And it is as everyone present at this meeting individually realises, and puts it to good use in a collective form, that so shall the bread-winners of the Tin-plate Workers' families reap the benefits that proceed from that principle.

In applying that principle industrially, he argued, the tinplate workers and their families would come to enjoy its benefits domestically.

A wider union of family, firm, nation and Empire rested on an implied social contract between masters and men. It drew on a distinctive local tradition reflected in other more famous Birmingham political institutions, such as Thomas Attwood's Political Union and

On the Operative Tin Plate Workers' Society's banner Unity, symbolised by the fasces or bound sticks, is flanked by the figures of Hope, left, and Justice, right, under the all-seeing eye of Providence, and encircled by the Society's reassuring motto: 'United to Support but not Combined to Injure'. Courtesy People's History Museum Manchester.

Joseph Chamberlain's Birmingham Caucus. The historian Trygve Tholfsen summarises its key features:

> The respectable artisan was expected to display the appropriate virtues to his social superiors, who were to extend every assistance and to recognise his achievement. He was to be civil and deferential in his relations with the middle classes; thrifty and self-reliant in his economic activity; scrupulously non-proletarian in his observance of the moral code; zealous in the pursuit of education and intellectual self-improvement; decorous and rational in demeanour and behaviour. His reward was the coveted cachet of respectability, which could be conferred only from above.

The rules of the Operative Tin Plate Workers' Society pledged its members to follow a decent, honourable and sober life. They undertook to give due notice before quitting their employment, finish off work before they departed, work for only one employer at a time, and get home in the evening by seven o'clock during winter and nine in summer. A member who lost his job through drunkenness or wilful misconduct lost the right to assistance from his brother unionists.

JH Hopkins, founder of the Hopkins family business, was a Baptist, and a supporter of the Baptist Missionary Society and the Religious Tract Society. His sons, in a pattern often replicated among the industrial bourgeoisie, became more worldly and conservative as they became richer. In the 1850s John Head Hopkins had lived in Ladywood, close to his works, but by the 1860s he had moved to a fine house in Edgbaston, the elegant villa suburb carved from the estate of Lord Calthorpe. His elder son John Satchell Hopkins, who inherited the management of the firm, and who was the brain behind its modernisation in the 1860s and 1870s, became Anglican and Conservative, while younger son Alfred was a progressive Liberal with interests in science and art. By the 1870s they all lived within a few blocks of each other in Edgbaston.

Yet, while they had left Ladywood behind, the Hopkins family continued to honour the old compact between masters and men. 'Our firm is of opinion, and has been during all these fifteen years, that a unionist workman is on average well worth 10 percent more than his non-unionist fellow,' Alfred declared. 'The fact of his being a unionist is a guarantee of his steadiness. In our trade the unionists are a highly respectable body of men, thoroughly trustworthy, and I believe excellent examples of the British workman. I have never had the slightest difficulty or trouble with them.'

In 1875 Thomas Davison led negotiations with the employers and with brother tinplate unionists in Wolverhampton to achieve a ten per cent increase in the prices paid to workmen. It was, as we would now say, a win-win result: Thomas had won the gratitude of his fellow workers and the esteem of his employer. Soon he was made a foreman, a promotion that required him, under the union's rules, to resign his membership. He probably needed that promotion. By 1871 Thomas and Mary were living in Rawlin Street, Ladywood, about fifteen minutes' walk from his job in Granville Street. The

Ladywood in which he lived has now disappeared. In the 1960s its low-rise terraces, corner shops, gospel halls and pubs were razed to make way for grim concrete towers of high-rise council housing. Former residents of Old Ladywood mourn its passing on a website that combines old photographs with memories of a sometimes tough but cohesive working-class community.

In 1881, when the census-taker called at their new house in Rann Street, the Davison family had grown to six: four boys—John, William, James and Thomas—and two girls, Elizabeth (Cissie) and Hannah. Hannah would die, aged two, in 1882 and another son, Alfred—an afterthought as they say—was born in 1885. Their house, a single-fronted terrace—two-up, two-down plus two cramped dormer bedrooms under the roof—would have been a squeeze for a family of eight, although adequate by the standards of the time. All the boys would follow Thomas into the metal trades or ancillary businesses, John as a warehouseman and ironmonger, William as a tinplate worker, Jim as a clerk and later a commercial traveller, Tom as an electrician and machinist, and Alfred also as a commercial traveller. Thomas's contacts, as a foreman and manager, may have helped to open the door to employment for his sons.

Success and Disappointment

In 1891, J. H. Hopkins and Sons became a listed company and Thomas took up a manager's position. The Davisons moved again, to Berkley Street, close by the works, possibly to a house owned by the company. Although he had joined the 'staff' of the company, Thomas's relations with the 'men' remained close. In the early 1890s, his close knowledge of the pricing system and intercession with the company's principals helped to secure his old mates a further five per cent increase in prices. 'This was entirely due to Mr Davison and put thousands of pounds into the pockets of our Members,' the union acknowledged.

There were signs, however, that as he moved into the lower ranks of Birmingham's middle class, Thomas's political allegiances had begun to change. The company's head, AN Hopkins, was an Edgbaston councillor and an avowed Liberal. But his elder brother, and former head of the family firm, John Satchell Hopkins, was the longtime chairman of the Birmingham Conservative Association and a fellow parishioner of Thomas's at St John's Ladywood. Under his leadership, the Conservatives had made inroads into the seemingly impregnable Liberal stronghold, establishing a network of local conservative associations and workingmen's clubs. In 1893 Thomas's name appears, once only and as an apology, in a report of a meeting of the St George's Ward Conservative Association. How eager a participant was he? Had he joined simply as a gesture of loyalty to his old boss? Or were his convictions, always moderate, shifting in a more conservative direction? If so, he may not have been alone. Since the 1860s there had been a realignment of political forces in the city. He was perhaps following in the wake of, and emulating, the most famous Birmingham politician of the era, Joseph Chamberlain. Son of a metal screw manufacturer and in his youth a champion of municipal socialism, by the 1890s, Chamberlain, the leader of the Unionist Party in the House of Commons, had joined a coalition with Lord Salisbury's Conservatives.

At first, the newly incorporated Hopkins and Sons expanded and prospered, but from the mid-1890s American tariff barriers and general recession bit into its profits. British exports of tinplate plummeted from a peak of over £7.1 million in 1891 to £2.7 million in 1898. By 1895 Hopkins shares had fallen to less than a quarter of their issue price. There were boardroom disputes over dividends and bonuses. Then, in 1898, disaster struck. Early in the year, company chairman John Satchell Hopkins died suddenly at the age of seventy-two, and by its end the business had been wound up. Its assets were sold to Joseph Sankey and Sons of Bilston and the Granville Street property where Thomas had worked for thirty-six years was sold.

The Hopkins family fortunes had been insulated from those of their company (John Satchell Hopkins left an estate worth £31 087) but old employees like Thomas Davison were more vulnerable.

Under the rules of the union, he had already lost his modest superannuation, and with the collapse of the company his expected £100 a year pension was also 'cast to the winds'. In modern parlance, he was retrenched without entitlements. The win-win he negotiated in 1875 had become a lose-lose in 1898. So when his old friends and workmates gathered at the Crown Inn in Broad Street in June 1900 to present him with his portrait and 'a handsome marble clock', it was with as much pity for his predicament as 'esteem of his many excellent and sterling qualities'.

'Mr. Davison was a model foreman and manager,' his fellow unionists agreed. 'True to his employer, true and just to the men.' In believing that he could serve both masters and men, Thomas was a man of his time and place. The mid-Victorian era brought a temporary suspension of class warfare, and many working families enjoyed a season of economic prosperity. In Birmingham, with its mixed economy and many paths to success, Thomas's belief in class cooperation seemed vindicated by his own experience. As Britain's Empire expanded, it opened markets for Birmingham's bedsteads and bicycles, guns and grates, frying pans and coalscuttles all over the world. Compared with his own childhood in Caldewgate, Thomas's sons enjoyed brighter prospects.

In the 1890s, however, Birmingham entered harder times. As its markets contracted, its political unity was fractured. After the collapse of Hopkins and Sons, and the loss of his pension, I wonder whether Thomas's long-held faith in the unity of Capital and Labour was not shaken. There is little outward evidence, though, that it changed his outlook or way of life. Among the tinplate workers, he remained a revered figure, his life celebrated by a biographical portrait in their 1917 *Annual Report*. A 'regular and devout' churchman, he continued to walk every Sunday to Evensong at Erdington parish church in a Victorian top hat and frock coat. In his own eyes at least, he was a gentleman.

In 1910 Islington Wesleyan Chapel's Grand Imperial Bazaar celebrated the imperial fervor and missionary zeal among Birmingham's Wesleyan community. Courtesy Islington Wesleyan Church records in Local History Collection, The Library of Birmingham.

CHAPTER 6

Towards Australia

OF ALL THE characters in this story, the most elusive is my grandfather, John Potter Davison. I never knew him. He died six years before I was born, and my father, who was twenty-three when his father died, seldom spoke of him, although affectionately when he did. Compared with my maternal grandfather Vic Hewett, who profoundly shaped my life, John Davison, from whom I got my second given name, seems a shadow. I know little of what he did, said or thought. The few surviving photographs depict a mild, bespectacled, unsmiling man in a Sunday suit, with a Methodist hymnbook sometimes tucked under his arm. He seems to hide behind his glasses, avoiding my gaze, defying my attempts to know him.

Yet John was the author of the most radical change in the Davisons' history. In 1912, at the age of forty-three, he closed his business, uprooted his wife and four children, said goodbye to his father, mother, sister and brothers and, with only twenty pounds in his pocket, embarked for a country they hardly knew on the other side of the world. None of his children knew why he decided to emigrate.

As I have gradually retraced his steps, however, I have begun to discern the outlines of an explanation.

As the eldest son of Thomas, John seemed destined to follow his father and brothers into the metal trades and onto the upper rungs of Birmingham's working class. He attended St John's elementary school, attached to his father's church in Ladywood, and apparently trained as a gold electroplater in the jewellery business. By 1891, however, when he was twenty-one, he was working as a warehouseman. Gold plating looks like a small step up from his father's tinplating trade, but warehousing, an unskilled occupation, seems a step down, unless it was an apprenticeship for his next move into the retail business. When his father Thomas left his manager's job at Hopkins and Sons, he was sixty-two years old and facing old age without a pension. John meanwhile was approaching thirty and hoping to marry. Both needed an income and metalware—Birmingham's specialty—was all they knew. In 1899 they became partners in Thomas Davison and Son, a retail ironmongery business in High Street, Erdington.

It must have seemed a mutually advantageous arrangement. Thomas could train his son in the business and gradually hand over the reins as his own financial needs grew smaller and John's increased. But from the beginning the relationship was complicated by other allegiances. John had abandoned his family's traditional Anglicanism to join the Islington Wesleyan Chapel in St Martin's Street, Ladywood. This shift, so insignificant to us, mattered more in an era when Church and Chapel were important social markers. Sixty years later, John's sister Cissie, who remained Church, deplored John's defection, which she associated with the influence of Ada Cardall who John married in 1899, the same year as he began a business with his father.

The Cardalls were longstanding residents of Ladywood, drawn from the same stratum of Birmingham's respectable working class as the Davisons. They were originally Shropshire folk. Ada's seventeenth-century forebears came from the village of Aveley, about forty miles from Birmingham in the Severn Valley. Her grandfather

Luke, born in another Shropshire village, Hinstock, was already living in Ladywood and working as a wire-drawer in a local factory by 1841. Her father Joseph followed Luke into the metal trades as a brass burnisher, while Ada, the eldest of his ten children, worked as a 'wrapper' in a brass foundry, perhaps alongside her father. In 1881 the Cardalls were living in Ruston Street, Ladywood, just along the street from their spiritual home, the Islington Wesleyan Chapel. Years later, they were remembered as 'one of the families that were the pride of Islington in the old days'. In marrying Ada, John was inevitably drawn into the Cardalls' religious sphere.

Ada, however, may not have been the only reason he became a Methodist. He was already a keen member of the Islington Wesleyan Bible Class five years before they wed. It is as likely that he met her through the chapel as that he joined it for her sake. Methodism was not traditionally strong in Birmingham—a city where the Church of England and Old Dissent had dominated—but it made rapid strides during the second half of the century, planting new mission churches in working-class communities like Ladywood where its comprehensive program of evangelism, education and social uplift gave it an edge over the more traditional offerings of the established church. Adult Sunday schools and Bible classes, like the one John attended, were a Birmingham invention, first established by the Quaker anti-slavery reformer Joseph Sturge, whose statue stood at Five Ways, near the Islington Chapel. Under its charismatic superintendent Jabez Barnes, proprietor of a local brass button factory, the Islington Adult Sunday School had attracted more than a hundred pupils and evolved an impressive program of recreational and cultural activities, including swimming, running, football, musical and literary clubs. The Pleasant Sunday Afternoon, a popular form of Sabbath recreation combining sacred music and stirring addresses on the great questions of the day, was another Midland invention adopted by the Wesleyans.

Broader than Anglicanism in some respects, Methodism was narrower in others. Its worship services, Bible classes, prayer meetings, choirs, missions, bazaars and tea meetings were an austerely teetotal alternative to the temptations of the pub, the racetrack and the music hall. 'The drunkard shall not enter the Kingdom of God,' a speaker at the opening of the chapel warned in 1863. The Jesus who associated with drunkards and sinners chose his company less carefully than the Wesleyans of Ladywood. Light, spacious and tastefully ornate, the Islington Chapel contrasted with the grimly utilitarian factories and terraces in which its members passed their weekday lives. During the 1880s it was extended and embellished with galleries, pipe organ, stained-glass windows, vestries and annexes large enough to accommodate 1450 worshippers. It epitomised the 'Forward Movement', Methodism's answer to the alienation of the industrial city.

In becoming a Methodist, John was embracing a distinctive culture, with its own sense of time and history. Some of that culture would be transmitted to me, along with the ancestral clock, so I beg the reader's indulgence for a brief digression into its origins. From its beginnings, Methodism's promise of personal and social renewal drew a strong response among the working people of England, including

Islington Wesleyan Chapel interior, Harvest Festival, 1911. Islington became one of Methodism's strongest congregations and, for John and Ada, a spiritual home. Courtesy State Library of South Australia.

those experiencing the first tremors of the Industrial Revolution. The name 'Methodist' was first coined by outsiders to mock the disciplined spiritual life adopted by its leader, John Wesley, and his Oxford friends, the self-styled Holy Club, but it stuck because it captured something essential to the Methodist outlook. As a loyal son of the English Church, Wesley diligently observed the feasts and fasts of the traditional ecclesiastical year. He followed a strict personal regimen of reading, prayer and reflection. These traditional observances, however, were coupled with a powerful psychological drive to capture every moment of his life for the service of God. 'Redeeming the time', a phrase he took from the Letter to the Ephesians, became one of his watchwords. In a sermon he exhorted his followers to 'buy up every fleeting moment from the hands of sin and Satan, out of the hands of sloth, pleasure [and] worldly business'.

In the New Testament, 'redeeming the time' referred to the end-time of God's opportunity (*kairos*), not to the measurable time of calendars and diaries (*chronos*). Like some other early Methodists, Wesley believed that Christ's second coming was rapidly approaching. Believers should therefore redeem what little time remained to save the lost. But in his sermons and other writings, Wesley gave the idea of redeeming time a more modern, pragmatic twist. For example, he recalled purchasing an alarm clock in order to discover, experimentally, the minimum number of hours he required for sleep. Wasted time, he insisted, is among the worst of sins: it harms the slothful person economically, physically and spiritually. In the hours lost to unnecessary sleep, a man might 'bring money, or money's worth, to [himself] or others'. In his spiritual economy, time and money were scarce resources to be carefully counted and conserved. 'Gain all you can. Save all you can. Give all you can,' he urged.

The main benefit of redeeming time was supposed to be spiritual. But Wesley recognised that it yielded a temporal dividend as well. 'The Methodists in every place grow diligent and frugal; consequently they increase in goods,' he noted in the 1780s. In his famous study of the Protestant ethic and the spirit of capitalism, the sociologist Max Weber noted how exquisitely Wesley's teachings on the husbandry of time and money met the requirements of an industrialising society, a point developed and debated by many later historians.

When Wesley died in 1791, Methodism was on its way to becoming a separate denomination. A century later, when John Davison joined the Wesleyan Islington Chapel, the movement had lost some of its evangelical urgency but none of its moral intensity. The ideal Methodist was well defined in a series of articles on the qualities required of a local, or lay, preacher: he should be self-denying, industrious, punctual, methodical and orderly. 'We recommend the young preacher to fix an hour for going to bed at night, and to do the same for rising in a morning; and to keep time punctually, except in rare cases, both for retiring to rest and getting up.'

Among ministers of a more philosophical turn of mind, Wesley's injunction inspired deeper reflections about the nature of time and progress. 'Time claims kindred with all existence,' the Rev. Richard Smetham observes in a long essay in the *Wesleyan Methodist Magazine*. 'Its touch is upon everything. It will bear to oncoming generations the influence of your daily life. It gathers up the accumulating forces of all generations, and sends them surging through the great heart of society.' In redeeming time, Smetham suggests, the Methodist was cooperating with the progressive spirit of the age while also anticipating the end of time itself. Economy of time was even more important than economy of money. 'Time is always coming, always going. You may treasure up your wealth, but you cannot treasure up your time ... If you lose your time, it is lost forever,' writes Smetham.

By the 1880s some Methodists worried that their church was losing its connection with the labouring poor and becoming 'much too exclusively the sect of the lower middle class'. The congregation of the Islington Chapel included working-class locals like John and Ada as well as carriage folk from comfortable suburbs to the north and west. John's Sunday school superintendent Jabez Barnes, who employed 150 men, was such a person. Wesley had ridden thousands of miles on horseback, preaching in the fields to unchurched agricultural workers, miners and factory hands, but the atmosphere of the Islington Chapel was respectable and self-improving rather than plebeian. It nourished values and ambitions that inevitably led its faithful to look beyond Ladywood.

The faith and fellowship of the Islington Chapel would become the foundation of John and Ada's marriage and a significant influence on their decision to emigrate.

A Family Business

John and Ada, at thirty and twenty-seven respectively, were of an age to marry, yet there are signs that Ada and her parents had qualms about the match. On Christmas Day 1899, his wedding day, John signed 'a deed of gift of furniture in contemplation of marriage' assigning all the 'furniture, plate, linen, china, glass, pictures, books, musical instruments and other articles of domestic use and ornament' in the house at 16 High Street to Ada 'as her separate estate and property free from the control, interference and engagements' of her prospective husband. A modern reader familiar with the idea of prenups might misconstrue this agreement as insurance for Ada in case the marriage broke down. Its primary purpose, however, was probably more immediate: by placing the couple's small personal property in Ada's ownership, it shielded it and her from the financial hazards of her husband's business. While Thomas, Mary and four of their adult children lived in the spacious three-level dwelling above the main business premises at number 218 High Street, Erdington, John and Ada occupied the smaller three-room residence over a second shop, a quarter of a mile away at number 16 High Street.

Implicit in the deed of gift was the Victorian ideal of marriage as a union of equal partners, each with their own spheres of activity. Factory owners like the Hopkins family observed that ideal by separating the factories and offices where they worked from the villas and gardens of nearby Edgbaston, Birmingham's premier suburb, where their wives and daughters presided. Farmers, artisans and shopkeepers, like John and Ada, who lived where they worked, found it harder to physically separate the spheres. Ada worked alongside John in the shop. John's deed of gift, whether it was offered spontaneously or at the insistence of Ada and her family, recognised her as the mistress of their upstairs household. It also hints at something their children later observed: that Ada, a forceful character, was at least John's equal in running the household and business.

The list of items attached to the agreement gives a picture of the couple's assets at the time of their marriage. They actually had no plate or linen, and their furniture—a bedroom suite, dining room suite and kitchen table and chairs—was sparse and frugal. There were thirteen pictures and 'a quantity of books' but no bookcase. They appear to have had only three rooms: a bedroom, dining room and kitchen above the shop. Oh, yes, and a Vienna clock (striker). That clock, a wall-mounted, eight-day, self-regulating model, a junior version of John's father's long case Hodgson clock, was probably the most valuable article in the household.

In March 1902 John and Ada's first child, Dorothy, was born; her death three years later from meningitis left Ada bereft. Her next child, Phyllis, born in 1903, would come to feel that she could never win the love her mother had somehow exhausted on her dead sister. With the birth of Frank in 1904, the quarters above the shop were becoming crowded and the needs of the family may have outgrown the income from the business. John and Ada may also have wanted to make their own way in life independently of their parents. In 1905, they moved five kilometres across town to Moseley Road, Balsall Heath, where John took over Sandbrooks' Ironmongery. Frank Davison later described him as 'manager' of the business, and the 1911 census shows him as a 'worker' rather than 'employer' or 'self-employed'. Perhaps the previous owner, Leonard Sandbrooks, remained the legal owner or retained an interest, while John worked to buy him out. The arrangement seems to have involved other members of the family, including Ada and Cissie, working in the shop, and John's younger brother Jim, a commercial traveller, who did the books and may have been a sleeping partner.

John and Ada's children retained fond memories of their life on Moseley Road. In his seventies, Frank could still picture his father standing behind the counter dressed immaculately in shirt, tie and black apron while his mother arranged wheelbarrows and watering cans on the pavement outside. At Christmas time she made an elaborate window display of toys and dolls. Frank recalled the pungent smell of paraffin oil and firelighters, the tactile pleasure of scooping handfuls of putty from a large barrel and the sound of double-decker trams rattling down Moseley Road on their way to the terminus. At dusk he looked out for the municipal lamplighter as he passed from door to door, touching each gas lamp with his magic wand. Occasionally an organ grinder parked outside the shop, and the children watched wide-eyed as a monkey dressed in a comical costume danced to the organ's honkytonk strains.

Proprietor John Davison, dressed in collar and tie, suit and apron, at the door of Sandbrooks Ironmonger's Stores, Moseley Road, Balsall Heath.

Moseley Street was the main shopping street of a working-class community. Socially it stood higher than Ladywood but lower than Erdington. The Davisons' neighbours, Mrs Pusey the greengrocer and Mrs Smith the general storekeeper, were friends as well as fellow traders. They looked after each other's children and patronised each other's businesses. Long before people spoke of takeaways, the Davisons purchased suppers of fish and chips and tripe and onions from the kitchens of nearby shops. Frank and Phyllis attended the Tisdale Street primary school, the Band of Hope in the nearby Congregational Church and Sunday school at Moseley Road Wesleyan Church. In winter they built snow forts in the side street and skated on an ornamental pond in Balsall Heath. The nearby Balsall Heath Municipal Baths and Public Library, an imposing monument to Birmingham's Civic Gospel, promoted healthy bodies and minds in a community where many homes had neither baths nor books. Frank remembered basking in its arcaded indoor swimming pool, with a stream of warm water bubbling up under his chin, and sitting in the library waiting for his requested book to appear in a special frame near the inquiry desk.

In 2018, more than a century after my father left Birmingham, I looked for the shop and dwelling on Moseley Road where he was born. Balsall Heath now borders the city's famous 'Balti Triangle'. Four-fifths of its residents are Muslims, and along Moseley Road tripe and onions have made way for curry and kebabs. The Moseley Road Methodist Church, rebuilt in modern style after German bombs destroyed the old Gothic pile, is now a Muslim Faith and Culture Hub. My grandparents' shop on the corner of Moseley Road and Runcorn Street has gone, alas, replaced by an ugly modern doner kebab seller. Amidst so much that had changed, I was astonished to discover that their hardware business actually survives in an almost identical Victorian building across the street. Its shop windows are filled with the same jumble of brooms and ladders, pots and kettles as theirs. I chatted to the proprietor, Mr Saifee, and later sent him a photograph of my grandfather standing in the entrance. Apparently,

Moseley Road, with its busy foot traffic and clanging trams, lived brightly in the memory of the Davison children long after they had departed for Australia.

not long after the Davisons departed, the business, still calling itself Sandbrooks, moved to its present site. 'When I took over Sandbrooks thirty years ago I reinvented the shop,' Mr Saifee explained.

Loosening the Moorings

The Davison children recalled their life in Moseley Road so fondly that I wondered why they all left it. 'Just what the circumstances were that decided mum and dad to emigrate to Australia I really cannot say,' Frank wrote sixty years later. 'I was too young to know what was going on in the adult world ... so even if I had some knowledge then it has now been forgotten.' In this, the Davisons were not unusual, for while public archives are full of letters and shipboard diaries describing the experience of migration, few throw light on the writers' motives for embarking. We are left to reconstruct the migrants' motives from the outside by putting ourselves in their circumstances. Sometimes, historians suggest, the decision to migrate overseas was the last in a sequence of moves within the home country, a gradual loosening of moorings. Sometimes the migrant was inspired by the example of a friend or family member who had left before them. Sometimes the decision rested on a careful balance sheet of positive and negative considerations: the push to leave the old land (declining economic opportunity, family friction, religious or political oppression) and the pull towards the new (better economic prospects, family reunion, political or religious liberty). But it was not always a coolly rational one: both the decision and the destination could be tipped by other factors, such as the propaganda of emigration agents, a love of adventure, the availability of passage money or an emotional impulse.

Some of these factors probably influenced John and Ada's decision. For example, there was actually more migration in their family history than I first realised. Thomas's 172-mile journey from Carlisle to Birmingham may seem no distance to us, but in an era when transport was expensive and regional differences were strong he had migrated almost as irrevocably as if he had crossed the Atlantic. Ada's family, the Cardalls, had travelled only forty miles from their ancestral home in Shropshire, but all five of her father's sisters and brothers had converted to Mormonism in the 1870s and left for Utah. More significantly, on 15 May 1906, her younger brother, 28-year-old toolmaker George Cardall and his bride Minnie Oldfield, left Liverpool for Montreal where they settled and raised a family.

George and Minnie were among a growing number of young Methodists leaving Britain for Canada, Australia and New Zealand in the early twentieth century. The historian Robert Wearmouth identifies 1906 as the high-water mark of British Methodism, the year when its membership peaked and its evangelistic fervour began to wane. Part of the reason for its decline, according to the Methodist Conference, was 'the vast stream of emigration now leaving our shores'.

There was something in the spirit of Methodism that encouraged migration. Historians have long debated the social implications of John Wesley's famous declaration, 'The world is my parish.' In the high noon of British imperialism, that missionary spirit became entwined with the civilising mission of the Empire. 'Methodism is an imperial body,' an Australian Methodist paper noted in 1899. 'Wherever you find Englishmen in Europe, Africa, Australia, and America, you will also find Methodism. And Methodists everywhere are loyal—intensely, enthusiastically loyal.' Nowhere were the Methodists more patriotic than in Birmingham, the political base of the liberal-imperialist Joseph Chamberlain. In 1910 the Islington Wesleyan Chapel hired the Birmingham Town Hall for four days to run a Grand Imperial Bazaar with stalls representing the various colonies and dominions, all with the objective of raising £8000 for an ambitious church extension scheme.

In 1907, Robert Perks, a Methodist millionaire and MP with business interests in Canada and the United States, founded a Methodist Brotherhood to 'assist Methodist emigrants or Methodist travellers to any part of the globe'. Perks envisioned a global network of Methodist cooperative labour bureaus, dispensaries and loan societies. The scheme finally adopted by the British Methodist denominations had the more modest aim of linking prospective emigrants with fellow Methodists prepared to offer employment and accommodation in the new land. In Victoria, Australia, the Methodist Conference enthusiastically endorsed the plan, appointing a committee of prominent ministers and laymen, enlisting Methodist businessmen prepared to offer newcomers employment, and appointing one of its ministers, the Rev. George Lloyd, as a chaplain to arriving migrants.

The brotherhood was launched just as the Victorian Government introduced a generous scheme of assisted immigration. 'It was hoped to settle 30 000 British people in Victoria,' Victorian Agent-General Sir John Taverner told the British press in 1910. He urged 'the people of this country [to] help us as far as possible in trying to keep our people under their own flag'. Taverner recognised what Australian immigration agents had known for decades: that it took something extra to persuade British emigrants to make the long, expensive and usually irrevocable journey to Australia rather than the shorter one across the Atlantic. During the late nineteenth century, almost three-quarters of the emigrants leaving the United Kingdom had gone to the United States. But in the first decade of the twentieth century, as America diversified its intake from northern and southern Europe, British emigrants turned in greater numbers first to Canada and then, as the flow to that country abated, towards Australia. In going to Australia, Victorian authorities pointed out, the emigrant could remain under the British flag without braving the North American winter.

Victoria favoured immigrants with agricultural skills ready to further its plans for closer settlement. Those with urban or industrial skills and family or friends already in Victoria qualified for concessional fares on a less generous basis. The nominated migration scheme was ideally adapted to the aims of the Methodist Brotherhood whose network of hospitable employers and congregations stood ready to welcome their brothers and sisters in the faith. Between 1911 and 1915 over 150 000 assisted immigrants came to Australia, 43 000 of them to Victoria. Seldom noticed by historians, it was the largest influx of assisted immigrants between the gold rush and the end of World War II.

Conditions in England were changing in ways that made emigration an attractive prospect. Real wages were declining and unemployment was rising. 'It was more work that was wanted,' Austen Chamberlain, Joseph Chamberlain's son and political heir, declared in 1909. If the unemployed could not find work at home they should look to 'their kinsmen across the seas'. In the winter of 1912 a coal strike cut gas supplies, throwing more than 250 000 workers out of employment. Industrial unrest, political turmoil in Ireland, suffragette protests and constitutional conflict between the Liberal government and the House of Lords added to 'the sense of an impending clash'. I do not know how my grandparents responded to these events, but if John was like his father Thomas, a believer in the old Birmingham ideal of class harmony, he may have found them unsettling.

In May 1911 Ada gave birth to her fourth child, my father, George Henry. He was probably named after her brother George, the Canadian immigrant, whose first son, another George, was born around the same time. The accession of the new King George V in 1910 may also have popularised the name. With a growing family, a crowded household, a shaky economy and an uncertain political situation, John and Ada may have feared for their future in England. Their anxiety was probably compounded by events within their own family circle. In 1910, John's brother William, a tinplate worker, died at the age of thirty-nine from tuberculosis, leaving a wife and two daughters aged four and seven. A year later, Ada's unmarried 29-year-old brother, Harry Cardall, a furniture salesman, also died. Another of John's brothers, James, a commercial traveller, would die three years later, also aged thirty-nine, from heart and lung disease, leaving a widow and three children. Jim, as he was known, was the most successful of the Davison boys. In a studio photograph taken around 1911 he cuts an imposing figure, taller, handsomer and better dressed than his father and brothers, with an air of authority

The death of 39-year-old commercial traveller Jim Davison, the most successful of Thomas's sons, was the third such premature death among John and Ada's siblings.

enhanced by a well-clipped military moustache, a pretty wife and a brood of well-dressed children. They lived together with a live-in servant in a substantial detached house, 'St Ives' in Church Road, Sutton Coldfield, a middle-class suburb on Birmingham's leafy northern perimeter. After his death, only John's unmarried siblings Cissie and Thomas, both in their early thirties, remained with their elderly parents in Erdington.

This sequence of premature deaths throws new light on my grandparents' decision to emigrate. If Jim was a sleeping partner in the Moseley Road business (he appears as the leaseholder in local rate books), did his worsening health jeopardise its future? Did fears of premature death and dreams of better health in a sunnier climate enter my grandparents' calculations? Was the apparent failure of John's younger siblings to attain marriage and domestic independence a sign of the family's deteriorating prospects? If my father had no wish to revisit his English origins, was it because he sensed that it led back to an unhappy place where he would not want to be?

Even with all these disappointments, John and Ada may not have emigrated without the encouragement of others in their circle. In August 1912, their 43-year-old friend Walter Mansfield, a coachbuilder and fellow member of the Islington Wesleyan Chapel, departed for Australia with his wife Elizabeth and three sons. 'We are in the best of health and have no regrets we came out here,' he later wrote. 'I have been fortunate in getting work all along and have not been out of work for more than a week at a time.' He was employed at the Victorian Railways workshops at Newport as part of a team building a magnificent new railway carriage for the governor's ceremonial tours of the state. News of his success may have encouraged John and Ada, another middle-aged couple, to follow him. Walter may even have taken the initiative, as other recent emigrants did, by offering to nominate them for assisted passage; in doing so, he pledged to offer them temporary accommodation when they landed and to look out for employment prospects among his Methodist friends.

The plan gained further impetus when another member of the Islington Chapel community, Harold Harding, also decided to apply for assisted passage. A 26-year-old joiner, Harold was one of the brightest lights in the Islington community: a soloist in the choir, a local preacher and a Sunday school teacher. In 1911 he became engaged to Ada's younger sister Edith Cardall. Harold, it was decided, would accompany his prospective in-laws on the voyage while Edith would follow him out and marry him when they had all settled in Melbourne.

As a qualified tradesman, Harold was probably eligible for an £8 assisted passage but John, who was older, lacked a trade qualification (he appears on the passenger list as a 'labourer') and came only as a nominated migrant, probably paid £12 together with smaller sums for Ada and the children—in all, about £20. Years later, John told his son Frank that he arrived in Australia with only £20 in his pocket. If £40—the equivalent of about four months of a tradesman's wages—was all that my grandparents had saved from a decade of hard work, it suggests as much desperation as hope in their decision to migrate. In balancing the ledger of positive and negative considerations, the desperation—declining business prospects and precarious health—was mostly on the Davison side while the hope—represented by George Cardall, Walter Mansfield, Harold Harding and the Methodist Brotherhood—came from the Cardalls and the Islington Wesleyans. Was my grandfather the originator of the decision or, as seems likely, a reluctant participant in a plan initiated by Ada and her family? If Cissie believed that John had been led astray by Ada, was this the seed of her grievance?

Royal Mail Steamer *Orontes*, undated photograph by Allan C Green.
Courtesy State Library Victoria.

CHAPTER 7

Voyage and Landfall

On 8 November 1912 John and Ada Davison and their four children, accompanied by Harold Harding, boarded the SS *Orontes* at Tilbury. On the train from Birmingham, eight-year-old Frank leant out of the window as the locomotive, racing through the countryside, spewed jets of steam and specks of soot into his eyes. They stayed a few days in a Salvation Army hostel to say farewell to London relatives and visit the sights of the city, probably for the first and last time. At 10.30 a.m. on the day of their departure, friends and family were ordered to leave the ship. 'Painful scenes,' Harold wrote in his diary. At 11.30 a.m. the vessel departed, sailing down the Thames estuary in bright sunshine. As night fell, it left the shore, passing a British Indiaman, its bright lights shining against the black sky.

The *Orontes*, launched in 1902, was a 9000-ton passenger liner capable of carrying 200 first-class, 200 second-class and 600 third-class passengers. John, Ada and Harold joined about sixty other assisted emigrants bound for Victoria, mostly farm labourers, mechanics, blacksmiths, painters and domestics. As third-class passengers, they had none of the benefits of domestic privacy: John and Harold would share a cabin with other male passengers while Ada and the children occupied a small cabin of their own. Ada was seasick for much of the voyage; Frank recalled it as a 'nightmare trip'. The food, according to Harold, was 'plentiful and good but roughly served'. Porridge with milk and sausages and mash for breakfast, boiled mutton with suet pudding for dinner and plenty of bread and jam and tea in between was a typical day's fare. Frank, again, was more candid: the children simply hated the food and only the kindness of first-class passengers who gave them fruit and other fresh food from their table made it tolerable. Their mendicant status probably worried the children less than their elders.

Harold, who kept a journal of the voyage, was an outgoing character who revelled in the opportunities afforded by the ship's concerts, games and religious services to learn, discuss and perform. The program was led by the ship's chaplain, a Church of England clergyman and 'a very good man' according to Harold, despite his tendency to look down on nonconformists and to give less than full measure in his sermons. The voyage, as Harold described it, was a long open-air lesson on religion, politics and geography. He compared notes on biblical history with a Greek Orthodox gentleman, relived the Israelites' miraculous crossing of the Red Sea and took up the cudgels with 'a loud voiced fellow airing his views on Socialism and Atheism … and gave him a good doing'. He came prepared for the concerts with a repertoire of solos in a nautical vein, such as 'Rocked in the Cradle of the Deep' and 'When the Ebb Tide Flows', selected to remind his audience of the perils of the voyage and their need for eternal salvation. Yet while bringing his fervent Methodism with him, his journal displays an attractive openness to everything the voyage offered.

They were crossing the world at the very zenith of the British Empire. In their imagination, the route from London through Gibraltar, Toulon, Naples, Port Said, Suez, Aden, Colombo, Fremantle and Adelaide became an expedition into the mysterious

East and back again to 'Western civilisation'. At Gibraltar they caught a glimpse of the rock-like impregnability of British power, while in Toulon, 'France's Portsmouth', they viewed the fleet of England's principal ally primed for the looming European conflict. Neither there nor in Naples could the Davisons afford to take a shore excursion, so it was not until the *Orontes* reached Port Said that they at last 'stretched our legs and made our first acquaintance with the Oriental'. Wandering through the town, 'pestered' by street sellers, the tourists were both shocked and intrigued by the sight of 'Europeans and Asiatics' mingling freely, drinking, smoking and gambling without apparent restraint. The sight of a long procession of 'Arabs and Niggers' carrying coal in wicker baskets into the ship's hold was a shocking revelation of the cheapness of human life and labour in the East. Later, in Colombo, they reacted to the sight of rickshaws with similar unease. 'It is very degrading to a European to be dragged about by his fellow man,' Harold reflected.

Passing through the Suez Canal, they met another liner, the SS *City of Birmingham*, returning to Britain. 'Good Old Brum!' they cried out as it drew alongside. 'Don't you wish you were coming our way?' a passenger on the other vessel inquired. 'No fear' was the general reply. Among their fellow passengers there were several couples, apparently 'ordinary working people', returning to Australia after taking a holiday in England, a discovery that encouraged Harold to hope he might return himself someday.

Approaching the Western Australian coast, Harold's thoughts turned 'back again from the Oriental to Western civilisation'. 'I suppose this is the Promised Land,' one of his fellow passengers remarked hopefully. 'A land of milk and honey!' another exclaimed. 'We are looking forward to a life of usefulness and success,' Harold confided in his journal. A former Queensland Government minister gave a lecture on the prospects that awaited them in the new land. Before they entered it, however, they had to undergo an examination by Australian quarantine inspectors. 'They are very particular about receiving unhealthy people,' Harold noted. In Victoria, farmers had begun to complain of the disappointing physical quality of the men sent under the assisted immigration scheme. 'On the average the Victorian is a fitter animal and so a better citizen than the Britisher,' their paper, the *Weekly Times* declared. When they all lined up for the examination, two passengers—a pale and sickly house painter with a bad cast in his eye and a bespectacled man with a nervous tic—were pulled aside. To their relief, Harold and the Davisons all passed. If John had divulged his family history of premature deaths I wonder if they would have got through. Ashore in Fremantle, they celebrated their arrival at a local cafe with a pot of tea, bread and butter, and tinned pineapple.

A Last-Minute Reprieve

'THE GREAT DAY has arrived at last,' Harold exclaimed on the morning of 16 December as the *Orontes* steamed up Port Phillip Bay. He was among 200 passengers disembarking in Melbourne. 'All is bustle and excitement' aboard, he observed as the ship docked at Port Melbourne. Those who had friends to meet them called out to the shore. 'We almost envy those who have come to claim their sweetheart & wives,' Harold confessed, adding that 'still our turn will come, & then we wonder who will meet us'. George Lloyd, the Methodist immigration chaplain, welcomed them but soon departed, perhaps because the *Orontes* had arrived simultaneously with another liner, the *Demosthenes*, which discharged an even larger complement of assisted immigrants. Then a man sent by John's cousin arrived with the disappointing news that he could not help them find employment.

Their hopes were sinking when they were spotted by 'young Walter' Mansfield, son of their old Birmingham friend and sponsor Walter Mansfield. Elizabeth, Walter's wife, disappeared below decks to look for Ada. Help had arrived in the nick of time. 'We had nowhere to go so they offered us a home until we get one & what a blessing it is to sleep on land again & in a house,' Harold wrote with evident relief. John and Ada, their four children and Harold would share the modest house in Ascot Vale with the five Mansfields while they found their feet in Melbourne. This moment—their rescue from homelessness by old Islington Methodist friends—would live long in the Davisons' memory. My father, who was only eighteen months old at the time, retold it in his own 'memoirs' as though he had seen it all himself.

As their sponsor, Walter Mansfield had agreed to help them find accommodation, but housing was in short supply. There are hints that the Davisons may have come close to outstaying their friends' welcome. 'The house was not a very big one,' Frank recalled, 'and as can well be imagined with our six [people] things must have been very crowded with the inevitable tensions generated.' John applied unsuccessfully to several local firms for work in his old occupation, selling hardware. He also tried for work in country towns, with mixed results. 'I know he must have had work here and there,' Frank believed, 'because he was away from home for periods at a time.' The buoyant employment conditions that Walter Mansfield encountered were fast disappearing. 'Thousands are weekly entering the country, and thousands are being weekly dumped on the labor market,' *Labor Call* reported in April 1913. As a 43-year-old Englishman, without local references or a desirable trade, John faced an uphill battle. The Promised Land of milk and honey was proving to be a land of bread and dripping. John's feelings are not recorded but I wonder if he began to regret his decision to emigrate. Eventually, it seems, Walter Mansfield came to the Davisons' rescue again by helping John find employment as a painter in a local carriage works, Walter's own line of work. This was the occupation he followed, with stints as a house painter, railway carriage cleaner and odd jobs man, for the rest of his life. Prepared by his Methodism to redeem every moment, he may have found himself with more time on his hands than he expected or wanted.

The Davisons settled close to the Mansfields in a rented timber cottage at 57 Scotia Street, Ascot Vale, about five kilometres north-west of the city. Ascot Vale straddled Mount Alexander Road, the main route to the Bendigo diggings, and from the best allotments near the railway station it spread east and west into the valleys of the Moonee Ponds Creek and the Maribyrnong River. Ascot Vale had taken off during the late 1880s, when the prominent land boomers James Munro and James Mirams developed a large triangle of land as a 'Temperance Township'. Munro and Mirams were leaders of the Victorian temperance movement—the suburb banned hotels and offered cheap land and housing finance to its working-class residents. 'The population consists chiefly of a superior class of working men, attracted by the means afforded for owning their residence, with the certainty of having the public house kept at a respectful distance,' the Melbourne *Age* reported in 1890. 'Probably there is no other place in the colony holding the same number of workingmen with the same degree of respectability.'

It is easy to see how my working-class Methodist grandparents could have been attracted to such a place. But the Temperance Township, along with its promoters, had taken a big tumble in the 1890s depression and by the time John and Ada arrived the name was all but forgotten. They settled in a rented jerry-built timber cottage in a narrow, unmade street, still without gas or sewerage, on flood-prone land near the Maribyrnong River and the municipal rubbish dump locals called the 'Rattery'. They had brought little furniture and for a time they had to improvise with packing cases as tables, cheap wooden chairs and stretcher beds.

'We have found a corner in the Master's vineyard and are now at work there,' Harold Harding wrote to his Islington Chapel friends on New Year's Day 1914. He had found a steady job and was looking forward to the arrival of his fiancée Edith Cardall later that month. No longer a New Chum, he was proud to be 'a Colonial of twelve months' standing'. However, while there was much he liked about his new home, with its 'glorious sunshine and picnics', there was also 'much that we could very well do without'. The 'painful newness of the country' and the 'entire absence of old buildings, churches, etc.' troubled him. More irksome still was the 'over-bearing self-confidence' of the average Australian. 'He is intensely democratic, and almost like the Continental in his pleasure-loving propensities,' Harold observed. 'Taken on the whole, he is, I think, sound of heart and generous of nature, but *not too religious*.' Not religious enough was what he meant. While they had been fortunate to land in a '*real live* church', he found many other churches, including some Methodist ones, 'cold and lethargic'. He worried, too, about the 'lack of reverence' shown by Australian children towards their indulgent parents. The decay of parental authority was a regular theme of Wesleyan preachers back in England, but in Australia, Harold believed, the problem was worsened by the democratic ethos of the whole country.

Harold's letter home unveiled a more censorious side than his shipboard journal. His impressions are as revealing of him and his English readers as they are of the Australians he encountered. So, for example, when he deplores the irreligious, excessively democratic Australian we catch a glimpse, not only of the typical Australian, but also of the diffident, deferential, misunderstood New Chum. When he censures the 'overbearing self-confidence' of the locals, he hints at rebuffs and put-downs he may have experienced at their hands. An Australian reader may dismiss him as a combination of those odious types, the wowser and the whingeing Pom. Whingeing, we think, reveals the migrant's failure to count his blessings, to jettison unjustified assumptions of superiority, to live as the locals do and to keep his complaints to himself. We cut the whingeing Pom less slack than migrants from other lands; because he speaks English we assume he should easily fit in.

Harold was living with my grandparents at 57 Scotia Street when he wrote his letter. His views were probably close to theirs. Because they were my grandparents and I know the difficulties they were facing, I'm inclined to look beyond their complaints to the disappointments that lay behind them. Becoming Australian was hard work. It required newcomers to give up some of their old selves and to accept as normal much that they first saw as strange, or even repugnant. When, like John and Ada, they were already in the second half of their lives, the adjustment was harder. If they looked down on the Australians, perhaps it was because they had been looked down on themselves. 'There was, at that time, a build-up of ill-will towards English migrants,' their son Frank recalled. At Moonee Ponds West State School, his elder sister Phyllis was teased for her English accent, while Frank was called a Pommy and chased home by stone-throwing roughs from the nearby Flemington racing stables.

For friendship and support they relied mainly on other Methodists and English immigrants. 'The folk at the church were very friendly to us,' Frank remembered. The 'real live' Ascot Vale Church, while not as big as Islington Chapel, offered a similar program of spiritual, intellectual, musical, recreational and missionary opportunities. One of the attractions of church activities was that they were cheap and people contributed only what they could afford. Harold Harding and Walter Mansfield quickly assumed leadership positions as local preachers and Sunday school teachers; John Davison, always more diffident, sang in the choir. Their children attended the Sunday school and two of them would marry young people they met there.

Their neighbours in Scotia Street included two other recent Methodist immigrants, Fred Todd, a 31-year-old carpenter, and John Wilkinson, a 26-year-old bricklayer, both from Lincolnshire, who had arrived a few months ahead of the Davisons. Both were to prosper, Todd as a successful master builder and property developer, and Wilkinson as a builder and garage owner. When my father started out in business as a plumber in the early 1930s, John Wilkinson took him aside and said, 'George, you need a motor vehicle.' 'But I haven't any money,' my father protested. 'No harm in looking,' Wilkinson replied. They spotted an old motor van and, over Dad's objections, Wilkinson bought it. 'Just pay me back when you can.' Todd and Wilkinson remained revered names in my parents' household. John Wilkinson died in his early fifties but his wife Margaret remained a family friend. Fred Todd lived on into his nineties. As a boy I watched him arrive at church on Sunday mornings, a quiet, dapper figure driving a big black Daimler from his home 'Mar Lodge', an old farm homestead in West Essendon.

My grandparents' experience illustrates the importance of religion in the story of Australian immigration and settlement. The churches provided a lifeline and a spiritual home for the immigrants. In turn, the immigrants supplied the churches with new recruits from their homeland. While the migrants kept coming, the churches continued to grow; when the flow ended, the churches also lost part of their raison d'etre. The decline of mainstream Protestantism since the 1970s has largely coincided with the decline of British migration.

'He bids us build each other up,' goes one of John Wesley's most famous hymns. The little acts of spontaneous charity among John and Ada's fellow Methodists amounted to much less than a reliable safety net. Help flowed mainly to fellow believers who shared the Methodists' austere personal morality. Yet perhaps a hand up from a fellow immigrant, extended within a shared ethic of Christian fellowship, was more acceptable to giver and receiver alike than the cool impartiality of the welfare state. Today, the mosques and temples of Middle Eastern and Asian immigrants continue to play a vital part in the movement of newcomers into Australian society. When I hear 'Old Australians' opposing the erection of a new mosque or urging newcomers to leave behind their homelands, I call to mind my grandparents who continued, to the end of their lives, to live within the Methodist Church and to call England Home.

In coming to Australia John and Ada had burned their bridges, but England was never far from their minds. The pangs of homesickness were often intense. Soon after they arrived Ada received a picture postcard from her sister-in-law Louie Davison, Jim's wife. 'This is the village of Aveley four mile past Arley where we have been this Easter,' she wrote. (Aveley, the ancestral village of the Cardalls, was an economical day trip from Birmingham on the Severn Valley Railway.) 'The weather is lovely just like the summer. We got lovely lots of primroses and water lilies, should like you to have some.' Only a few months later came the dreadful news that Jim, John's brother and business partner, had died.

In July 1914 came happier news: Ada's youngest sister, 26-year-old Nellie, was engaged to 53-year-old Rowland Scurrah. The Scurrahs were Methodist aristocracy. Dr John Scurrah, Rowland's father, was one of the founders of the Islington Chapel and Rowland, an accountant, was its treasurer. Nellie would be going to live in an imposing house with a live-in servant in Streetly, a wealthy suburb on Birmingham's northern edge. 'I suppose when you get this you will be Mrs Scurrah,' Ada wrote with undisguised envy. 'I think it's lovely where you are going to live just where I should like to live if I had my choice. Mother will be able to come and see you it's not like coming right away like we have.'

The Call of Empire

By the time Nellie received Ada's letter, all their hopes and plans had been capsized by England's declaration of war on Germany. England's war was Australia's too and distance from their homeland only increased the immigrants' anxiety. In Melbourne as in England, the 'intensely, enthusiastically loyal' Methodists were at the forefront of efforts to bolster military recruitment. In August 1915 the Rev. Thomas Woodfull, superintendent minister of the Ascot Vale congregation and chaplain of the Flemington recruitment camp, addressed a Pleasant Sunday Afternoon service at Wesley Church. Between 900 and 1000 of the 6000 men in the camp, he reported, were Methodist lads. 'It is evident that our Church is not in any way holding back in its contribution to the call of Empire,' the *Methodist Spectator* boasted.

At forty-five and with four dependent children, John was ineligible for military service. But 28-year-old Harold Harding felt the call of duty more intensely. He was young, devout, patriotic and probably homesick. The majority of recruits were young single men in their early twenties; only about one in six was married and about a quarter were over thirty. He and Edith had married early in 1914 and before the year was out she was pregnant. When eventually the military authorities issued a call-up, they exempted married men with children. Most people would have excused Harold for not enlisting. Even if he had wished to join, however, he could not. At five foot three and a half and with a chest measurement of only thirty-one inches, he did not meet the stringent physical requirements for enrolment in the first battalions of the Australian Imperial Force (five foot six and thirty-four inches). Australian observers, including the war correspondent and historian Charles Bean, praised the magnificent physique of the bush-bred Anzacs, often contrasting them with puny city-bred English Tommies, like Harold. Yet one in five recruits to the AIF, including heroes like John Simpson Kirkpatrick, 'The Man with the Donkey', was actually English-born.

Harold Harding's daughter Margaret was only seven months old when he enlisted in the AIF. His widow Edith was living with the Davisons when he died in action in November 1916. They later returned to Birmingham.

By the time the Hardings' daughter Margaret was born in June 1915, the drums of war were beating more insistently. After their withdrawal from Gallipoli in December 1915, the Anzac troops were redeployed to France where the Allies were locked in a bloody, inconclusive war of attrition. Millions of men in uniform—French, English and German—occupied a double line of trenches stretched along a 700-kilometre frontier between the North Sea and the Alps. They were waging war on a scale and brutality never seen before. As the casualties mounted and recruitment flagged, the Australian authorities stepped up the pressure on eligible young men to enlist. Posters appeared at suburban stations asking 'Will they never come?' Dials on public clocks issued the urgent command 'Enlist Now'. In Moonee Ponds the Rev. Thomas Woodfull appealed to the young men in his congregation to enrol in a holy war against the godless Hun. To enlarge the pool of potential recruits, the authorities lowered the physical requirements: in June 1915, the height requirement was dropped to five foot two.

On 2 February 1916 Harold walked to the Ascot Vale recruitment depot and joined the 21st Battalion of the Australian Infantry Force. The 21st had been formed early in 1915 at the Broadmeadows camp on Melbourne's northern outskirts. Most of Harold's fellow recruits were tradesmen from the city's inner and north-western suburbs (its red and black badge was in the colours of the local Essendon football team) and included a number of older men and British immigrants like Harold himself. On 4 April, after six weeks' basic training at Broadmeadows, they boarded the troopship *Euripides*. They arrived in England just as the war was reaching a critical moment. Frustrated by the Allies's inability to break through the German lines, the Allied command under Field Marshall Earl Haig resolved to mount an all-out summer offensive along the river Somme north of Amiens. Success would depend on the Allied artillery smashing the German defences so that the infantry could penetrate the barbed wire and take the enemy trenches. While he trained and waited to join the fray, Harold visited Birmingham to see his parents and attended Sunday worship at Islington Wesleyan Chapel.

Within hours of the first attack on 1 July it was obvious that Haig's plan was flawed: 20 000 Allied soldiers died and a further 40 000 were wounded in just twenty-four hours, the most calamitous day in the history of warfare to that time. Yet the generals pressed on with the attack. The First Australian Division joined the battle at Fromelles on 19 July but the Second Division, including the 21st Battalion, was held back until the end of the month when it attempted an assault north of Pozieres. 'Pozieres has been a terrible sight … an insatiable factory of ghastly wounds,' Charles Bean wrote in his diary. Lieutenant Leo Hine of the 21st Battalion left a searing account of their ordeal:

> All the time there is the drawn out whine and nerve shattering crash of the shells. Sometimes they come singly along the trench, and sometimes they come in a perfect tornado. To the man sitting in the trench, it is Hell. He sees this one blown to pieces, that one buried, another shockingly mutilated. One of the most pitiable of sights is that of a man suffering from shell shock, his nerves shattered, and, in some cases, his reason destroyed. He crouches on the ground shaking like a leaf; and, at the sound of an approaching shell, he whimpers like a frightened child. I saw one man driven mad by the sight of his two mates blown to pieces, and deprived of his speech by the one shell. And so it goes on, day in and day out; the hellish din, the choking gas shells, the stench of the dead, and the expectation of death by the next shell. Strong men who went in come out nervous and physical wrecks.

The exhausted Anzacs were finally taken out of the line on 5 September. They had suffered 24 139 casualties since 19 July. More than half the 21st Battalion, which had comprised twenty-four officers and 651 soldiers, were dead, wounded or missing; only eleven officers and 491 other ranks remained ready for service.

On 15 September, the day before he left for France, Harold made a will, leaving 'all my goods and money' to Edith. By the time he joined his unit in Belgium on 28 September, its ranks had been only partially reinforced, to thirty-five officers and 798 other ranks. On 19 October it was again ordered into the line, instructed to relieve the 22nd Battalion near Gueudecourt, just a few kilometres from the Belgian border. Winter was approaching. Autumn rains had turned the battlefield into a quagmire and the shell craters into icy ponds. The conditions, according to Charles Bean, were the most difficult ever faced by the AIF. The battalion's orders were to hold the front line 'at all costs' and, if forced back, to be 'in instant readiness' to resume the attack.

On 3 November they pushed out from Buire into the sea of mud and occupied forward lines towards a labyrinth of German trenches known as 'The Maze'. A 'violent enemy bombardment' on the night of 5 November killed five men and wounded sixteen. With their left flank now exposed, the troops were ordered the next day to strengthen the battalion's defences by digging a new trench towards the enemy's lines. It was while they were engaged in this task that Harold Harding was killed, the battalion's only fatal casualty of the day. He had been a soldier for ten months but had perished, without firing a shot, after only two days in the field. A few days later his battalion was withdrawn from the line without having gained a yard of enemy ground.

Counting the Cost

Breaking the news to the families of 'the fallen' was the dismal responsibility of clergymen of the soldier's denomination. It probably fell to the Ascot Vale Methodist minister George Lloyd—the same George Lloyd who had met Harold on the *Orontes* in 1912—to knock on the door of 95 Athol Street, where Edith and her baby Margaret were staying with the Davisons in their new abode. After Lloyd departed, John and Ada were left to console their thirty-year-old sister as she suddenly faced the prospect of bringing up her child in a strange country without the man she came to marry. She was joining the immense international sisterhood—three or four million strong—of women who lost their husbands in the Great War, at least one-third of whom had children.

Harold's death devastated his friends on both sides of the world. A memorial service at Ascot Vale Methodist paid tribute to his earnest and winning personality. The boys in his Sunday school class were deeply affected by the tragedy. 'Time alone will prove the amount of good which Harold's influence has wrought upon the lives of the boys who were brought into contact with him as their teacher,' his friend and fellow immigrant Walter Mansfield wrote to their friends in Birmingham. Members of the Ascot Vale Methodist choir inserted a tribute to their 'esteemed member' in the Melbourne *Argus* with the subscript 'Greater love hath no man than this—that he lay down his life for his friends'. These were the words of Jesus, whose death was the model of self-sacrificial love that many Christians, including Harold, aspired to follow. His old congregation in Birmingham hailed him as 'one of Islington's finest' and included him in a roll call of 'Our Heroes', although they had no information about his heroic deeds, perhaps because there were none. Heroism and noble self-sacrifice were comforting names for what must otherwise have seemed senseless slaughter and incalculable loss.

Historians have often remarked on the muted presence of religion in Australian public commemorations of war. Men and women who had seen their world blown apart often seemed to recoil from the certainties of Christian faith. Australians, it is also suggested, are a laconic people, less inclined to religious sentiment than the English. Seen from that perspective, Harold Harding and his family may look more English than Australian. Yet the absence of Christian symbolism in the public Anzac commemorations may reflect a reluctance to open up sectarian differences rather than a rejection of religious belief altogether. In the intimate setting of home and church, Australians at that time often drew, as Harold's family did, on the words of scripture and the consolations of faith. On the threshold between the two, as in his death notice and epitaph, their language was often coded, alluding both to the interior life of personal belief and the public world of patriotism.

To serve without counting the cost was the highest form of patriotism. Yet if Harold did not count the cost, his family must often have wondered how different their lives might have been if he had not given up his. He had come to Australia anticipating 'a life of usefulness and success'. He was talented, popular and earnest. He might have used his trade as a joiner to follow Fred Todd and John Wilkinson into the building business. Who knows, he might one day have lived in a big house like Fred's and driven a Daimler to church. Or his fervent faith and eloquence might have drawn him into the Methodist ministry, magnifying his influence for good. He and Edith would surely have added to their family, giving more cousins to my father and his siblings.

No one lost more by his death than Edith. All she received from the military authorities were his few personal effects: a Bible, a devotional book and a wallet. In August 1917 she wrote to acknowledge them. 'There are others which should come,' she noted, mentioning in particular 'a wristlet watch with name engraved'. 'I would be very pleased if you could make investigations for me, as the watch would be very valuable to me.' Harold's engraved wristlet watch was probably a recent gift, perhaps from Edith herself. He had lost his old timepiece, a pocket watch and chain, back in 1912 on the voyage to Australia when it was pilfered from his cabin. Wristlet watches were the modern fashion. They became the dominant style during the trench warfare of 1914–18 when attacks were synchronised to the second and soldiers needed to tell the time instantly without having to fumble with fobs, chains and lidded watchcases. Beyond its utility and cash value, however, Harold's watch would have been valuable to Edith as a memento of the man himself, as sure a guide to his character, as a tradesman and Methodist local preacher, as his Bible.

Materially, Edith was not left well off. Harold's will was probated at £61 and from the Australian Government she received a small gratuity and a war widow's pension—a pound a week and ten shillings for Margaret. Before the war, they had lived in an attractive timber house in Walter Street (it recently sold for well over a million dollars) but afterwards she could no longer afford a home of her own. For a while she shared a terrace house near the Ascot Vale train station with a labourer and his wife, but was soon back with the Davisons, contributing eighteen shillings board from her thirty shillings a week pension for a share of their already overcrowded home in Athol Street. 'She has no debts but finds it a struggle to get along,' the Essendon Repatriation Committee reported in December 1918. Moved by the situation of women like Edith, the Repatriation Commission had recently recommended an increase in the pension of war widows with a dependent child from thirty shillings to fifty-one shillings a week. Edith applied for, and was duly granted, the increase.

She later obtained a position as housekeeper on a dairy farm at Port Campbell in western Victoria. The farmer, Wilhelmina Ward, a Red Cross activist, was the widow of another dead soldier, Trooper Christopher Ward of the Australian Light Horse. Wilhelmina's older half-brother Henry Cairns, an executor of her husband's will, lived just around the corner from the Davisons in Ascot Vale and may have suggested the arrangement. Although sympathy for each other's loss may have drawn them together, living on an isolated farming property with another grieving woman cannot have been easy. Perhaps only desperation would have persuaded Edith to take up the opportunity. At any rate, it did not last.

In 1922 Edith returned with Margaret to Birmingham to join her widowed mother and two unmarried sisters in their old home in Kenilworth Place, just a kilometre from Islington Chapel. Like many other single women, she survived by sharing the little she had with others in her situation. There she lived for the next twenty-eight years until her death in 1950. Her Australian family did not forget her. Over seventy years after Edith died, her great-granddaughters are still in touch.

My grandfather John Potter Davison did not go to war but the crisis did not leave him unmarked. By the time Harold died, Australia was bitterly divided over the question of military conscription. On 28 October 1916, when Harold was preparing to enter the battlefield, prime minister Billy Hughes conducted a plebiscite on the proposal to conscript young men of military age for overseas service. Methodists generally voted yes, although a minority, who believed that patriots should be volunteers, voted no. The fiercest opposition to conscription came from the trade union movement, and from Melbourne's charismatic Catholic Archbishop Daniel Mannix, whose fiery rhetoric stirred Irish memories of English oppression and Protestant doubts about Catholic loyalties. As a leader of the Protestant Federation, the Rev. Thomas Woodfull of Moonee Ponds led the attack on Mannix: 'Archbishop Mannix had deliberately set himself out to discourage the loyalty of the people … It was a betrayal, despotical and horrible.' Inspired, perhaps, by Woodfull's example, and by Harold's death, my apparently mild grandfather joined the Protestant Federation. It is one of the few things I know about him. My father mentioned it, a little shamefacedly, as evidence of how completely relations between Catholics and Protestants had changed during his lifetime.

Looking back, my political sympathies are with the anti-conscriptionists, but if I put myself in John's shoes, I can understand why he felt as he did. He was probably angry—angry about Harold's death and what it meant for them all, especially Edith, but perhaps about other things as well. He had come to Australia believing it was part of a Greater Britain, only to find there were Australians unwilling to come to Britain's aid. Anger, it is said, is often a response to grief. Harold's death was the last and worst in a series of disappointments the family had faced since leaving England.

At last, in November 1918, the guns fell silent and peace was declared. On 21 November, ten days after the Armistice, the Methodists of Ascot Vale gathered in a service of thanksgiving. The interior of the church had been decorated with a 'very fine display of flags and flowers'. A lay preacher, Mr Kelly, whose only son had been killed in the conflict, led the morning service, which began with the doxology and ended with Te Deum Laudamus. In the evening, the Rev. Henry Richardson continued to sound a note of thanks for the 'great victory that has been won by the British Empire and her Allies, thanks to the brave lads who have fought and bled, thanks to the brave and patient mothers who have given their boy in the great cause'. I am sure that the little colony of recent English immigrants—John and Ada Davison, Edith Harding, Walter and Elizabeth Mansfield, along with the Todds and the Wilkinsons—would have been there in strength that day, joining heartily in the thanksgiving and trusting that the all-wise Providence who had brought them victory would also deliver them into better times.

Lower-middle-class Essendon grew rapidly through the early twentieth century along Mount Alexander Road and the Broadmeadows railway line. Its best streets were near the transport corridor. The Davisons lived on the flat near the Maribyrnong River.

The Borders was a region where extended families, or 'surnames', each had their own homelands. East Teviotdale was dominated by rival branches of the Ker family. The Davisons clustered close to the Cheviot Hills, near Forster, and the English Border. Courtesy Joseph Bell of Chorley, Lancashire, England, UK.

Elizabeth Anne ('Cissie') Davison, 1878–1968, was the fifth of Thomas and Mary Davison's seven children and the only surviving daughter. Attractive and vivacious, she worked alongside her father and brother John in their Erdington ironmongery business until 1919, when her mother died and Cissie became housekeeper for her father and unmarried brothers.

By 1929, the Davison household in Erdington had shrunk to ninety-year-old widower Thomas, his fifty-year-old daughter Cissie, and 43-year-old son Alfred. Three other brothers had died prematurely so, when Alfred married in 1932, Cissie was alone and homeless.

Carlisle marketplace and town hall. The sundial on a seventeenth-century market cross measures pre-industrial time while a four-faced mechanical turret clock above the town hall, gifted by mayor John Richardson in 1800, announces the arrival of the industrial age.

Cummersdale Mill, Samuel Bough, 1844, Tullie House Museum, Carlisle. William Davidson's employer, the textile printers Stead McAlpin, purchased the water-powered mill in 1835, later adding the steam-powered printery whose tall chimney appears in the distance. The station of the newly opened Carlisle and Maryport railway is faintly visible in the left foreground.

Archivist Alan James demonstrates the technique of creating hand-printed fabrics with designs cut on wooden blocks practised at the Stead McAlpin works for almost two centuries.

With his frock coat, clenched fist and penetrating gaze, tinplate worker Thomas Davison projects the authority of the model trade union leader. His wife Mary (nee Shepherd) had followed him to Birmingham from Cumberland.

By 1900, when his workmates presented this photographic portrait to Thomas Davison, he was 62 years old, still bright eyed, but facing retirement without his expected pension. Mary, with her spectacles, lace cap and open bible, is the picture of the Victorian matriarch.

Ada Cardall, eldest child of brass burnisher Joseph Cardall, met her husband John Davison, eldest child of Thomas and Mary Davison, at Islington Wesleyan Chapel in the 1890s. John's casual pose belies his startled expression and contrast with the determination in Ada's eyes and mouth.

John and Ada Davison and their children (from left) Frank, Grace, baby George and Phyllis posed, probably at the rear of their shop in Moseley Road shortly before their departure for Australia in June 1912.

Engaged couple George Davison and May Hewett shortly before their marriage in 1940.

Ada Davison in 1947 with children Frank, Grace, and George, next to sister-in-law Cissie, and nine of her eleven (eventually fourteen) grandchildren. Absent was the family of her first-born, Phyllis.

George and May Davison with children Graeme, Helen and Janet in the front garden of 16 Banchory Street, c. 1962.

Oxford bound. The author farewells his girlfriend Barbara Grant on the deck of the P&O Liner *Orcades,* September 1964.

CHAPTER 8

The Years between

MIGRATION IS A lottery. The big winners are usually not the adults who decide to leave their homeland but their children. John and Ada Davison didn't fare much better in Australia than they had in England, maybe even worse; the real beneficiaries were their four children, Phyllis, Frank, Grace and my father George. That is certainly what the children believed. Looking back from comfortable middle age, they praised their parents' courage in leaving the Old Country to give them a better life in the new. By then, they were enjoying the long wave of prosperity that followed World War II. They owned their own homes and cars, watched television, kept their food in refrigerators and saw their children passing through high school into secure, often professional, jobs. This, they believed, was the Promised Land their parents had glimpsed from afar, and wished for them.

But I wonder if they were right. Their good fortune may have vindicated their parents' decision to emigrate but it did not explain it. In the 1950s a researcher asked assisted British migrants sailing to

Australia why they were migrating. Most men said it was to improve their personal prospects, although their wives were more likely to say it was for their children's. Many years later when historians asked a group who emigrated at about the same time to recall their reasons for leaving, their answers were different: now, most migrants, men as well as women, said they had migrated for their children. With the benefit of hindsight, they had apparently revised the memory of their intentions to agree with its best outcome: the better lives enjoyed by their children. We don't have direct evidence of John and Ada's intentions but perhaps, like their friend Harold Harding, they originally expected lives of 'usefulness and success' for themselves, and not just for their children.

After all, those better times took a long time to arrive. My parents and their siblings achieved modest comfort only after weathering two world wars and a global depression. If their lives in 1950s Melbourne were better than their parents' in Edwardian Birmingham, it was because the whole Western world eventually became more prosperous. If they had stayed in England they may also have shared the general prosperity of the postwar years. John and Ada's fortunes may even have improved during World War I when Birmingham's armaments industry boomed. When Frank visited his Birmingham relatives in 1929 they gave him such a good time, with motor tours of the surrounding countryside and lunch at a gentlemen's club, that he probably felt like the poor Australian relation. By the 1950s his English cousins were also driving cars and watching television, if not yet owning their own homes.

To understand my parents' outlook, then, I need to forget the happy ending of their story and consider their difficult early years. They were products, not of the boom after the second war, but of the hard years following the first. Their experience was different from earlier and later waves of British migrants. In the 1850s, 1880s and 1950s Australian living standards were rising, pushing new migrants up the social scale and consolidating their good fortunes. In the quarter century following the Great War they actually fell. Australia ended the war loaded with debt and did not quickly recover. By the mid-1920s living standards had barely regained prewar levels, and with the onset of the Great Depression they fell again. In the nineteenth century Australian incomes were higher than in similar societies, like the United States, Canada and Argentina, but in the 1920s they were lower. Australia again became a lucky country in the 1950s and 1960s only after a long run of indifferent luck.

In the midst of the Great War politicians had promised a land fit for heroes. When peace came they spoke expansively of an Australia Unlimited. But the reality for most young people in the 1920s was of an Australia Limited—a land of dimmed hopes and narrow horizons. What welfare expenditure the state could afford was directed towards the heroes, the returned servicemen who certainly needed and deserved it. So, for example, there were state-sponsored schemes for soldier settlement and war-service homes. My grandparents were ineligible for any of these. Their children, coming of age in the late 1920s and early 1930s, belonged to what was often later called 'the depression generation'.

As a child, I was conscious of the difference between the world in which my parents grew up and my own lucky youth. Of course our parents were glad for us. Our good luck was the deferred reward for their endurance. But the luck came with the tacit expectation that we should be grateful for it. Being young and not really knowing any world but our own, our parents' occasional homilies, illustrated with stories of depression hardships, made little impression. Every now and then, especially when one of us became too demanding or ungrateful, my father, usually the mildest of men, would remind us of the material contrast between his childhood and ours.

There was little sign that hardship made my parents more disillusioned or alienated, but it certainly made them more frugal and risk-averse. Knowing little of what they had endured, we mistook their desire for security for a failure of imagination, rather than the sane recognition of life's uncertainty that we would learn only when our own lucky streak ended.

Crowded House

My father George, the youngest of John and Ada's children, was seven when the Great War ended. He recalled little of the war itself, or of his dead uncle, Harold. But one of its effects—the presence of his widowed aunt and cousin Margaret in the household at 57 Athol Street—was among his earliest memories. How they all—three adults plus five children ranging in age from infancy to early teens—fitted into a single-fronted cottage with just two decent bedrooms is a mystery. In the eyes of some of their fellow Methodists, it may even have been a cause for pity or censure. Overcrowding, after all, was considered both unhealthy and immoral. As devout Methodists, they would have been shocked to be regarded as slum-dwellers, not because their housing was satisfactory but because they had overcome its limitations. When he looked back, my father was grateful to his parents for the 'happy secure home environment they provided under difficult circumstances'.

They had brought very few possessions with them from England so they improvised with the few they had. They threw a cloth over a large sea chest to make a dining table and inserted shelves in shipping crates for dressing tables. They hung rails and curtains beside fireplaces for wardrobes and fitted legs to spring mattresses to make stretcher beds. John made a tiny bench under the kitchen window where, on Saturday nights, he repaired and polished the family's shoes in preparation for Sunday services. Ada cooked the family's meals on a wood-fuelled stove, which also heated the house, and prepared Sunday roasts in a gas oven fed by a penny-in-the-slot meter. She stored food in a cupboard with perforated sides and kept butter in a cooler placed in the hearth to catch the breezes trapped by the chimney. They washed clothes and dishes in a tiny annex (scullery) beside the kitchen while the family took turns to bathe in a bathroom with hardly enough room to stand up beside a tin tub filled from a cold tap and hot water carried from the kitchen stove.

This four-roomed cottage in Athol Street, Moonee Ponds, was home to the Davison family for more than fifteen years. In 1920, John and Ada and their four children, (clockwise) Phyllis, Frank, Grace and George, shared the house with Ada's widowed sister Edith and her daughter Margaret.

John and Ada occupied the matrimonial bedroom and their daughters Phyllis and Grace shared the second, leaving their sons Frank and George to sleep on stretcher beds on the front verandah behind a roll-down canvas blind. How Edith and Margaret squeezed in I do not know, but perhaps they camped in the living room. (A tiny, windowless room, nominally the third bedroom, was used as a store.) On cold and rainy nights the boys were forced to gather up their beds and sleep in the entrance hall. They continued to sleep on the verandah even after the family moved to a more spacious house in Washington Street. Sleep-outs were a feature of many houses in that era, when eugenists fretted about the physique of a nation reared in narrow alleys and airless rooms. I slept in one myself until I was in my teens.

Just along the street was the Moonee Ponds West State School. Even before he enrolled there, George liked to stand at the gate and listen for the school bell. 'That's the first bell, hurry up, you will be late,' he would remind his brother and sisters. Towards midday it would sound again. 'That's the bell, the children will soon come home for lunch,' he reminded Ada. The school bell was like 'the timekeeper for the whole community', he recalled. When he became old enough, he was excited to be asked to pull the bell-rope himself.

His memories of the classroom and playground were less fond. Sitting in rows on backless wooden seats, chanting and scratching letters and numbers on a slate, he found 'dull and uninteresting'. In the playground, handicapped by his diminutive stature, he was usually among the last to be 'picked up' for football or cricket teams. The competition was keen, for his contemporaries included the future Essendon football champions Dick Reynolds and Jack Kidd. Nobody who knew him in later life would have thought him unintelligent. He was probably not the only child to find the classroom tuition of that time unappealing. He was never a keen reader, except of the daily newspaper—always the broadsheet *Argus* or *Age* rather than the tabloid *Sun*—nor a fluent writer. Experience, including some hard knocks, keen observation, imitation and discussion, were his education.

Going to Work

As he reached Sixth Grade, George discussed with his father what he might do in life. John, who lacked a trade ticket, had struggled to find regular employment in Victoria. He had seen fellow migrants with trade qualifications sail past him. He was determined that his children not repeat his mistake and insisted that they all get a trade. 'When a boy leaves school in Victoria,' a contemporary explained, 'it is easier for him to get a job at what then appears to him to be a big salary than to get a job at which he will be taught a skilled trade.' A fifteen-year-old boy employed as a messenger, factory hand or 'improver' could earn a pound a week, but as soon as he reached adulthood and a man's wage he was sacked. This trap—the Dead-End Job—was what John wanted his children to avoid. Neither he nor my father had much interest in an academic path. 'Higher education,' they agreed, was both 'unnecessary' and 'out of reach'. All of George's children would one day go through high school into professional jobs but in the 1920s, when scarcely one male in ten worked in a white-collar job, they were probably right to think it could be just another dead-end.

'I think you would be happier at a technical school,' John advised. 'You seem to be more suited to working with your hands.' 'Being good with your hands' was a phrase I often heard as a child. It did not mean that your mind was not engaged as well. The ability to draw or read a plan, and reproduce it in wood, stone, clay, textile or metal, using only hand tools, was something to be proud of. It was what the Davisons had been doing—as breeches-makers, calico printers, bootmakers and tinplate-workers—for more than a century. By the 1920s, the hand worker was increasingly thrown into competition with a machine, but for my father, like his Davison forebears, the qualities of a good tradesman—ingenuity, dexterity, precision, hand–eye coordination, honesty, hard work—aligned closely with their ideal of manly independence. Fifty years later, George was grateful for the 'perceptive' advice that set him on the path to 'a most satisfying and enjoyable working life'.

Instead of staying on at Moonee Ponds West, my father completed Seventh and Eighth Grade at the West Melbourne Junior Technical School. Leaving home at 'the first bell', he took a fifteen-minute walk to the Ascot Vale station and a ten-minute train ride to Spencer Street, arriving in time for the commencement of classes at nine. He was proud of his school and became a strong supporter of technical education, trained several apprentices himself, and later served on the council of his local technical school, becoming president in the year I went to university. In the 1960s, technical education was often seen as the inferior branch of education, in spite of its excellent results. Even in the 1920s, my father recalled, some teachers and parents would say, 'He's not too bright; better send him to the Tech.' But that was not his own experience or opinion, and a century on, with universities oversold and trade training neglected, I think he was right.

In becoming an apprentice, my father was undertaking one of the oldest forms of vocational education. Since the Middle Ages, parents had entered a contract ('indentures') with a master to teach their children (usually their son) a trade. In earlier times, they paid a sum of money ('premium') to the master and, while that practice had largely ceased by the early twentieth century, apprentices still earned only a reduced wage in recognition of their tuition. In insisting that his children learn a trade, John, whose own earnings were never great, was sacrificing his family's current income to advance his children's future prospects. A small advance in our eyes, it was a large one in his.

In August 1919, his eldest child, fifteen-year-old Phyllis, began a four-year apprenticeship as an 'order coat maker' with the large Flinders Street clothier Charles Lane. Making clothes was a traditional occupation for girls but it was notoriously badly paid.

In making coats to order for well-to-do clients, Phyllis was entering the more respectable side of the industry. She would learn all aspects of making a coat—designing, measuring, cutting, sewing, fitting—not just a part of it. The firm's location, close to the city's fashionable retail shops, may also have been attractive to her.

Phyllis and her parents signed an agreement with Lane to teach Phyllis her trade 'to the best of his knowledge and ability', while she promised to 'honestly faithfully and diligently serve and obey' her master. Lane could cancel the agreement at any time if she was 'disobedient to [his] lawful commands', 'seriously misconduct[ed] herself' or gave 'no promise of becoming a competent workman'. Beginning on 7s 6d per week, Phyllis's wages rose to a maximum of thirty-five shillings, or about two-thirds of the male clothing apprentice's wage, at the end of the fourth year. She worked five and a half days a week, or forty-four hours, with no provision for sick pay and only eight paid public holidays a year.

Most people then, including John and Ada, regarded women's employment differently from men's. 'A boy knows from birth he will be a breadwinner; that is his lot in life. A girl learns that in all probability she will marry,' an arbitration judge observed. Since most female employees lived with their parents, they were paid just enough to relieve the parents from their upkeep, but not much more. But in 1919 the president of the Commonwealth Arbitration Court, Justice HB Higgins, took a closer look at the situation of young women working in the clothing industry. In his 1907 *Harvester Judgment*, Higgins had defined the 'living wage' as sufficient for a man to support his wife and two children in 'frugal comfort'. What wage, he now asked, would meet the 'reasonably necessary requirements of a woman living in a civilized community?'

Higgins was torn between two objectives: giving equal pay for work of equal value and protecting the livelihood of the family man. He acknowledged that women's wages were too low: they made no allowance for train and tram fares, sickness or old age, union or lodge fees, amusements, church collection, stamps, journals, books or charity—or even for buying clothes. But the young women did not have to support a family—or so he assumed. So their wages should be higher, but not as high as men's wages.

Higgins was concerned with the young women's working conditions as much as their pay. After all, they were the future mothers of the nation. Was the factory, with its noise and vibration, its artificial light, its long hours spent sitting and stooping, its fatigue and headaches, harmful to their health and to that of the children they would eventually bear? To limit the risk, Higgins shortened their weekly working hours from forty-eight to forty-four and required a minimum three-quarter-hour lunch break. This concession to the supposed weakness of the female worker was also passed on to her male peers. But, by the same logic, he also refused to allow them to concentrate their forty-four hours into five working days, so depriving them of a Saturday holiday. Time, he implied, was a dimension of life to be ordered in accordance with public health and public good as well as personal preferences.

In 1920, Phyllis's brother Frank began his apprenticeship with a local printing and publishing firm, Lucas and Tabsley. Printing was a respected and well-paid trade. It attracted young men with literary and political interests, like Frank and my maternal grandfather Vic Hewett. The printers' union, the Melbourne Typographical Association, retained some of the traditions of a medieval craft society. But by the 1920s new technologies such as linotype machines and offset rotary presses were transforming the traditional forms of trade training. In 1921 a conference of employers, unions, educational authorities and the government agreed on a new system of trade training for printers which soon became the model for other trades as well. Apprentices now began their indentures only after the age of fifteen when they had completed their elementary education. They served for six years, instead of the traditional seven, but had to attend technical school classes in English and arithmetic and, in the later years of their apprenticeship, in printing at a technical college.

This was the modern plan my father was following when he enrolled in West Melbourne Tech. He seems to have thrived on it, steadily improving his marks and winning a studentship that paid all his fees, until in 1926 he began a five-year plumbing apprenticeship with Cecil Rodgers. Why he chose plumbing is unclear. Working with metal was a family tradition, and my father later spoke of the satisfaction he gained from cutting, shaping and soldering sheets of lead, copper and galvanised iron into three-dimensional forms. But obtaining an apprenticeship was a matter of patronage as much as choice or aptitude. The fact that Cecil Rodgers, a forty-year-old AIF veteran with Methodist connections, lived just a few doors from the Davisons in Athol Street may have been the decisive factor.

In many people's eyes, plumbing was—to speak plainly—a shitty job. Even today the plumber is often portrayed as the rough fellow who arrives at your door with a wrench and plunger to unblock your sewer, disappears under the house or into the back lane for a few moments and later presents you with an enormous bill. He does the dirty work you would not be prepared to do yourself but gets little admiration for it. Even in a society where many people worked with their hands, plumbers had to overcome the stigma of their association with the most basic human functions.

A contemporary photograph of a plumbing class at West Melbourne Tech depicts apprentices practising the ancient craft of beating and shaping lead, the metal from which the trade took its name (in Latin, plumbum), under the watchful eye of their instructor. In the 1920s lead had largely given way to galvanised iron, brass and copper in many phases of the trade and by the time my father retired they had all been replaced by plastic. Teacher and pupils are dressed respectably in shirt, tie and waistcoat, sometimes with a fob watch. On the wall, amidst samples of T-joints and S-bends, is a framed motto: 'When people are educated to know the importance of sanitary plumbing in relation to their health and happiness they will respect the plumber for having instructed them in these things and the business of plumbing will be elevated to that place in public

In the 1920s apprentice plumbers at West Melbourne Technical School learned the ancient skills of working with lead, the malleable metal that gave the trade its name. Courtesy Public Record Office of Victoria.

estimation now enjoyed by the learned professions.' The writer was correct: the engineers and plumbers who rid cities of their human filth did more than the doctors to cut the appalling mortality of nineteenth-century cities. My father was proud of his trade but as his kids we knew that we were still a few notches below the doctors and lawyers in public estimation.

The Long Years of Youth

In the 1960s people used to speak of a 'generation gap' between the baby boomers and their parents. One of the big differences was the length of time between the end of education and the beginning of marriage and full adulthood. In the late 1960s, when I married I was still engaged in formal education, but when my father married in 1940 more than fifteen years had elapsed since he left school. His brother Frank waited even longer to marry, almost twenty years. Their generation usually left school earlier than we postwar children, but they also married later, sometimes because depression and war intervened. In between, they lived with their parents, contributing to the family income, sometimes completing apprenticeships, and waiting until they could afford to marry and start families of their own. These waiting years were a long education in patience and self-denial, an experience beyond the comprehension of their children.

How they occupied this long waiting time was a topic of keen public interest. 'Much attention is at present being given to the Australian adolescent,' the Melbourne *Age* observed in 1929. In using the word 'adolescent', the writer was alluding to the anxieties famously raised by the American psychologist G Stanley Hall in his popular book *Adolescence* (1904). Hall feared that young people, especially young men, chafing against parental authority, would become demoralised and rebellious. Australian observers generally took a more hopeful view. Their young people were less likely than Americans to leave home for college education. Many, like the Davison children, undertook apprenticeships, a semi-dependent state that, it was argued, curbed their discontent. 'In metropolitan and provincial cities, in numerous suburban areas, armies of youths and maidens are to be seen making their way to evening technical schools and other educational institutions,' *The Age* noted approvingly.

Days of tiring work, lengthened by evening classes twice a week, left these youths with relatively little leisure. Their elders were eager to fill their idle hours with harmless fun, vigorous outdoor recreation and community service. 'The community seems delivered up to institutional work on behalf of youth,' *The Age* noted. 'The churches and closely related bodies, along with numerous organizations innocent of any ecclesiastical odor, are unselfishly seeking to cater for youth's physical well-being and wholesome pleasure.' When I scan my parents' photo albums I am struck by how much of their time seems to have been spent in the company of their own sex. Most youth organisations were run along single-sex lines—relations with the opposite sex, at least in my parents' churchy lower middle-class stratum of society, were more circumscribed than in my own youth. Propriety, modesty and prudence, built into the structure of their workplaces, churches, sporting clubs and youth organisations, kept the sexes within sight of each other but mostly at a distance.

In 1917, soon after Harold Harding perished on the Western Front, twelve-year-old Frank Davison joined the new First Moonee Ponds Scout Troop. He and my father would devote much of their youth to the Scout movement. Their parents were active supporters, their sisters would marry young men from the Moonee Ponds troop, and Frank would marry the sister of two fellow Scouts. Scouting gave a muscular slant to their Methodism, nurtured lifelong friendships, introduced them to the Australian bush, consolidated their Australian identity and eased the transition from their parents' ardent imperialism to their adult internationalism. They were among the thousands of young Victorians drawn to the movement in the interwar years. In 1929 there were 18 000 Victorian Scouts, or almost one in five of their age cohort, probably the highest penetration of any voluntary youth movement before or since.

The Scout movement arrived in Victoria soon after it began in England. Its founder, Major-General Robert Baden-Powell, originally promoted it as an antidote to the effects of slum life on English working-class youth. 'Civilisation sapped a man's strength,' he declared; only a return to the wild frontier could restore it. B-P, as his followers affectionately dubbed him, toured Australia in 1912, hailing its harbour foreshores and leafy suburbs as ideal for Scouting. Competition from the Commonwealth's compulsory youth military training scheme at first slowed the movement's growth, but after the Great War it took off. First Moonee Ponds Scout Troop was founded in 1915 by local Methodist preacher Cecil Stevens. A 37-year-old bachelor, Stevens was patriotic, devout and charismatic in the earnest manly style of B-P himself. He stressed 'The Spiritual Basis of Scouting', an idea pithily expressed in the plaque he hung on the wall of his Scout Hall:

> Who teaches a Boy
> By the Master's plan
> Is shaping the life
> Of the future man.

A century on, many features of the early Scout movement seem foreign, even repugnant, to us. Its militarism and imperialism, its patriarchal masculinity and muscular Christianity, belong to an Edwardian world we have left behind. Some historians detect a strain of misogyny and repressed homosexuality in its bachelor leaders' love of young men. But to my family, Stevens was a 'shining example' of Christian manhood. When he resigned as scoutmaster, discouraged by a lack of support, my grandfather persuaded him to stay on. After he died in 1942, George and Frank led the appeal to install a plaster relief of his profile in the new Scout Hall they built on land he had acquired. In the 1950s, I visited the First Moonee Ponds Scout Hall with my parents for a square dance, an American craze then at its peak. The interior, with its dark wood panelling, stone fireplace and effigy of the saintly Cecil Stevens, made a strong impression. A combination of the barrack, the shrine and the den, it is an evocative relic of the early Scout movement.

During the Great War, the Scouts acted as junior auxiliaries of the Red Cross and military authorities. Some of its leaders were returned soldiers, and uniforms, badges, salutes and drill were essential parts of its program. As soon as the war was over, however, they repudiated the idea that they were 'Australian soldiers in embryo'. '[The movement] does not aim at making good soldiers; it aims at making good citizens,' Governor-General and Chief Scout Lord Foster insisted. Scouting was a Great Game, a form of rugged play that instilled good citizenship more effectively than the classroom or the parade ground. Years later, Frank Davison exulted in the 'jolly days of our very early scouting':

> Fresh to the 'game', with the romance and adventure of it filling the needs of our tingling young souls, a thirst for the thrills of life—how we played those games: 'Attack and Defence', stalking, tracking, and the long-awaited and much-longed-for camps full of fun and jolly comradeship.

New Scouts, or 'Tenderfeet' as they were known, promised to do their best to do their duty to God and the King, and to obey the ten points of the Scout Law. One law in particular left its mark upon my father: 'A Scout smiles and whistles under all difficulties.' As a boy, I could always tell when my father was approaching by his cheerful whistle. He was a singer, too, with a fine tenor voice, but whistling was his everyday domestic music. He taught me to whistle but I notice that younger people look at me strangely when I do. I seldom hear anyone whistling nowadays. People carry their music with them in phones and earplugs rather than making it themselves and sharing it with others. Nothing, I sometimes think, so separates my father's age and ours as the decline of whistling, a simple form of musical and psychological self-help that buoyed people's spirits in hard times.

'There was nothing like a bit of camp life in summer for making boys men,' B-P believed. It took the Moonee Ponds boys two days to pull their trek cart—a light, two-wheeled vehicle laden with tents, ropes, billycans and their own packs—to their usual campsite at Eltham, breaking the journey overnight beside the Darebin Creek. They pitched their ex-army tents on a friendly farmer's land near the junction of the Yarra and Diamond Creek. There they filled their summer and Easter holidays with swimming, boating, football, cricket, stretcher drill, fire-lighting, singsongs, campfire concerts and 'heart-to-heart' talks by their inspirational leader. A quince tree laden with ripe fruit lured the best swimmers across the swift-flowing river. Stevens confiscated the proceeds of their first raid for the camp

Frank Davison joined the Boy Scouts when the movement was in its infancy. He later became a Rover Scout, Scoutmaster and eventually District Commissioner.

kitchen but locked the gate to their little Eden after one boy nearly drowned. Camping was adventurous, companionable and, importantly, cheap. Frank and George embraced it with an enthusiasm they passed on to us.

On 26 April 1926, Frank and his mate Ron Horne were returning from an Anzac Day weekend hike when their train collided with a motor van packed with homecoming picnickers at the Boronia level crossing. The passengers' raucous singing had drowned out the whistle of the approaching train and the van was halfway across the line when the locomotive hit. The driver escaped injury but nine of his passengers were killed and fifteen injured. Frank and his companions, who had been travelling in the second carriage, immediately set about rendering first aid, cutting into the wreckage to release the wounded and improvising splints with their staves and scarves. 'They worked wonderfully, I do not know what we would have done without them,' an eyewitness recalled. Public figures, from the prime minister down, hailed their heroism. The Moonee Ponds Scout Troop won fame and a medal in recognition of Frank and Ron's part in the effort.

Scouting was just a phase in the lives of most boys. Frank and George Davison, who joined early and rose to become Rovers and Scout leaders, were an exception. While still in his early twenties, and despite his diminutive stature—his nickname among the Rovers was 'Small'—Frank began to play a role in the wider Scout movement. Inspired by Stevens, he led a Cub Pack for boys at the Royal Park Neglected Children's Home. The boys, distractible and rebellious, were locked with their leaders in a large room, with ex-soldiers guarding the doors. Capturing their interest and winning their trust was 'difficult work', yet Frank evidently got through to some who were still writing to him years later, sometimes from prison and other dark places.

The growth of the movement—the number of Cubs had increased tenfold in less than a decade—quickly outran its supply of leaders. In 1927 Frank addressed a 'Great Rover Moot' at Wesley College's Adamson Hall. 'Scoutmasters were not offering in sufficient numbers, and therefore they had to look within, rather than without, the movement for leaders,' he contended. 'In this respect the rovers could do big things in little ways to help heal the breach between capital and labour.' The unity of capital and labour was a tune straight out of his grandfather's Birmingham songbook. In Australia, as in Britain, the movement flourished most among the lower middle and respectable working classes: First Moonee Ponds included the sons of clerks, commercial travellers and teachers as well as butchers, wheelwrights, quarrymen and labourers. Scouting appealed to the outlook of a lower middle class that was simultaneously deferential to its social superiors and benevolent towards its inferiors. 'A Scout is a friend to all and a brother to every other Scout, no matter to what other social class the other belongs,' the fourth Scout Law decreed. 'A Scout must never be a snob,' the *Australian Scout's First Book* (1931) added. By the time I joined in the 1950s, the law had been revised to embrace every other Scout no matter what their 'country, class or creed'.

The lower middle class gets generally bad press from Australian historians, despite the fact that many were born into it. Some ignore it, even though it comprised as much as a quarter of the population. Others, influenced perhaps by Marx's dismissive view ('the most reactionary [class], for they try to roll back the wheel of history') despise it. One leftist historian, Stuart Macintyre, writes more sympathetically of 'the anxious class'—lower white-collar workers, self-employed tradesmen, minor professionals, shopkeepers and the like—caught uneasily between their slender means and their moral and social aspirations. Over the generations, my own family moved back and forth across the divide between the respectable working class and the lower middle class. Were they anxious? If so, perhaps their anxieties were eased by their involvement in movements like Methodism and Scouting that straddled class divisions and promoted self-respect and altruistic service above wealthy display. Were they 'reactionary'? In my observation, they were as likely to break to the left as to the right. Certainly Marx's expectation that the lower middle class would quickly sink into the proletariat was wide of the mark. The wheels of history rolled slower than he expected. Indeed, others have argued that the temper of Australian society as a whole was essentially lower middle class. If that was so, then the Davisons were not marginal but mainstream.

Frank finished his apprenticeship in 1926 and worked for several job printers before joining the *Herald and Weekly Times* in 1927. He became a specialist in setting the large type for the paper's headlines on a Ludlow Typograph, a machine that straddled the old world of hand compositing and the 'hot metal' technology of the linotype machine. Now on a man's wage, he saved enough by June 1929 for the

£125 fare aboard the P&O liner *Baraldine* carrying the 200-strong Australian Contingent to the World Scout Jamboree at Arrowe Park near Liverpool. The Scouts were travelling with eighty Anzac 'Pilgrims', the first of many Australians to 'return' to the shores where their sons had died. On embarkation, they were sorted into patrols drawn from the various states. 'This tended to weld us together into an Australian outlook, rather than into States with just a narrow State outlook,' Frank noted. Eager to impress their English hosts, they spent the long hours afloat brushing up on their scoutcraft.

In August they joined 80 000 other Scouts living under canvas at Arrowe Park. Marching behind a giant kangaroo mascot, the Australians gave a good account of themselves. Frank wrote:

> I think I can say, without in any way boasting or exaggerating, [the Australian Contingent] was equal to … any other Contingent present. The idea among the chaps seemed not for self-advertisement, but for Australia. Most of the chaps were big in stature, rough in speech perhaps, but the way they made friends everywhere and the unsolicited praise received was a testimonial of no mean measure to the popularity of the Australians.

Frank, the short, reserved, polite and half-assimilated English immigrant, seems to be commending his alter ego, the big, rough-spoken, outgoing Australian, to the minatory Englishman who still resided in the minds of many Australians.

After the jamboree, Frank participated in a Cubmaster training course at the British Scout headquarters at Gilwell Park, investigated English schemes for the reform of delinquent youths and visited his family in Birmingham, the scene of that memorable encounter with his grandfather Thomas when the old man exclaimed: 'Listen, our ancestors!' He made a brief tour of the Continent before returning to Australia in November. What had most impressed him, he told his friends at First Moonee Ponds, was 'a feeling of the bigness of Scouting and of its wonderful possibilities for International and

Inter-racial brotherhood'. This was 'not merely as a passing idea, but a thoroughly fixed and definite object to be achieved'.

No sooner had it become a 'fixed and definite object', however, than that hope began to fade. Unknowingly, Frank was returning to an Australia perched on a precipice. Through 1929, amidst mounting economic and industrial woes, the conservative government of prime minister Stanley Melbourne Bruce was sliding towards electoral defeat. On 12 October, as Frank neared Australian shores, Labor's James Scullin became prime minister. Two weeks later, a catastrophic sell-off of shares on the New York Stock Exchange—the 'The Wall Street Crash'—signalled the beginning of the Great Depression. Everywhere, it seemed, at home and abroad, class and national antagonisms were on the rise again. For the Davisons, the timing could hardly have been worse. Just as John and Ada entered old age and their children looked towards marriage and families of their own, their prospects took an abrupt turn for the worse.

John Davison poses with his sons Frank and George and fellow English immigrant Bob Buck on the verandah of 49 Washington Street, the house he and Ada purchased in August 1929.

CHAPTER 9

A Tale of Two Houses

JOHN AND ADA longed for a home of their own. It was a dream well beyond their reach in Birmingham, where renting was the rule. But since colonial times, owning your own home had been one of the main attractions of migrating to Australia. I don't know whether my grandparents conceived the ambition before they left England or after they arrived in Australia. Most of their neighbours in Athol Street were renters like themselves, although several of their immigrant friends had bought their own homes. When they arrived in 1912, about half of Australia's householders owned or were buying their own homes. But from the first, despite their straitened circumstances, John and Ada seem to have been eager to follow them.

In May 1920 John put a deposit on a block of land on the Glenroy Heights estate, half a mile east of Glenroy Station, five stations up the line from Ascot Vale. 'Ideal building land', '21 trains daily' and 'assured large profits' the advertisements promised. He began paying off the balance at ten shillings a month. Did he really intend to build there and move his family out so far? He kept up the payments for a few years but not until the 1950s, twenty years after he died, did the suburbs catch up with the speculators. His eldest son Frank would then buy his own block and go live in Glenroy. Eventually the Victorian Housing Commission purchased John's remaining equity for £50, less than he originally paid for it.

Another decade would pass before John realised his dream. As a young man he had taken out a £100 policy on his life with the Prudential Insurance Company. Prudential specialised in selling life insurance, previously a middle-class concern, to the respectable working class. Its logo, the Rock of Gibraltar, was a reassuring symbol of the company's solidity. Through all his ups and downs, John somehow kept up the premiums. At last, in August 1929, on his sixtieth birthday, the policy matured. 'Well Mum,' my father recalls him saying, 'we will put a deposit on a house of our own.' The timing was hardly favourable. John's own health was precarious, and economic storm clouds were gathering: the housing market had peaked and would soon begin to fall. He could not know, of course, how long the coming depression would last, or that his own remaining time would be so short. But perhaps these uncertainties only made him more determined to rescue something tangible from his eighteen years in Australia.

Number 49 Washington Street, a plain, twenty-year-old timber cottage in an unfashionable street ten minutes' walk from Essendon station, was no dream house. But with six good rooms, a bathroom, washhouse, lean-to lavatory, return verandah, and a shed opening on the back lane, all set on a forty-by-150-foot allotment, it was more than twice as spacious as their single-fronted rented cottage in Athol Street. In April 1930, John paid his £100 towards the £885 purchase price, borrowing the rest from the vendor, Winifred Olley, the wife of a local builder, at seven and a half per cent interest. He pledged to pay it off at thirty shillings a week until he could secure finance from a bank or building society.

'Thus,' my father recalled, 'in the midst of an economic depression the Davison family … occupied with much pride the first home of their own. [John] thoroughly enjoyed those four years living in his own home.' Soon, however, John's health took a turn for the worse. The congestive heart failure that claimed his younger brothers was catching up on him. In September 1933, aware that his days might be numbered, he made a fresh will.

His sister Cissie, now alone in the house in Erdington, decided to sail out and join him. She arrived at Station Pier aboard the SS *Ormonde* on 15 January 1934 with the Davisons' ancestral clock in her baggage. A photograph taken in the backyard of 49 Washington Street captures their reunion. Cissie, Ada and Grace smile bravely into the camera while John, wearing his best suit, sits in a wicker armchair, his misty eyes fixed on the great beyond. In the bleak days that followed, Ada, Grace and Phyllis took turns to sit by his bed, holding his hand as his heart stopped and started. On 3 March it stopped altogether, never to beat again.

They buried him in Fawkner Cemetery. His epitaph, 'Safe Home in Port', hints at the storms he had weathered since leaving the land

A poignant reunion. In February 1934, newly arrived Elizabeth (Cissie) Davison poses with her dying brother John, sister-in-law Ada and niece Grace in the back garden of 49 Washington Street.

the family still called Home. His Home now was a heavenly one, his earthly one only as safe as the thirty shillings a week he had pledged to Winifred Olley. Melbourne house prices fell less precipitously than in the 1890s depression, but enough to push the Davisons into negative equity. Lending institutions were loath to foreclose unless borrowers fell so far into arrears they could not recover; under the *Financial Emergency Act* of 1931, the interest on borrowings was reduced and mortgagees were protected from foreclosure. But as unemployment increased, there were times during the early 1930s when only one of the Davison children was in work. Unlike tenants, they could not easily downsize, split up or move to where jobs were more plentiful. Intentionally or not, John had bound them in mutual dependence. Their home was bondage as much as boon.

Even before John's death, the Davison household had begun to shrink. In 1932 Phyllis married Alan Porter, a watchmaker and fellow Rover Scout. Their wedding reception in the First Moonee Ponds Scout Hall was a frugal affair, in keeping with the times. Second daughter Grace, a typist, became engaged to another Ascot Vale Methodist and Rover Scout, Bert Horsburgh. Bert's employer, the National Bank, discouraged employees from marrying until they reached a salary of £260 per annum, high enough to keep up respectable appearances and resist the temptation to embezzle. Only in 1936, when they were both twenty-seven and Bert became a branch accountant, were they free to marry. Meanwhile, Cissie also left for the country, where she worked as a live-in nurse.

I wonder how Ada reacted to her husband's death and coped with life afterwards. My father hardly mentioned her in his 'memoirs' and there are only glimpses of her in the stories passed down on the female side of the family. The impression they leave is of a forceful character, perhaps the dominant partner in her marriage. She could certainly be demanding: Grace remembered her barking to her dawdling husband—'Hurry up, John'—as she set off for church without him. In later life, if Grace spoke sharply, Bert chided her: 'Now … Ada.' My own hazy memory is of a staid, severe old lady inhabiting a dark and unwelcoming house, a sharp contrast with my maternal grandparents' bright, warm and welcoming one. How much of that severity, I now wonder, was the woman who came to Australia, how much the one left after the bereavement, homesickness and hardships she endured afterwards?

Surviving the Depression

The obligation to care for Ada and Cissie fell mainly on her boys, Frank and George. To pay off the house they probably stayed longer at 49 Washington Street than they may have wished. Frank lost his job at the *Herald and Weekly Times* in 1931 and then attempted to start his own printing business in Moonee Ponds before joining *The Star*, a short-lived afternoon tabloid published by the morning *Argus* in 1934. When the *Star* folded in 1936 he stayed on with the *Argus*. He also continued to rise through the ranks of the Boy Scout movement, succeeding Cecil Stevens as group Scoutmaster of First Moonee Ponds in 1933.

George finished his plumbing apprenticeship in 1931, 'just as the depression hit'. 'I couldn't get a job anywhere,' he remembered. The building industry, which had boomed in the late 1920s, was hardest hit, and even two years later, when the economy had begun to pick up, plumbers in their twenties had an unemployment rate of over fifty per cent, twice that for married men in their forties. Unemployment in Essendon was lower than in the neighbouring factory suburbs of Footscray and Brunswick and only half that in Fitzroy and Collingwood, but young single men were at the back of the queue for the meagre 'sustenance' work provided by the local council. I doubt my father ever joined that queue, although such was the shame of unemployment he might not have admitted it if he had. The only bitter memory of these years he relayed, at least to me, was his anger at the condescending attitude of patrons at a Melbourne Town Hall concert where he picked up a few bob as a program seller.

With no alternative, he decided to go into business on his own. He had saved about £100. So he put on the phone, got a few tools together and fitted a toolbox to the back of his pushbike, before turning the shed at the rear of 49 Washington Street into a workshop. 'I decided to advertise a bit,' he recalled. He fitted a painted sign into the bike's triangular frame, made another to put beside the road where he was at work, and paid for a larger one on the side of a shop near Essendon station. Years later, commuters could still glimpse the distressed paintwork: 'George H. Davison Licensed Plumber FU5385'.

In the early years of the Depression, George cycled round Essendon with my grandfather, looking for leaking gutters to repair and paint. Later, he followed the Board of Works turncocks as they shut off burst water pipes and served repair notices on householders. As the gang departed, he would knock on the householder's door and propose himself for the job, then pedal back a day or two later carrying lengths of water pipe and a pick and shovel on his shoulder. Once, he rode six miles from Essendon to Richmond, one hand on the handlebar and the other steadying his precarious load: 'I wonder how I did it.' In the days before pneumatic drills, digging down through the bitumen and clay to repair a burst pipe was exhausting pick-and-shovel work, often carried out in mid-summer when the pipes were under the most pressure. But he could ill afford to decline it.

The second-hand vehicle that fellow British immigrant and Methodist John Wilkinson helped my father to buy was a Rugby panel van previously owned by the film company FT Productions, the namesake of which was Frank Thring. The bike was pushed to the back of the shed but when war broke out and petrol rationing began, Dad reclaimed it for the daily three-mile ride to the Maribyrnong Munitions Factory. Years later, when I demanded a bike of my own, we pulled the old one apart, replaced its worn-out tyres and ball bearings and gave it a fresh coat of royal blue paint. Its old-fashioned foot brake was no match for the fancy handbrakes and gears on my mates' new Malvern Stars but it got me through high school.

In his later years, George was interviewed by his grandchildren about his experiences in the 1930s as they researched school projects on 'The Depression'. The stories he told them—of cycling round his neighbourhood for work, eating bread and dripping, turning away beggars because the family had nothing to give, making their own fun because they couldn't afford the kind you paid for—are standard images of the Great Depression. Those experiences were real enough, and there is no doubt that my father's life choices were curtailed, and his values shaped, by the ordeals of that time. But asking someone 'What did you do in the Depression' may elicit a quite different response from asking, say, 'What did you do in your twenties?'—even though, for my father, they were chronologically identical. The 1930s was the decade when he became an adult, made new friends, formed his religious and political outlooks, explored the Victorian countryside and fell in love. None of these experiences was unaffected by the Depression, but they were not defined by it alone.

The Challenge of the Church to the New Age

When they moved to Essendon, the Davisons changed churches. North Essendon Methodist was one of the denomination's strongholds, a stepping stone for talented ministers on their way to the church's highest offices. Prominently located on Mount Alexander Road, its most striking feature—a large rose window—adorned an otherwise unremarkable red-brick Gothic facade. Since opening in 1888, at the peak of the Melbourne land boom, its congregation had grown steadily, along with the lower middle-class population of the surrounding area. My maternal grandparents, Vic and Emma Hewett, arrived from Williamstown just before the Great War and became prominent members, Vic as a local preacher and Bible class leader and Emma as a stalwart of the Ladies Guild and the Sudan Mission Auxiliary.

Just as the Davisons arrived, the congregation welcomed a dynamic new minister, 45-year-old Rev. Cyril Walklate. Walklate, the grandson of a convict, had grown up in Tasmania, trained for the ministry in Melbourne, and was serving in Gippsland during World War I when his brother was killed on the Western Front. He offered himself as an army chaplain but was rejected on medical grounds. Impelled by a mixture of grief, guilt and anger, Walklate threw himself into prime minister Hughes's campaign for conscription with such ferocity that his opponents drove him from a public meeting, pelting him with eggs.

When the guns at last fell silent and they began to count the human cost of the war, many Methodists recoiled from their bellicosity in 1917. Cyril Walklate now campaigned for peace as ardently as he had previously fought to send men to war. He dreamed of a Christian social order that would abolish the greed, militarism and class division that had caused the conflict. 'Society should be established on Christian principles,' he declared in 1934. 'In so far as our social order rendered the teachings of Jesus impracticable, then it should be altered.' With the pacifist H Palmer Phillips and the slum reformer Oswald Barnett, he became a leader of Methodism's radical wing. 'Communists today … offered a definite plan to the world which could be countered only by the adoption of a Christian policy,' he contended.

Since Wesley's day, Methodism had combined calls to personal salvation and social reform. Individual Methodists often leant more towards one or the other, although both were authentic sides of their tradition. Among my father's generation of young Methodists, the idea of a Christian social order offered a glimmer of hope in a dark time. The rise of the dictators and the coming of World War II dashed those ideals and in retrospect we may consider them delusory. Yet during the 1930s they had much wider influence than a reader of most Australian histories would suspect. Their successes, such as Oswald Barnett's housing reforms, are remembered, but their failures, like his equally ardent Christian pacifism, are forgotten.

Walklate combined his ministry at North Essendon with leadership of the Anti-Sweating League. Methodists had helped form the league in the 1890s to combat the exploitation of low-paid factory outworkers and revived it in 1931 to defend unemployed workers, evicted tenants and struggling home-purchasers. Walklate combined Christian socialism with old-fashioned Methodist moralism. He condemned exploitative capitalists and unscrupulous landlords as well as Sunday traders, bookmakers and sly-grog sellers. One Sunday afternoon he stood outside his church counting the commercial vehicles on Mount Alexander Road to bolster his claim that Sunday trading was out of control. Working on Sundays, he believed, not only broke the Ten Commandments but a law almost as holy: the Eight-Hour Day.

Perhaps nothing in my parents' and grandparents' Methodism now seems so strange as their strict, some would say pharisaic, observance of the Sabbath. My grandfather Vic Hewett, a local preacher, walked three miles from his house in North Essendon to lead a service in Flemington rather than take the tram. Melbourne's dismal Sundays, when you couldn't shop, play sport or get a meal or a drink in a hotel, shocked international visitors and embarrassed emancipated locals. Yet Methodists were proud to belong to 'the quietest city in the Empire'. Its quietness testified to its social peace and justice as much as to its piety and sobriety.

They were acting out a distinctively Methodist idea of time. Our post-industrial regime of flexitime, staggered peak hours, insecure casual work and 24/7 shopping has completely obliterated their fixed timetables of work, worship and play. Part of their thinking was still anchored in the Jewish Sabbath, a divinely ordained calendar of work, worship and play, but they were also erecting defences against the insecurity of a capitalist order which left the worker constantly at the beck and call of the boss.

At the heart of their vision was the Christian family, headed by an upright, diligent, securely employed and fairly rewarded working-man. 'Sweating'—unregulated, unscheduled, ill-paid and insecure work—threatened that moral order. 'The average working man of to-day was daily in fear of receiving notice of dismissal,' Walklate wrote as unemployment peaked in 1932. He advocated equal pay for women but his primary concern was for the workingman with family responsibilities: 'Provision should be made for every man over the age of 21 to secure such a position as would enable him to marry and rear a family in reasonable comfort.' In a letter to prime minister Scullin, he proposed that the basic wage should be raised to recognise modern conditions, including the wage earner's need to repay a mortgage. 'Young couples now have to choose between the childless or one-child home, with its comforts, or the mean houses and economic stress inseparable from the possession of children.' To 21-year-old George Davison, an unemployed tradesman with aspirations to marriage, and a mother with a mortgage, this was a persuasive point of view.

North Essendon Methodist was where my father, George Davison, met my mother, May Hewett, eldest of the five daughters of Vic and Emma Hewett. The story of their courtship and marriage is so intertwined with the life of that congregation that I find it hard to disentangle them. My parents remained members of the church for the rest of their lives—more than ninety years in my mother's case. Soon after his father died in 1934, George became a member of the Young Men's Society led by Vic Hewett, who became a father figure to many young men, including my father. The attraction may have been mutual. The young men were like the sons my grandfather hoped for but never had. I also wonder whether my father was attracted to my mother partly because she was Vic's daughter.

Readers of *Lost Relations* have already met Victor Stephens Hewett. Born in Campbell's Creek on the Victorian goldfields, he grew up in Williamstown where his father, an engineer, worked for the Victorian Railways. Vic finished his apprenticeship as a printer just as he qualified as a Methodist local (lay) preacher. By the time he encountered my father in the mid-1930s, he was the manager of one of Melbourne's leading quality printers, the Speciality Press. Books were not just his livelihood but his passion. He was the epitome of the artisan autodidact, a dedicated reader, bibliophile, book collector and philatelist, with a special interest in Australiana.

With reading and discussion, his youthful evangelicalism had broadened into a more expansive social gospel. 'The church is assailed from all quarters,' he told his flock of young Methodists. 'Has the church any survival value? What is its nature?' He continued:

> Just as a watch is to keep time so the church must have a purpose ... Mere extension of membership or reunion is an [in]adequate aim. Its task is to redeem the world's life, to think less of itself and more of the world ... Mr Hewett claimed that a Christian cannot accept any social condition that is hurting people & he is necessarily revolutionary and bound to protest against wrongs.

Vic valued his Methodist heritage, esteeming Wesley the social reformer perhaps more than the evangelist, and encouraging his young men, including my father, to apply the Christian message of love, hope and justice to the urgent questions of the time.

A Methodist Courtship

By the time my parents met, Vic and Emma owned an attractive weatherboard house in Edward Street, one of Essendon's better streets, a few blocks up the hill from the Davisons. With their five pretty daughters, ranging in age from mid-teens to mid-twenties, the family probably cut more of a figure in the North Essendon congregation than the widowed Ada Davison and her two diminutive tradesman sons.

Vic and Emma were devoted parents. Their daughters portrayed Emma as the stricter of the two and Vic as the more indulgent, especially as he grew older. My mother (Emma) May, the eldest, was shy, almost timid, and conscientious to a fault as older children sometimes are, especially if their parents expect a lot of them. She became more confident with age, especially as my father encouraged her to 'come out of herself', as they say.

I did not think of my mother as well educated, although by the standards of her time and sex, she was. After primary education at Essendon State, she attended Essendon High School. It was then quite new, one of only five state high schools in the whole metropolitan area, all of them north of the Yarra except for Melbourne High. The private fee-paying schools had successfully lobbied the government to keep them out of their heartland in the south-eastern middle-class suburbs, an imbalance not redressed until well after World War II. Frank Tate, a long-serving director of education, established the first high schools in country towns to equip young Victorians for a life on the land. The metropolitan high schools had a different mission: to prepare city children for the burgeoning white-collar occupations: teaching, the public service and commerce.

Their headmasters, earnest middle-aged men in three-piece suits, had usually worked their way up from humble beginnings. James King, headmaster of Essendon High in my mother's time, boasted that his school had brought secondary education 'within reach of those who are not blessed with an abundance of this world's goods'. Some of his students, he predicted, 'will pass on to the University for higher studies, others will become shining lights in the business world, whilst all, even the educational failures, will become better citizens of our fair Commonwealth'. His successes included the left-wing journalist and historian Brian Fitzpatrick, Melbourne University Professor of Geology Maurice Tattam, and leading criminal barrister Ray Dunn.

Just to get into Essendon High was a kind of success: my mother and her younger sister Joyce were among only six per cent of Victorian children aged between twelve and sixteen to enjoy a state high school education. Only about half of them progressed as far as the Intermediate Certificate (Year 10). (Essendon High's record was no worse in this respect than that of the 'elite' private schools: just half the boys at Scotch College and Melbourne Grammar reached Intermediate and only one-third of the girls at Methodist Ladies College.) Even so, King and his successor James Hill, father of the communist lawyer Ted Hill, were dissatisfied with their school's retention rate. 'Equality in educational opportunity must be practised as well as preached,' Hill insisted. He constantly chastised parents who did not keep their children at the school for at least four years.

Most Essendon High boys followed the 'professional' stream that led on to university, teaching or the public service, while most girls, like my mother, younger sister Joyce and aunt Grace Davison, followed the 'commercial' stream, supplementing their studies in English, Arithmetic, French, History and Geography with practical classes in typing, shorthand, and commercial principles and practice. May left Essendon High in 1926 after five years' study, including a two-year course in typing and shorthand. 'She is a very well behaved girl, capable, earnest and painstaking and should make a successful typiste or junior clerk,' King wrote. She applied for a junior position at the Eagle Star Insurance Company, missed it, but accepted a temporary position at thirty shillings a week with the prospect of permanency.

By the 1920s the fashionably dressed 'typiste' had become a familiar figure on Melbourne's streets, the epitome of the 'modern girl'. Her appearance in the previously all-male environment of the bank and commercial office stirred anxieties, both economic and sexual. 'Male clerks are a vanishing race,' a contemporary observed. The pen pusher was losing out to the more efficient, pliable and inexpensive typist. The clean, modern office was a more attractive place to work than the factory or home. The city streets, with their nervous movement, crowded footpaths and glittering shop windows, added to its charms. Some of the glamour was illusory. Typing could be tedious and the pay, while better than that offered by factory work or domestic service, was low by male standards. It was essentially a young woman's occupation—two out of three typists were under the age of twenty-four. 'They readily relinquish their jobs to marry,' one contemporary stated. The good grooming, 'knowledge of money values' and 'obedience to routine' they learned in the office were said to prepare them well for their ultimate destiny as wives and mothers.

My grandfather loved the city and all his daughters became modern city girls, May and Joyce as typists, Gwen as a milliner, Marge a shop assistant and Florence a commercial artist. All would eventually become wives and mothers, but they looked back fondly on their youthful years in the city, with its fashionable shops, theatres and cinemas. For the rest of her life, my mother always dressed well and liked nothing better than putting on her hat and gloves, getting on the tram and spending a day 'in town'. In the early 1930s a street photographer captured her, dressed to the nines, striding confidently beside her father along a city street. I cherish it as an image of the independent 'city girl' she was before she willingly merged her identity with my father's.

Elegantly dressed city girl May Hewett and her father Vic are caught mid-stride by a Melbourne street photographer in the early 1930s.

One of the attractions of typing was the opportunity to meet eligible young men. In romantic fiction, the pretty typist married the boss's son; in the sensational press, she fatally succumbed to the wandering eye of the boss himself. Her sexual allure evidently unsettled the masculine atmosphere of the old-style office or bank. Managers debated whether they should engage a pretty typist or a plain one. One employer eliminated the first five applicants for a new position as either too superior, vague, designing, sullen or anaemic, and settled on the sixth whose good teeth, nice smile, neat dress, moderate intelligence and pleasant, but not glamorous, looks promised dependability without distraction.

My mother served almost fourteen years in the typing pool at the Eagle Star under the watchful eye of its supervisor-chaperone, the terrifying Miss Hall. If she had an office romance, we certainly never heard of it. With the coming of the Depression the volume of insurance business subsided and the typing pool began to empty. My mother recalled the ripples of anxiety that spread among her work-mates as each round of retrenchments was announced. She kept her head down and by the time the Depression lifted, she had survived, now in her late twenties and still unmarried. She had been quietly putting by what she could from her modest salary; her savings, rather than my father's, furnished their home.

Just when my father and mother began to 'go out' I do not know. By the mid-1930s he was a regular member of my grandfather's Bible class and of the camping parties he led at the Methodist campsite at Ocean Grove. He became a member of 'The Wanderers', a male quartet that performed at church socials and occasionally on radio. Jack Hanna, already a cartoonist for the *Herald* newspaper, drew a caricature of my father, clad in overalls and swinging a pick, for the Methodist Men's Society Banquet. He was probably one of the few tradesmen in the society; others, like future mathematics professor Rupert Leslie, university administrator Harry Shurey, medico Noel Chenhall and chemical engineer Ron Ride, had already embarked on professional careers.

Cartoonist and fellow member of The Wanderers quartet Jack Hanna drew this caricature of plumber George Davison for the menu card of a North Essendon Methodist Young Men's banquet. Along with, left to right middle row, Warwick Hanna, George Davison, Rupert Leslie, Harry Shurey and Jack Hanna, they took part in Methodist Young Men's Camps at Ocean Grove.

In the era before mass higher education, the Methodist Men's Society, like Young Catholic Workers, the YMCA and the Communist Party, were poor men's universities, providing opportunities for education, discussion and action on the great issues of the day. My grandfather gave occasional talks on literary subjects, like the poetry of WB Yeats, the novels of HG Wells and—his favourite—Henry Lawson, 'The Apostle of Mateship', but he also led discussion of religious topics, like the historicity of the Bible. My father's main role, however, was to lead the sessions of community singing that opened each meeting. Whether they remained in the church or not, its members were equipped by the society to think, write and speak clearly and persuasively.

My father pursued my mother for a long time, perhaps years, before she surrendered to his gentle, persistent wooing. 'I chased her and chased her until she caught me,' he used to say whenever the subject of their courtship came up. She may have hesitated to marry a short, unprepossessing man in overalls, two years younger than herself and with uncertain prospects. All her sisters would marry older, white-collar businessmen and move across town. She alone would stay on in Essendon where her parents lived and my father based his business. Whatever doubts her parents may have had about the match had evidently dissolved by the time they became engaged on Christmas Day 1938.

That Christmas, three months after Neville Chamberlain returned from Munich announcing 'peace in our times', was a brief interval of hope in a darkening time. The topics discussed by my father and his friends in the North Essendon Methodist Men's Society—'The Death of Collective Security', 'Christianity and the Crisis', 'Hitler over Russia', 'Peace with the Dictators'—convey their rising anxiety. Many younger Methodists, influenced by the radicals Palmer Phillips, Oswald Barnett, Cyril Walklate and Moonee Ponds minister William Warnock, were drawn towards Christian pacifism. Total abstinence, the stance Methodists traditionally adopted towards the 'social evils' of alcohol and gambling, they also applied to war. If all

Christians followed Jesus's teaching to love their enemies and resist evil, then, Barnett argued, 'war will soon cease to exist'. That others were unlikely to follow their example did not seem to discourage them, any more than my grandfather's boycott of Sunday tram services discouraged other passengers.

During the Great War, Methodists leant heavily towards conscription for military service, but in the late 1930s the church's position was more equivocal. War was evil but citizens were obliged to render service to the state. Those whose conscience forbade taking up arms should 'assist in defence in ways that would save life and minimise suffering'. At North Essendon the church's pronouncement provoked vigorous debate. 'The views of members varied appreciably and were submitted with vigour,' the minutes of the Men's Society noted. Where my father and grandfather stood is not recorded. From the books I found on my grandfather's shelves after his death, which included works by Norman Angell, Mahatma Gandhi and Toyohiko Kagawa, I know that he sympathised with many of the pacifists' arguments.

Putting myself in his shoes, I can see why he 'hated war'. He had seen eleven young men of the North Essendon congregation march off to the Great War and not return. 'We are not yet certain that the present civilisation has survived the last war. It is very doubtful it could survive another war,' he wrote around this time. While my father was too young to remember the war itself, he remembered how it had blighted the lives of his Aunt Edith and cousin Margaret. It is not surprising that they all, including Australia's political leaders, clung to the hope of appeasing the dictators until—or some historians would say until well *after*—their unappeasable appetite for war became obvious. In 1938 Australians did not know everything we now know about the evil at the heart of the Nazi regime, but enough, surely, to realise that it was impervious to the passive disobedience that had enabled their pacifist heroes to humble the British Empire.

My father and mother were no sooner engaged than the hope of peace in their time evaporated. By mid-1939 the Robert Menzies government, driven by public sentiment and the deteriorating situation in Europe, had abandoned its support for appeasement. War now seemed inevitable. My parents preferred to focus on the future they could control rather than the one they couldn't. Three months before the declaration of war they bought a house of their own. Several of their siblings became engaged and married around this time but they were the only ones to buy a house before 1945.

In mid-1939 EG Goddard, a real estate agent who employed my father for occasional repair jobs, mentioned one of his rental properties was coming up for sale. Number 16 Banchory Street was a five-room Californian bungalow on the Deeside Estate, just a few minutes' walk from Washington Street. Matt Atkinson, a local builder, had erected it for his own family in the mid-1920s but later moved to the eastern suburbs and let it out; now he wanted to sell. 'I feel sure you will like the house,' Atkinson wrote in reply to my father's request for a copy of the plans. 'I was in it again a few years ago, and remarked to my wife what a big comfortable house it was.' By today's standards it was a modest house—a lounge, dining room, kitchen, two bedrooms, sleep-out, external washhouse and lavatory—and the tenants had let it run down. But its location was ideal and my parents *did* like it, so much so that sixty years later they were still contentedly living there.

The asking price was £800 but all George and May could pay down was £100, too little to secure a bank loan. 'Try old man Hood,' Goddard suggested. William Hood, a local businessman, was known to lend a bit of money on mortgages. 'How much do you need?' Hood asked when Dad knocked on his door a few days later. 'Seven hundred pounds.' 'Well, look in that drawer.' Dad took out two bank passbooks. 'How much in that one? And in the other? That should be enough, shouldn't it?' So the deal was done. Hood advanced the £700 at six per cent interest—a little over the five per cent bank mortgage rate—repayable at £1 5s a week.

Historians, including me, have often marvelled that so many people of modest means, unlikely to win the approval of a financial institution for a loan, somehow managed to get homes of their own. Big financial institutions like banks and building societies favoured well-to-do borrowers, but working-class borrowers often relied on networks of lenders, based on local knowledge and family- or faith-based connections. Winifred Olley, who lent the money to John Davison for 49 Washington Street, and 'old man Hood', who financed my father and mother, were typical of their kind. In the world before credit ratings and professional qualifications, getting a house or a job depended not on what you knew, but who.

A thick file of letters, bankbooks, pencilled budgets, invoices, receipts and lay-by dockets attest to the care my parents took in what they obviously regarded as the most important transaction of their lives. They budgeted their expenses down almost to the last penny: £13 for a bedroom carpet, seven guineas for the hall, £18 for the maple lounge and dining suites, £25 for the bedroom suite with a large circular mirror, £20 for kitchen and bathroom renovations. There was just enough left, they thought, for a wireless. But they had forgotten one little item: £10 for legal fees. 'Bang goes the radio,' my mother cried in exasperation as they left the solicitor's office.

There was one other sensitive matter my father had to resolve. Since their father's death, he and Frank had lived with their mother, paying most of the bills including the mortgage. Now as they both prepared to marry, she would be on her own with nobody to pay the bills. My father proposed letting out the rooms he and Frank vacated to tenants. 'I did not want to give up my rooms,' Ada complained to Frank. 'I have been looking forward to a bit of home. I have been wandering about for months, one place and another.' But there was no alternative. Ada kept her home but only a bit of it; the rest she had to share with strangers.

George and May married at North Essendon Methodist on 26 January 1940, four months after Hitler invaded Poland. Frank was best man and Mum's younger sister Marge, also soon to marry, was bridesmaid. A little over nine months later I was born. While I was gestating, however, the world beyond 16 Banchory Street was fast becoming more dangerous. In May, German troops burst through the Ardennes, and in less than a month France had fallen and the British Expeditionary Force had retreated to Dunkirk. 'I am afraid to look at the papers,' Ada wrote. 'It seems dreadful, it looks as though they will soon be in England.' By mid-year, Japanese troops had begun their southward advance through China and the Battle for Britain had begun. On 18 November, when I was born, firebombs were falling on London and Australian troops were fighting in North Africa and preparing to defend Singapore.

Nobody, at that perilous moment, could have foreseen that I had been born into the luckiest and most consequential generation in the history of the planet.

North Essendon from the junction looking south, c.1954. Triangular Lincoln Park occupies the centre of the picture, while to the upper right, amidst rows of Californian bungalows, is the author's childhood home, 16 Banchory Street. Airspy photograph, courtesy State Library Victoria.

CHAPTER 10

Revving up

EVERY GENERATION THINKS it is special. It easily confuses the curve of its own life-course with that of the world around it. So when I wrote that I was born into the most consequential generation in the history of the world, the reader may have wondered whether I had succumbed to that delusion.

Yet I'm not alone in my belief. Historians confirm that the years following World War II have had no parallel before or since. Australia doubled its per-capita income, and thousands of ordinary families like mine were lifted out of unemployment and insecurity into relative affluence. Some European countries grew faster but they began well behind Australia and had still to catch up by the 1970s. The farther we get away from these years, the more extraordinary they seem. We reach for hyperboles to convey their astonishing impact: 'The Long Boom', 'The Golden Age' and 'The Great Acceleration'.

When I review the long arc of the Davisons' history from the Scottish Borders to mid-twentieth-century Australia, I perceive a gradual quickening of the pulse of change, as my forebears move from country to city, from agriculture to industry, and from precarious subsistence to modest comfort. The life my father enjoyed by the 1930s was very different from that of his Scottish and English ancestors, yet over the *longue durée* from 1780 to 1940 there were continuities—in their working and religious lives, for example—that would be abruptly broken in the following years. It was as though the whole of society then shifted to a new gear, and time itself moved forward at an increased tempo.

When did these golden years begin? In histories and popular memory, they are associated with the baby boom, the years after 1945 when returning soldiers married and settled down, priming the demand for jobs, migrants, cars and houses. The Australian economy embarked on a quarter-century of uninterrupted prosperity. The shift coincided with the advent of a new suite of technologies and, as we now know, with our move onto a path of carbon-reliant economic development that would ultimately prove unsustainable. Yet for many Australians, including my own family, the good years actually started earlier, during the war itself, when military recruitment, the demand for wartime supplies, and the mobilisation of the home workforce soaked up the remaining unemployment and boosted the wages of skilled workers. During the first world war, Australia's GDP fell, but during the second, it rose strongly. War, not peace, started the engine of prosperity.

Yet, while economic conditions improved, people's habits and outlooks changed more slowly. 'In many of its essential features, daily life in the first decade after World War Two would have been thoroughly familiar to men and women of fifty years earlier,' writes the European historian Tony Judt. Only after the mid-1950s, he suggests, did the new affluence begin to be seen and felt in people's lives. Like Judt, who grew up in postwar London, I was born into a world of ration books, string bags, ice chests, horse-drawn carts, wood fires, overcoats and woollen gloves. My parents continued to practise the frugality and thrift that got them through the Great Depression well into the postwar years. It took a while for them to realise that their luck had changed for good. I grew up in a more constrained environment than the baby boomers, the generation accustomed to affluence from the beginning.

Wartime

World War II was a People's War. It involved a larger proportion of the working population than World War I, both in uniform and in reserved occupations, although the proportion of Australians killed or injured was barely half that in the first of these conflicts. For those in the armed forces and their families the war brought years of fear, danger, hardship, separation and sacrifice. But for others—including my own family—it ushered in the most prosperous years of their lives. The pre-boomers were arguably even luckier than the boomers, for when the war ended they were already poised to take advantage of the peace.

'Dad, what did you do in the war?' The question often arose around Anzac Day when my classmates wore their father's medals to school. My father's answer was vague. He was one of the 431 000 men—almost as many as the 554 000 in uniform—who served their country on the home front as workers in reserved occupations. In an age of total war, victory depended as much upon the efforts of those who built the tanks and planes, and manufactured the bombs and bullets, as it did on the bravery of those in uniform. The nation's leaders prohibited men with essential skills from enlisting in the armed forces, but it did not give them the same honour as those who volunteered to fight. The Anzac Legend, which made the fighting man the epitome of Australian patriotism, was a serviceable myth in a time of war, but it marginalised those who served in other ways. My father's service entitled him to a badge for the duration of the war but no medals afterwards. British workers in reserved occupations were often vilified as physical or moral weaklings, unpatriotic shirkers or effeminate cowards. If similar attitudes prevailed in Australia—and the subject still awaits a historian—it may explain my father's reticence. He did not complain about this, and nor do I, for the men and women in uniform often took risks and made sacrifices that my own family was not required to make.

Despite my father's ambiguousness, I think I can reconstruct how he may have thought. When war was declared in 1939, he was ineligible to enlist because, like his uncle Harold Harding at the beginning of World War I, he was just five foot three and did not meet the physical requirements for military service. Under manpower regulations proclaimed in September 1939, plumbers were also listed among the occupations deemed essential on the home front and excluded ('excused' might be a better word) from military service. By the time the physical requirements for recruits were relaxed in 1942, my father was thirty-one and married with a child—me. Before the year was out, my mother was pregnant with my sister Helen, born in August 1943. Their third child Janet was born in 1946.

As the Pacific war effort ramped up, and the need for troops increased, the authorities pruned the list of reserved occupations, but plumbers over the age of twenty-five remained on it. In August 1942, under orders from the Manpower Directorate, my father began work at the Maribyrnong Munitions Factory. He cycled from Essendon, listening for the whistle that warned of the approaching start of the working day. He joined the Plumbers' Union—the factory was a closed shop—and made tentative efforts to participate in its affairs. But the old guard of the union was then engaged in a pitched battle for control with the communists, and his contribution, he told me much later, was not appreciated. It was his only experience of factory employment and union politics and he quit both at the first opportunity. In late 1944 the Manpower authorities granted his request to resume working as a subcontractor with the builders McDougall and Ireland on a Housing Commission estate in Coburg and later with the State Electricity Commission on its hydro-electricity project at Kiewa in Victoria's north-east.

So I can understand why he did not have a simple answer to my question. Had the authorities denied him the opportunity to fight?

If he had really wanted to enlist, he could probably have got around the regulations, as others did. Was he shielding behind the Manpower regulations to avoid enlisting? Perhaps even he did not know the answer. If the authorities had drafted him into a form of civilian service that aligned with his family responsibilities, he may have seen no reason to challenge it, especially if it also squared with whatever remained of his pacifist beliefs.

In 1942, as the threat of a Japanese invasion loomed, he volunteered as a local air-raid warden—Essendon Aerodrome was a busy military airfield and a possible target for Japanese bombers. He dug an air-raid shelter in our backyard and patrolled the streets at night to ensure that his neighbours were observing the blackout. From a pacifist's point of view, helping to make bombs may have been morally indistinguishable from dropping them, but it was in line with his church's advice to those unable or unwilling to bear arms to 'assist in defence in ways that would save life and minimise suffering'. Helping his neighbours avoid the enemy's bombs, however, and rescuing them from the chaos if an attack occurred, were forms of service perfectly in line with his convictions.

In balancing the claims of country, conscience and family he was surely not alone. Of the other members of The Wanderers' quartet, only two enlisted. Harry Shurey declined to bear arms and joined the field ambulance. He was imprisoned after the fall of Singapore and spent the rest of the war in Changi prison camp, barely surviving the ordeal. Jack Hanna enlisted in the army but spent most of the war in its educational services drawing cartoons for its magazine *Salt*, while the fourth member, the mathematician Rupert Leslie, whose high academic attainments exempted him from military service, completed his university studies. All were single men in their twenties, an age cohort twice as likely to enlist as men in their thirties, such as my father.

Whatever justification my father had for not enlisting, there is no doubt that his family was better off for it, emotionally and economically. We did not endure the anxiety and insecurity that other families experienced, nor the bereavement my childhood friend and neighbour Jim Coomes was to suffer when his father, along with the crew of his RAAF flying boat, went down over the Atlantic. When Dad left Maribyrnong, he was earning about six pounds a week, not much more than soldier's pay. But he and my mother lived frugally and by 1944 they had reduced the debt on their house to £460, just over half of the original purchase price, and transferred the mortgage from William Hood to a bank. Many servicemen returned to an acute housing shortage and sharply rising house prices, but by 1950 my parents had almost paid off their house, which was now worth more than twice what they'd paid for it. They did not plan it that way but their experience illustrates the disparity between the fortunes of the pre-boomers and those who got a start only after the war was over.

In the late 1940s my father spent many hours providing free advice and labour to family members and friends building their own homes. In the evenings he helped them with the paperwork for estimating, ordering and securing clearance for building materials. Saturdays were often spent helping his brother Frank build his new house at Glenroy or making mud bricks with an old friend from North Essendon Methodist who was building at Montmorency. These 'love jobs', as he called them, were perhaps his way of helping to offset that disparity.

A Clock Baby

Like others of their generation, my parents had to wait for marriage and parenthood, and when I was born they were both past thirty. My mother was the eldest child in her family and I was the first boy born into it for many years. I had grandparents and unmarried aunts who also delighted to take care of me. So, while we lived quite frugally and I had few treats or toys, I wanted for nothing in the way of attention and loving care.

Outside my family, the most influential person in my infancy was probably Sister Muriel Lee. Every week or so, my mother pushed my pram up Lincoln Road to the North Essendon Baby Health Centre. Determined to ensure that their children got the best possible start in life, local residents had campaigned for the centre, which Mayor Cr Robert Gilbertson opened in December 1938. Its modern cream-brick design, hygienic green-and-white interior, and dedicated weighing room and measuring tables were the last word in scientific infant care. Clad in her white cap and starched uniform, Sister Lee was a faithful disciple of the most famous contemporary expert on infant care, New Zealand's Dr Truby King. Childless himself, King was zealous for the welfare of other people's children. He regularly toured Australia to spread the gospel of scientific parenthood. Babies, he believed, needed a firm hand, and his regime placed a heavy emphasis on punctuality, regularity and discipline.

As soon as we were discharged from St Andrew's Hospital, my mother and I visited the Health Centre to get our instructions from Sister Lee. She wrote them in her firm hand in a little blue book:

Feed regularly
Sleep alone
No dummy
Keep out in fresh air
Givc sun kicks daily
Give boiled water daily.

As a conscientious first-time mother, Mum took these instructions to heart. She breastfed me by the clock every four hours, and worried if I did not put on enough weight. If I cried in the night, I was not supposed to be taken into bed with my parents. I could be cuddled, but not too much. Pacifiers such as dummies, or the various patent remedies for crying babies, were also discouraged. By eighteen months I was expected to be toilet-trained. To ward off disease—we were living in the aftermath of severe outbreaks of polio and diphtheria—I was required to have plenty of sun, fresh air and exercise. The little blue book tabulating our Health Centre visits and recording my weight showed steady progress. Mum was entitled to feel she was doing well, but somehow she never did.

My sisters, in their turn, followed our path to the Health Centre, where Sister Lee remained in charge into the 1950s. The ethic of restraint underlying her program struck a chord with my parents. Mum demonstrated her love for us by curbing her own impulses as well as ours. We were not kissed and cuddled as the children of later generations were. Nor were we praised lest it go to our heads. 'You're not the only pebble on the beach,' I hear my father say. Sometimes the pebbles would have liked less company. Other people of my generation tell similar stories. And yet we knew, without a doubt, that we were loved.

It was a year on from the end of World War II that an American doctor, Benjamin Spock, challenged this parenting regime in his bestselling book *The Commonsense Book of Baby and Child Care* (1946). He encouraged mothers to trust their instincts. His book would sell over fifty million copies worldwide, though it was not widely read in Australia until the early 1960s. By then, many mothers had already opted for a more relaxed approach. By the time I became a father in 1969 we were encouraged to do what came naturally. What made people ready for a change was a shift in the society at large, not just in its nurseries. The 'Clock Baby', as the Australian journalist Margaret Sydney called it, was a product of a time when the whole society was restrained by depression and war. The 'Permissive Baby' appeared just as everyone became more prosperous and relaxed.

I was a 'Clock Baby'. So were millions of others, free spirits as well as repressed ones. How much did our infant training mould us? Being an optimist, I tend to discount the influence of Dr King and Sister Lee. To think our beginnings explain everything about us is surely as mistaken as to believe they explain nothing at all. And yet I wonder. Years later, to my deep embarrassment, my mother recalled that my first words were, not 'Daddy' or 'Mummy' but 'Tick-tock'!

16 Banchory Street

Memories of my childhood are inextricably connected to 16 Banchory Street, Essendon, the modest bungalow my parents bought in 1939 and where my sisters and I grew up. To remember the house as I first knew it is to enter into a different mental as well as physical world, for my parents' conceptions of home and family were not today's. The desires they brought to their homemaking were inscribed on its fabric, and as I mentally revisit each room I am reminded of patterns of activity and thought long past.

Today, almost from the moment they leave school, young people are urged to 'get a foot in the property market'. They may buy an investment property and let it out while they continue to live with their parents, or purchase a renovator's opportunity and camp in it while they prepare it to sell. From the beginning, they see the house as a step on the ladder of wealth accumulation, more than a place to put down roots and imprint with their personalities. But that was not how my parents thought when they began their life together at 16 Banchory Street.

Having bought their home, I doubt they gave further thought to its monetary value. A house, in their minds, was first and foremost a home, or rather the location for one, since a home was more than just a house. Towards the end of his life, my father reflected on his attachment to 16 Banchory Street. It was 'futile', he believed,

> for people to build too much emotion into bricks and mortar … I like to tell myself that it wouldn't matter too much if we had to move out of this house for some reason or other—though it has memories and everything else … It's served its purpose, it's only a house. That's a glib thing to say but whether you'd be able to do it [leave the house] or not I don't know.

As it turned out, he would never discover the answer to that question. He lived at 16 Banchory Street almost until the day he died.

Not long after my parents came to live there, the politician Robert Menzies gave a series of wartime radio addresses entitled 'The Forgotten People'. My father was one of those 'forgotten people'—a self-employed tradesman, part of the home-loving, middling stratum of society whose interests, according to Menzies, were often overlooked by the parties of Capital and Labour. When Menzies spoke of home as a human and spiritual, as well as material, idea, my parents would have nodded in agreement. 'The foundation of sanity and sobriety … the concrete expression of habits of frugality' were words that resonated with their own sobriety and frugality. 'Human nature,' Menzies declared, 'is at its greatest when it combines dependence upon God with independence of man.' My parents would have agreed with that too, while adding that their home was an expression of sociability as well as independence. They made no sharp division between their home and its neighbourhood and took Jesus's commandment to love their neighbours quite literally.

When they bought it from Matt Atkinson, their house was surrounded by a shoulder-height, hoop-wire fence. Most of their neighbours also had hedges and fences, sometimes bearing little enamel plaques that read: 'No Hawkers or Canvassers'. These were relics of the Great Depression when people took refuge from the appeals of workless men selling things door to door. We didn't have such a sign ourselves; my father and grandfather, after all, had once been among the unwelcome callers. Dad replaced the hoop-wire fence with a lower, more modern one of timber and cyclone wire. Eventually, when it showed signs of wear, he removed it altogether, leaving the house open to the street.

Others were beginning to do the same. The defensiveness of the interwar period seemed to be receding. By the early 1950s the street was full of children running in and out of each other's backyards. Their front gardens were becoming a stage for floral display. In wartime, only productive gardening was encouraged, but afterwards front gardens became more decorative, as people surrounded their well-clipped lawns with borders of mixed annuals—marigolds, snapdragons, sweet peas and chrysanthemums—or bulbs, like gladioli, irises and dahlias. Our next-door neighbours, Mr and Mrs Hicks, won admiration for their brilliant summer shows of red and orange dahlias and zinnias. Our own horticultural efforts were comparatively modest. Dad hated roses—he had tangled with their thorns too often on the job—and Mum preferred hardy perennials like geraniums and gardenias, which required little attention. The silver birch they planted in the middle of our front lawn eventually grew so large it crowded out almost everything else.

Our house was one of several 'Calbungs' or Californian bungalows in the street. This American-derived timber house design came to dominate Australian suburbs in the 1920s, which is when Banchory Street was subdivided. It was more modern and spacious than the houses in which my parents had grown up, with a lounge, dining room and kitchen, two bedrooms and a sleep-out along with an out-door laundry and lavatory. Crossing the front verandah and entering

George and May Davison on the verandah of 16 Banchory Street, early 1960s.

the front door, with its distinctive diamond leadlight windows, you met the most striking feature of the house: a welcoming arch of stained Californian redwood mounted on pillar-like umbrella boxes. Today a purchaser would lovingly restore such period features, but my parents had little regard for them and embarked on a program of ruthless modernisation. They demolished the arch, replaced the leadlight windows with frosted glass, painted over the stained architraves, tore down the cream embossed wallpaper and encased the red-brick fireplace with a cement render. They wanted a lighter, more open look, like the modern houses my father was helping to build.

The 'lounge room', as we always called it, looked onto the street through an attractive bay window. In *The Presentation of Self in Everyday Life*, the sociologist Erving Goffman contrasts the 'front stage' of our lives, where we perform for others, with the 'back stage', where we can simply be ourselves. The lounge was the front stage of our home and my mother kept it 'nice and tidy' to present our best face to the world. Having such a room was a step up for the family: my paternal grandparents had not been able to afford one in their previous houses in Athol Street or Washington Street. A three-piece club lounge suite, purchased new from Nunan's in Puckle Street, Moonee Ponds, occupied much of the room. Nearest the gas fire was my father's chair, flanked by a chromium-plated Art Deco smoking stand. A lifelong teetotaller, Dad nonetheless had yet to kick his nicotine addiction. He rolled his own cigarettes, smoking them in a cigarette holder and tipping the ash into a cup-like receptacle on the stand. Smoking, he often said, was a 'filthy habit'. I suppose he confined it to the otherwise sacrosanct lounge room in order to save us from the fumes. At last he renounced it, rewarding himself with regular doses of confectionary. His favourite treat, Small's Club Chocolate for Men, came in a black-and-white wrapper depicting a smoker, much like his old self, reclining in a club armchair beside an Art Deco smoking stand.

In the opposite corner of the room was my mother's black pianoforte, a wedding gift from her mother-in-law Ada Davison.

From the early days of the colonies, a piano denoted lower middle-class respectability. Mum played it mainly for herself, sometimes for us, and occasionally for the Sunday night singsongs that were a regular feature of Methodist life. A framed print of working horses by the Australian artist Septimus Power, famous for his nostalgic scenes of rural life, adorned the mantelpiece, while my mother's collection of teacups, saucers and souvenir teaspoons took pride of place in the glass-fronted china cabinet. While the lounge was out of bounds during the week, an exception was made for Sunday afternoon tea, a relic of the high tea tradition my grand-parents brought from Birmingham. Around five o'clock my father unfolded a green-baize card table in front of the fire, which my mother covered with a damask table cloth, and we consumed the plates of egg and lettuce sandwiches, plain and fruit scones, alcohol-free fruit trifle and cream sponge my mother lovingly prepared for us. This was our weekly 'At Home', when relatives and friends might also drop in.

From the lounge, you passed through glazed double-doors to the 'dining room'. This was a misnomer since we usually ate our 'tea', as we called it, in the kitchen. The dining room was really our living room, the cosy back stage of the house. The dark wooden dining suite was pushed against the wall to make room for a sofa in front of the fireplace. In the afternoon after school, we stretched out on the carpet in the far corner of the room beside the four-shelf bookcase. *The Great War in Pictures*, *Our Silver Jubilee*, *The Australian Gardener*, volumes of the *Reader's Digest Condensed Books* and a second-hand set of Arthur Mee's *Children's Encyclopedia* were among the titles in our modest library.

Above the bookshelf hung a framed, printed copy of Rudyard Kipling's famous poem 'If'. In the 1940s it rivalled Gibran's 'The Prophet' and Minnie Haskins's 'The Gate of the Year' in popular esteem. Its stoic morality—trusting yourself when others doubt you, waiting but not being tired by waiting, dreaming but not making dreams your master, losing and starting again without complaining—resonated with the experience of a generation who had weathered depression and war. It concluded:

> If you can fill the unforgiving minute
> With sixty seconds' worth of distance run
> Yours is the Earth and everything that's in it
> And—which is more—you'll be a Man, my son.

I pondered these lines. To a child, they seemed more daunting than hopeful, but perhaps some particle lodged in my mind.

Next to the bookshelf stood a console radio, an Australian-made Fisk Radiola. Its stained cabinet, perspex dial and bakelite tuning knobs were then the acme of modernity. The Davisons were avid radio listeners and subscribers to the weekly radio newspaper, the *Listener-In*. We were creatures of the spoken and printed word rather than the coming world of video imagery. My father loved classical music and his favourite station was 3LO, the ABC's version of the BBC Third Programme. We children turned to the commercial stations for our favourite radio serials, *Hop Harrigan* and *The Air Adventures of Biggles*, then back to 3AR for the ABC's long-running children's program, *The Argonauts*. Around six o'clock, when my mother called us for tea, often in the midst of the popular serial *Blue Hills*, she threw a switch in the kitchen. Instantly the signal was transferred to a relay speaker above the kitchen table. Thanks to this simple device, punctual meals were guaranteed and hardly an instant of the broadcast drama was missed.

The kitchen was my mother's domain. She and my father shared a conventional view of their roles: he was the provider and protector and the decision-maker of last resort while she was the mistress of the house. They would have considered themselves equals, although later feminists might see their relationship as more patriarchal. So, for example, whatever my mother managed to save from the generous weekly amount she received from my father for housekeeping was her own. It was enough for her to dress well and accumulate a small portfolio of shares. She became a member of the Housewives' Association, just as he was a member of the Master Plumbers. Theirs was a deeply affectionate and companionable relationship. I never heard them raise their voices or disagree. He called her 'Pal' but they were soulmates, not workmates. I seldom saw my father 'lift a hand' in the kitchen except in emergencies; his cooking was strictly of the Boy Scout variety. My mother played only a limited role in his business, such as answering the phone and pacifying customers demanding to know when their leaking roof or burst pipe would be mended. In later years, as his married daughters developed careers, Dad sometimes wondered aloud why he hadn't encouraged my mother, who had a good head for business, to take a bigger role in his own.

Mum was a baker more than a cook. Her most creative efforts were reserved for the cakes, slices, scones and sponges she made for church or family afternoon teas. Her home cooking was comparatively plain. Her policy was to buy the most nutritious fresh meat and vegetables she could afford and to cook them well, until any resemblance to a living thing was extinguished. Strong flavours and exotic foods of any kind, such as garlic, curry or spice, were avoided. Dessert was considered an indispensable element in every evening meal, with tinned fruit and ice cream the default option.

After tea we usually retired to the dining room to sit in front of the fire listening to a quiz show or drama. Radio, unlike television, allowed us to continue with other activities while we listened. My mother might knit or sew while we did our school homework. From time to time she would summon one of us to stand like a human scarecrow as she wound a fresh ball from the skein of knitting wool stretched between our arms. My job was to tend the fire. If the flame burned low, I stumbled through the darkness to the woodshed to cut a few more sticks of firewood. Around 8.30 p.m., when the clock on the mantelpiece struck, we rotated in front of the fire, like piglets on a spit, to warm ourselves before we dashed to our beds. My sisters shared the second bedroom while I slept on the back verandah. Snuggling under the blankets, with my crystal-set headphones clamped over my ears and the wind rushing through the unglazed windows, I watched the sweeping searchlights from Essendon Aerodrome and the blinking neon of the nearby Circle Picture Theatre as it spelt out the letters H-O-Y-T-S.

By 1951, the house was just about paid off and my parents borrowed a bit more for a modest extension. The outdoor laundry and lavatory were demolished to make way for a third bedroom for me and an indoor laundry and lavatory. I now had my own desk and bookshelf. The sleep-out was glassed in to make a sunroom and the kitchen extended into the old pantry to give an outlook to the back garden, a gesture towards the sun-filled open-plan designs favoured by contemporary architects. After his Depression experiences, Dad hated painting, so I was invited to consult the Dulux paint chart and decorate the sunroom with lemon, lime and watermelon pink 'feature walls'. Of all these changes, the most appreciated was the advent of the indoor 'toilet', which ended the dark age of the chamber pot and our shivering midnight excursions to the outdoor 'lav'.

By the early 1950s our lives were becoming more prosperous, progress made visible in our growing stock of modern household appliances. The consumer revolution, as we now call it, was enabled by a massive expansion of household credit, but my parents, frugal as ever, purchased only what they could pay for outright. The bathroom and kitchen, where my father could employ his gas-fitting skills, were the first rooms to be modernised. He replaced the combined gas and one-fire stove with a modern gas stove and fitted new gas sink- and bath-heaters. In no time at all, they were replaced by a central gas hot-water service. With hot and cold running water, we no longer had to queue to use the bathroom or reuse each other's bathwater. In the kitchen, the ice chest made way for a second-hand gas Electrolux refrigerator. Now we could make our own ice cream from a three-milk recipe requiring multiple freezings and beatings, a treat my father rated highly. If a gas-powered vacuum cleaner or television had been available, we surely would have had it too.

More valuable from my mother's viewpoint was the installation of a Hoover single-tub washing machine, to supplant the old wooden washtubs, copper and wringer. The Hoover was teamed with a whizz-dryer, a water-powered centrifuge that extracted surplus water from the washed clothes before they were hung on our rotary clothes hoist. Then, in quick succession, came an Electrolux cylinder vacuum cleaner, a Sunbeam Mixmaster and an electric Singer sewing machine. An electric clock with a sweep minute hand replaced our green-and-cream bakelite kitchen clock. 'Electricity makes life easier' was the State Electricity Commission's slogan. Indeed it did, although each innovation raised our expectations of better, as well as quicker and easier, meals, clothes and other comforts. A domestic regime that had hardly altered for a century vanished in less than a decade. 'Labour-saving' technology eased or shortened some of the most tedious and exhausting household tasks. It enabled my mother to devote more time to lady-like activities outside the home. Neither of my parents anticipated, however, that they would pave the way for married women to re-enter the paid workforce, and may not have welcomed them if they had.

The electric age also introduced a new world of entertainment. My mother's younger sister Florence and her husband Bill, always more abreast of popular culture than my parents, were the first in the family to acquire a radiogram. My maternal grandparents had owned an old-fashioned wind-up gramophone, but its squeaky seventy-eight records of Melba and Galli-Curci were no match for the thrilling sounds that emanated from Florence and Bill's living room. Soon we had our own Astor radiogram. My father took out a subscription to the World Record Club, and once a month a new classical recording appeared in our letterbox. I picture him standing in front of the speaker waving his arms like Toscanini in time with the *1812 Overture* or the *Hallelujah Chorus*.

We were slower to embrace the attractions of television. Perhaps my parents feared it would distract us from our studies, or couldn't yet afford it, but they didn't buy a set until the early 1960s, when

Helen and I had left school. With its installation in a corner of the lounge room, the division between the front and back stages of the house began to blur. The lounge remained our best room, and the place for welcoming visitors, but now, all too often, their arrival broke into the imperious new timetable established by our viewing habits. Confirmed ABC listeners, we stuck to ABV2, although some of my father's viewing preferences were bizarre. He cared little for Australian football and cricket, but why a man of such peaceful inclinations so enjoyed the pantomime violence of *World Series Wrestling* still beats me.

After the revolutionary changes of the 1950s, not much changed at 16 Banchory Street for the rest of the century. Having achieved an acceptable level of comfort and convenience, my parents saw little need for further improvements. Ducted heating, flat-screen TVs, clothes dryers, computers, video recorders, mobile telephones—all the hi-tech, high-energy innovations of the late twentieth century passed them by. If they felt cold, they put on more clothes. The idea that you needed to heat or cool the whole house struck them as absurd. True, they made some small adjustments, such as the tape-recorder and CD player Dad bought for his music, and the machine for watching videos of their English grandchildren, but they had long since sent the false gods of consumerism packing.

The Backyard

Not far from us, in a smart, modern house on McCracken Street, lived a local celebrity, the aviator Charles Pratt. Pratt was born in New Zealand and learned to fly during the Great War before becoming the principal pilot for Airspy, a company specialising in aerial photography. Using the powerful cameras invented for military reconnaissance, Pratt photographed Melbourne from the air for more than forty years. His archive, now preserved in the State Library Victoria, is an incomparable record of the city's changing landscape.

One day in the mid-1950s, as he descended towards Essendon Aerodrome, Pratt turned his camera in our direction. As I peer into his photograph, the world of my childhood suddenly comes into focus. I am like an eavesdropper on my own past. The closer I look, the more my memory is stirred. Forgotten landmarks reappear in vivid detail. Along the spine of Mount Alexander Road, Essendon's main street, I spot the line of pumps outside Varcoe's Garage where my father bought petrol and oil. Nearby are Sanders grocery and Dench's butchery where my mother shopped almost every other day. North Essendon Methodist Church where we worshipped on Sunday looks across the tramline and palm plantation towards Christ Church where I attended kindergarten. Closer to my home I can see the broken-down swings and seesaws in Lincoln Park and the Circle Picture Theatre where we attended Saturday afternoon matinees. So exquisite is the detail that I can make out the crowds buying live chickens in the yard behind Kirk's Bazaar and read the Robur Tea advertisement on our corner shop. I can roughly date the photograph from the Holdens and Ford Prefects parked along Mount Alexander Road and guess the season from the winter hats and overcoats worn by two old ladies crossing the street.

What most strikes me now, as I look down on my neighbourhood, is how much of it was occupied by those unconsidered appurtenances of suburban life: backyards. Screened from the gaze of the casual passer-by, they are revealed to the aerial observer in all their glorious adhocery. Today, backyards have all but disappeared in new suburbs, but in 1950s Banchory Street, where houses were smaller and allotments larger, they occupied about half the average block. They were not dead spaces but vital parts of the household. As well as the usual laundry, lavatory and woodshed, they accommodated a range of other buildings and installations, such as workshops, 'bungalows', henhouses, dog kennels, pigeon lofts, bicycle sheds, garages, caravans, greenhouses, rubbish bins, compost heaps, potting sheds, children's playhouses, climbing frames, clotheslines, rotary hoists, vegetable gardens and fruit trees. They provided space for cricket pitches, football practice, motorcar maintenance, and a hundred kinds of extempore work and spontaneous play. Add them up and I suppose that more than half the things we did as kids occurred in our backyard.

My mother was also a photographer. She had a good eye for composition, and with the Kodak folding camera given her by her father she took hundreds of black-and-white images—mostly of her children, sometimes of my father, but almost never of herself. In 1942, when I was about eighteen months old, she took my photograph as I stood in the middle of our backyard. In the foreground is the mounded roof of the air-raid shelter that Dad dug to save us from Japanese bombers. Nearby is a small water tank to prevent us from dying of thirst if the enemy cut off our water supply. In the distance, our family car, a boxy 1928 Essex Super Six, occupies an open-sided garage. Rationing would soon make petrol unprocurable and the car would be put up on blocks. The rest of the yard seems quite empty.

With the coming of peace, as Dad's business expanded, the yard rapidly filled up with ramshackle timber buildings, tacked together from cast-off or second-hand materials. The garage was enclosed and progressively extended into a large workshop with benches, racks of galvanised pipe, coils of copper tubing, earthenware drainpipes, and old ammunition boxes filled with fittings and fixtures of all kinds. Two motorcar packing cases were knocked together to make a small home office, roofed with malthoid sheeting and lit through a small louvre window. Parking spaces were created for my father's new Chevrolet utility, trailer and family caravan. On the very last patch of unclaimed ground, he erected an outdoor bungalow, as extra sleeping accommodation.

Tradesmen, clients and materials entered through double gates at the rear of the property, where a bluestone lane led to the side street. With wartime rationing over, home building was booming. Most of my father's business came from three or four spec builders running up rows of almost identical weatherboard cottages along the unmade streets of Strathmore, Niddrie and Aberfeldie. They offered him more work than he could manage. At the top of the boom Dad employed a team of six or seven men, including an apprentice or two. He spent most evenings on paperwork and most days driving between jobs. 'I'd never do that again,' he remarked years later. 'You're paying other people to do what you should be doing yourself. I trained as a plumber and ended up being a bookkeeper and transporter running around after other people.'

One day, he had an epiphany. One of his children demanded his attention for a game or school project. 'I don't have time,' he replied impatiently. On reflection, his answer troubled him. There was something wrong if his business left him no time to answer his children's questions. He would rather earn less and have more time for his family, he decided. So he gradually downsized until he had just one employee, Hughie Maebus.

Hughie, the son of a local horse-trainer, was a year or two older than Dad. He lived with his wife and only daughter in a terrace house opposite the Essendon Oval, near his parents. We always called him 'Mr Maebus' but among his mates he was 'Yick', a nickname borrowed from an old employer, a Chinese market gardener. Yick was a sound tradesman and a hard worker, but his outlook on life was about as different from my father's as could be imagined. Dad never drank, gambled or swore, while Yick, I believe, had no such reservations. Among his mates his manner was rough but with women clients he was the very soul of charm and propriety. He lives in my memory as the epitome of an older type of working-class Australian.

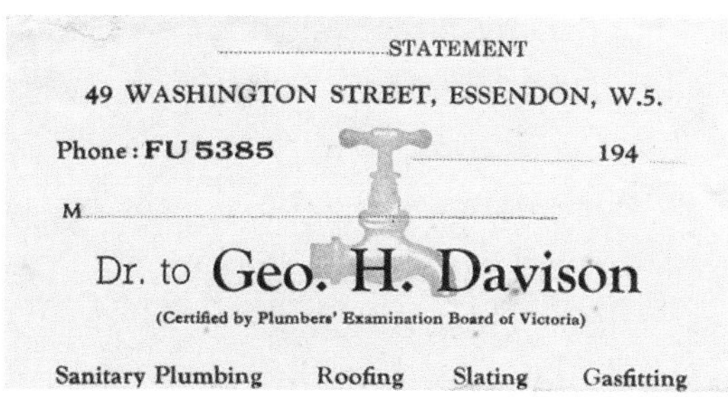
..........STATEMENT

49 WASHINGTON STREET, ESSENDON, W.5.

Phone: FU 5385 .... 194 ....

M..........

Dr. to Geo. H. Davison

(Certified by Plumbers' Examination Board of Victoria)

Sanitary Plumbing Roofing Slating Gasfitting

Every morning around eight, Yick arrived punctually at our back gate on his ancient bike. For more than thirty years, he and my father worked together amicably. But they never became business partners, for Yick preferred the security of a weekly wage. When Yick got into difficulties paying off his house, Dad stepped in and guaranteed his loan with the bank, undertaking to forward five pounds a week from his pay. Yick liked to reminisce about his early days working in Canberra and was proud of his part in building the national capital, but had never been back to see what became of it. One day Dad said, 'Let's go,' so they took the week off and drove up to have a look. When historians write about the Australian cult of mateship, I often think of Dad and Yick. Formally they were Boss and Worker, yet neither would have hesitated to call the other his mate.

Their workshop was a male domain but we children were always welcome to watch what was going on or to scrounge odds and ends. If my father was working at home, he might come inside for lunch or a cup of tea. Mum called from the back steps—'Teatime!'—but she seldom entered the workshop. As he returned to the house, Dad paused in the laundry to wash his hands and take off his overalls. Hughie usually ate his sandwiches in the workshop but occasionally joined my parents around the kitchen table. In the workshop they were always 'George' and 'Yick' but in the kitchen Hughie was 'Mr Maebus' and my mother was 'Mrs Davison'. In his late fifties, Yick's domestic life came apart. He also began to find plumbing more demanding physically. One day, frustrated by his inability to perform a task, he suddenly exploded, walked off the job and never returned. It nearly broke my father's heart.

I sometimes ponder my father's attitude to work. I admire his decision to put his family before material prosperity. In his famous study of *The Protestant Ethic and the Spirit of Capitalism*, the sociologist Max Weber contrasts what he calls the 'traditional' or 'pre-capitalist' attitude to work with the calculative, profit-oriented ethic that fostered capitalism. The traditionalist worked only to live as he is accustomed to live. It was the 'worldly asceticism' of Protestantism,

Weber argues, that gave capitalism its push to maximise profit. John Wesley was one of his examples. Yet my father, a model of the Protestant ethic, remained a stubborn traditionalist, happy to earn just enough to live as he was accustomed to live, provided he had time for other things. His attitude was a world away from the compulsive time-thrift of Kipling's 'If'. He always had time for us. He would turn up midweek at school sports days to watch us compete. He took us on camping or caravanning holidays in school breaks. It was he, not my mother, who took us to see the young Queen Elizabeth when she visited in 1954. He did it, not just for our good, but for his own, for nothing gave him more pleasure than being a father.

Departure Lounge, Essendon Airport, 1967. Photograph by Wolfgang Sievers, courtesy State Library Victoria.

CHAPTER 11

Taking off

GROWING UP IN the 1950s and 1960s, my sisters and I entered a wider world than our parents. We did not have to go far to outdistance them. They had grown up within two blocks of each other, moved just two blocks away to Banchory Street, and stayed there for the rest of their lives. My father's work seldom took him outside Essendon. My mother, who never learned to drive, shopped in nearby Mount Alexander Road, walking her purchases home in a shopping jeep. About a quarter of a mile from their home was the church they attended all their lives; most of their friends were fellow parishioners or neighbours. After arriving in Australia as a baby, my father did not travel outside Victoria until the 1960s and returned only once to the land of his birth, to visit my sister Helen who settled there. Towards the end of his life, when he wrote down some of his experiences, he entitled them 'The Memoirs of an Essendonian'. Essendon was his village and he was proud to be an old identity in it.

My parents may have been parochial but they were not insular, for within their community they were very outgoing. Other children were always welcome in our backyard, some of them seeking sanctuary from homes more troubled than ours. My parents offered hospitality to overseas visitors, including a Fijian Methodist and an American Rotary exchange student, but saw no reason to visit those lands themselves. In his eighties, my father was still acting as a voluntary taxi-driver for his elderly neighbours. Being a good neighbour, in my parents' eyes, was both a Christian responsibility and a source of pride and identity. A little of what they invested in their neighbourhood came back as custom for my father's business, much more in everyday kindness and esteem.

If I regard Banchory Street as more neighbourly than the streets of today, then it's probably because I still see it through their eyes. Of course, I'm also comparing two stages of my own life and two different parts of the city. In childhood, our lives are more circumscribed by locality than in adulthood, and even today Essendon people maintain that their streets are friendlier than the stuffy suburbs on the other side of town. Nor can I disown the nostalgia of an octogenarian for what he may misremember as a more innocent time. As hard as I try to discount them, there's no denying these biases. 'The interaction between collective and personal memories may be near impossible to untangle,' a historian of suburban neighbourhoods wisely observes. Yet, with all those qualifications, I think there *were* real differences between the neighbourhoods of the 1950s and today's.

In the early 1950s there were twenty-three households in Banchory Street, about half of them with sub-teenage children. I knew all their parents' surnames and their father's occupations, although not their first names, for we always addressed them as Mr and Mrs. I knew most of our neighbours' backyards and the interiors of quite a few of their houses. Banchory Street straddled the respectable working class and the lower middle class. Our next-door neighbours were Mr Nolan, a retired police inspector, and Mr Hicks, the foreman for a large plumbing firm in South Melbourne. Across the street were Mr Corr, an aeronautical instrument maker; Mr Scott, a builder; and Mr Cressey, a taxi-driver.

Until the mid-1950s housing was in short supply and several households, such as the Davys, Hughes, Hills and Fewsters, were multigenerational, with parents and children living with grandparents who had usually bought the house years earlier. Some of the men worked locally, like Mr Dodds the postmaster, and Mr Northcote, a bank accountant. Some walked, cycled or took public transport to nearby suburbs, like Mr Moylan, an auctioneer at the Newmarket saleyards. Only a few, like Mr Pattison, a clerk in the Taxation Department, worked in the city.

Their wives, without exception, were full-time housewives and mothers. Ours was not so much a 'dormitory suburb' as a day-time matriarchy of mothers' clubs, ladies guilds, tennis clubs and kindergarten auxiliaries. Most of the houses were weatherboard bungalows of similar size and quality and nearly all of them were owner-occupied. The only differences of social status were subtle. Most families lived modestly; only a few drove cars, let alone new ones, and only a few children, with bountiful grandparents, enjoyed expensive toys like rocking horses, Hornby electric trains and bicycles with gears.

Banchory Street felt like a community largely because the baby boom filled it with children. It's through their children, after all, that parents mostly connect. We were street kids in a day when the phrase had none of its pejorative associations. One of the saddest phrases in my grandchildren's vocabulary is 'play date'. The idea that you need to make a date to play, or that someone has to drive you to it, would have struck us as absurd. We played in the street and in each other's backyards, usually improvising our toys from whatever cast-offs or scrap materials we could find. 'Comin' down to ours?' I hear our neighbour Rob Davy calling out to my little sister Janet. Down to our backyard is what he means. In Charles Pratt's 1954 aerial photograph there were only three cars parked in our street, so it was safe enough to play cricket and kick-to-kick footy, or to drive our billycarts down the Braemar Street hill, without fear of being run over. In 1956 we ran our own Olympic Games, timing the running events by the sweep hand of my wristwatch. We had a local role model—world junior mile champion Ron Clarke, an Essendon High School boy who carried the Olympic torch into the MCG, lived just round the corner in Spencer Street.

The most pervasive difference in our little community was not class but religion. By the 1940s, the raw bigotry of the 1920s had softened, but living just a block away from St Therese's Catholic church and school, and with several devout Catholic families in the street, we were conscious of the largely unspoken divide between Protestant and Catholic. I recall only a few occasions of open prejudice or name-calling but mutual suspicion hung in the air like a miasma. The miasma thickened after the Labor split of the mid-1950s delivered the traditional Labor seat of Maribyrnong to the Liberals on Democratic Labor Party preferences, but lifted in the 1960s. In the 1940s and 1950s, religious observance was close to an all-time high.

Street kids. The author, in ill-fitting blazer, school friend Mac Hawkins, left, and sister Helen, centre right, with neighbours in Elder Parade, Essendon, c. 1947.

Many, if not most, Protestant children attended Sunday schools, whether their parents were churchgoers or not. The high days of the Davisons' year were the Sunday school anniversary, when my mother made new dresses for my sisters, and Melbourne Cup Day, when Methodists fled the city for a country or beach picnic and the innocent pleasures of raspberry vinegar, ham sandwiches and egg-and-spoon races.

Much of our leisure followed sectarian lines. The strongest teams in the local football and cricket associations belonged to Protestant churches, although many of the players attended church only once a year for a church parade. They played on Saturdays, leaving the fields vacant on Sundays for Catholics. The church teams were the main recruiting ground for the Essendon Football Club, then enjoying a golden era. The Bombers had the reputation of being a Protestant club, perhaps because of the strong links with these church-based clubs. My parents cared little for spectator sport but my aunt and uncle, who were passionate Essendon barrackers, took me to my first game when I was seven. Standing on a box under the scoreboard I saw Dick Reynolds play one of his last games. Later, on Tuesday and Thursday evenings, I stood outside the gate to the Essendon Oval with my autograph book—we never called it 'Windy Hill' in those days—to intercept famous players arriving for practice. Three of my Essendon High contemporaries would play in Essendon's 1962 premiership team.

Topography as well as history separated Essendon from the surrounding suburbs. Looking down through Charles Pratt's camera, you could see how it had expanded along its main thoroughfare, Mount Alexander Road. Mount Alexander was an old name for Castlemaine and the road, originally the main route to the goldfields, followed a north-westerly route along the high ground between Moonee Ponds Creek and the Maribyrnong River. Essendon's terrain was more undulating and picturesque than its flatter neighbours. Its light, sandy soil was better suited to gardens than the dark, glutinous clay of the basalt plain to the north. Ours was a residential suburb, unlike Brunswick, to the east, with its brickworks and boot factories, or Footscray, to the west, with its abattoirs, fertiliser factories, sugar refineries and ropeworks. Many of the captains of their industries lived in Essendon, which secretly considered itself better than its neighbours.

Essendon felt like a bounded community. To the south it was enclosed by Flemington Racecourse, the Newmarket livestock saleyards and the Showgrounds, to the east by Moonee Ponds Creek, to the west by the Maribyrnong River and to the north by the Essendon Aerodrome. Taking the train towards the city, you could close your eyes as you passed through Newmarket and Flemington and recognise where you were by the smell of sheep and cattle yards and tanneries. To the east we played in the valley of Moonee Ponds Creek, still flowing between its natural banks lined with willows, but littered with old car bodies, tyres and other junk—an abomination to the naturalist but delightful to a boy in search of adventure. Industrial pollution had also deprived the Maribyrnong or Saltwater River of its natural charm. In the 1920s oarsmen had competed in a local regatta and ferries sailed upstream to the Riverview Tea Gardens, but by the 1950s the regatta was defunct and the river stank. The sandpits overlooking the river were one of our adventure playgrounds until an avalanche almost killed one of my classmates.

The most exciting frontier, in my eyes, was to the north. Essendon Aerodrome—'The Drome' as we called it—was Melbourne's gateway to the rest of Australia, and the world. In the 1920s Melburnians flocked there to greet pioneering aviators, like Alan Cobham and Charles Kingsford Smith. When the winners of the 1953 London-to-Christchurch Air Race visited, I gatecrashed the reception to collect the crew's autographs. In 1954 we lined up along Mount Alexander Road to greet the young Queen Elizabeth as she rode from the Drome to the city, stopping at Essendon Town Hall to receive a loyal address. On Sunday afternoons, families gathered at the top of Bulla Road to watch planes taking off and landing on the north–south runway. Down the tarmac they trundled—twin-engine

DC3s, four-engine DC4s, lumbering Bristol Freighters and speedy Lockheed Convairs—before taking off, engines roaring just above us, into the great beyond.

We thrilled to the excitement of the dawning jet age. I made a scrapbook about the race between British and American military aircraft to break the world airspeed record. In 1953 RAAF test pilot Bill Scott broke the sound barrier over Melbourne in an Australian-made Sabre jet fighter. My friend Noel Fewster and I made a replica for the backyard entertainment of the kids of the neighbourhood. Dad salvaged a wooden trough, straightened the sides, extended the fuselage with galvanised iron, fitted a plywood cabin, wings and rudder, and painted it in RAAF grey with bull's eye roundels. Noel and I alternated in the role of test pilot, wearing the ex-RAAF helmets we'd procured from an army disposals company. To simulate the sound of the jet we installed Mrs Fewster's vacuum cleaner in

Banchory Street breaks the sound barrier. Pilots Noel Fewster and Graeme Davison wearing ex-RAAF helmets pose with homemade jet fighter and juvenile spectators at their summer holiday airshow.

the tail while the pilot provided a running commentary on our test dive through a microphone hitched to the family's pedestal radio. Citius, Altius, Fortius—swifter, higher, stronger: the motto of the Olympic Games—was our motto too. Breaking the sound barrier, like John Landy breaking the four-minute mile, offered statistical proof of our progress. Beautiful machines, we believed, would transport us to a better kind of life.

In 1950 my father traded in our old 1928 Essex for a brand-new Chevrolet utility. With its cream duco, sleek lines and wide chromium grille, it stood out from the boxier British cars that still dominated the market. He paid £1001 for it—£200 more than he and my mother paid for our house only a decade earlier. With a rack for carrying pipes and spouting, it became the workhorse for his business. With a canvas hood and the old Essex's horsehair seats in the back, it doubled as our family car. With a caravan hitched behind, it took the whole family on holidays to the four corners of the state. In summer we camped at Phillip Island and in spring and autumn at Bright, Marysville and the Grampians. We seldom visited places of historical interest. What interested us then was the future, not the past. Our holidays were full of excursions to open-cut coalmines, hydro-electric power stations, butter factories, woollen mills and other symbols of modern progress.

With our eyes fixed on the future, we seldom considered what we were leaving behind or trampling underfoot. The Methodism of the 1950s caught some of the optimism of the era. With Sunday schools full to overflowing, vigorous youth groups and modern cream-brick churches going up along the suburban frontier, it seemed for a moment that the ebb tide of unbelief had been reversed, or at least arrested. The temper of congregational life was expansive and outward looking, with ministers and youth leaders eager to confront the social challenges of the age. Methodists maintained their 'unswerving hostility to the drink traffic'. The only occasion when my mother took part in a political campaign was in 1956, when she doorknocked in support of the retention of Victoria's notorious six o'clock curfew on hotels. But along with the old moralism went a growing awareness of the injustices of class and race.

As Sunday school pupils, we gathered under a picture of a pale-faced, white-robed Jesus standing among black, white and yellow children and sang:

> Jesus loves the little children,
> All the children of the world,
> Red and yellow, black and white,
> All are precious in His sight,
> Jesus died for all the children of the world.

We read a little magazine, *Friends*, produced by the Methodist Board of Overseas Missions, with stories and photographs of the little black children being cared for in faraway places like Elcho Island and Yirrkala. But there were no black children among our own friends. We heard of the work of the Methodist Babies' and Children's Homes in caring for infants given up for adoption by their mostly white mothers. But we did not question why they had relinquished them. Why didn't we ask? Our progress was so rapid, and its pleasures so addictive, that we looked past tragedies and histories hiding in plain sight.

Occasionally something happened to alert us to thc miscry that lay just below the surface of suburban life. Among our friends was a family of three children, a boy and two girls, about the same ages as my sisters and I. They came to church with their father, a quiet man who sat in the back pew. Their mother, if she was still alive, was nowhere in sight. One afternoon as I was dawdling home from school, I glanced at the *Herald* banner outside a newsagent's shop. An appalling tragedy had occurred in our suburb. In the middle of the night, something in the quiet man had snapped and he had run amok, killing two of his two older children and seriously injuring the youngest. Our elders tried to shield us from the details but I had already read them in the newspaper. Mr Stenning, our Sunday school superintendent, struggled for words of comfort but nothing in our own experience could account for the sheer horror of it. There was no public funeral and the surviving daughter disappeared into the care of relatives far away. A silence descended, but years later, when one of us raised the subject, it was the one dark, indelible memory of our Sunday school years we shared.

As children we often played in Lincoln Park, an untidy five-acre triangle of land bounded by pines and eucalypts in the middle of our neighbourhood. We walked through it every Sunday on our way to church. I sometimes sat in a pew just under a window dedicated to the memory of Dr Lorimer Fison, a former missionary who was co-author of one of the classic accounts of Aboriginal kinship, *Kamiliroi and Kunai*. In my boyhood, Fison's unmarried daughter still lived in her father's big house on Richardson Street overlooking Lincoln Park. Recently I came across the reminiscences of George Bishop, an old Essendon man who recalled that in his youth, about thirty years before Dr Fison's time, the land between Mount Alexander Road and Lincoln Road was a regular meeting place for the Wathawurung and Djadjawurung people. After erecting a dark backdrop of boughs cut from trees, they made two large bonfires for their songs and dances. In the 1950s we built bonfires in Lincoln Park for our own tribal ceremonies: Guy Fawkes Day and Empire Day. Like Dr Fison, we regarded Aboriginal ceremonies as primitive magic rather than religion. It would not have occurred to us that we were walking across someone else's sacred place on the way to our own.

Where Should I Go, Dad?

I don't know why my parents sent me to Aberfeldie State School. It was more than a mile away and right on the edge of the built-up area. Perhaps it was because, while other schools were closer, Aberfeldie had a good reputation, and some of our neighbours' kids went there. My mother took me on the first day. Afterwards I made my own way, usually with other children, hurrying in the morning to beat the siren that signalled the beginning of classes and dawdling on the way home to collect butterflies, birds' eggs and cocoons. On 8 August 1949, when I was in Third Grade, I was hastening to school with my sister Helen when we met some of our classmates coming in the other direction. They brought the startling news that the entire school building had been gutted by fire. Their joy in anticipation of a long holiday was short-lived, for we soon learned that we were to be bussed three miles each day to Flemington Training School.

Flemington adjoined one of Melbourne's poorest suburbs, Debney's Paddock, identified by the Housing Commission as a slum. One day I was asked to take home a local boy who had taken sick—his mother opened the door onto a scene of squalor and wretchedness the likes of which I had never glimpsed before. We continued to

The postwar baby boom swelled class sizes and strained the supply of teachers. The author, top row third from left, was among the fifty children in veteran teacher William Corrigan's sixth grade class at Flemington State.

be taught by our own teachers but there were sometimes fisticuffs in the playground between the Aberfeldie and Flemington kids. My father, a man of peace, was dismayed when I came home one day with a black eye but cheered up when I told him that I had given my assailant a blood nose. Classes were large—often fifty students or more—and trained teachers were in short supply. Some tottering veterans of the Education Department were called out of retirement to relieve the pressure. Our Fourth Grade teacher Mr Cecil, who had probably trained in the early years of the Commonwealth, taught us to memorise snatches of sentimental Victorian verse and to write in old-fashioned copperplate with pens dipped in inkwells. Our classroom ceiling bristled like a dartboard with the steel-nibbed pens aimed skywards by generations of reluctant calligraphers.

'Where should I go, Dad?' I asked as I neared the end of my primary education. Thirty years earlier my father had posed the same question to his father John, who wisely guided him to a technical school and a respectable trade. 'It all depends on what you want to *be*,' he replied. 'But I don't *know* what I want to be,' I pleaded. 'What should I be?'

During the school holidays I often joined my father out on the building site. I fetched and carried, made billy tea and attempted simple tradesmen's tasks. I enjoyed being part of a man's world of physical labour, technical proficiency and good-humoured, sometimes bawdy, banter. I saw a different side of my father from the well-domesticated family man or the respectable Methodist who sat in the back row of the choir on Sunday mornings. I admired his quiet authority among the team of young plumbers and his easy rapport with the spec builders—Hec, Bill and Fergie—who ran the project. Perhaps he hoped that I would like his life enough to take it on too. 'George H. Davison, Licensed Plumber' was the sign on the rack of his new Chevrolet ute. There was enough space to add '& Son', my sister cheekily observed. But it was becoming obvious that I was not cut out for a trade. The manual dexterity that sustained five generations of Davison men had somehow stopped with me. 'You're all thumbs,' Dad would say as he watched my fumbling efforts to thread a pipe or solder a joint.

I was always near the top of my class at primary school but the subjects I enjoyed most, like English, History and Geography, seemed to lead nowhere in my father's world. So what *could* I be? A secure, superannuated government job like teaching or a respectable profession like pharmacy or engineering seemed to be what he had in mind. The Depression had taught him the hazards of working in a cyclical industry and he wanted me to avoid his error. You could do engineering at the Tech, he suggested, in what I now see as a last-ditch plea for his old school. Engineering was a step up from his trade but it was a profession a plumber could understand and admire. Civil engineers were the brains behind the roads and bridges, dams and power stations that we saw on our holiday trips around the state. They were the masters of the exciting new universe of material progress that we called 'modern'.

My mother had been quietly listening to our conversation. Was the Tech the only way to become an engineer, she inquired. To settle the matter, she called an old family friend, a civil engineer in the Harbour Trust. Yes, he confirmed, you could also go to high school and become a civil engineer. Our adviser, I know now, had been one of her admirers, which hardly raised the value of his opinion in my father's eyes; but it vindicated my mother and settled the matter. Mum probably realised that engineering was not my bent but was content to go along with my father's plan as long as it took me to her old school where other possibilities might open up. When Mr Corrigan, our Sixth Grade teacher, set an essay on 'What I Would Like to Be When I Grow Up', I knew what to write. 'I would like to be a Civil Engineer,' I began. 'This means doing such work as designing roads, bridges and parks. After leaving this school I would have to go to High School then matriculate.' I got ten out of ten for this effort.

High School, My School

Across the Western world, governments faced a steeply rising demand for education. Just as the baby boom hit the schools, students began to stay on longer. Parents were having smaller families than previous generations but investing more heavily in their education. These two forces—the 'bulge' and the 'trend', historians call them—lifted Victorian secondary school enrolments by 136 per cent during the 1950s. In England, children took a make-or-break examination at the end of primary school, the notorious Eleven Plus. Only about one in twenty went on to grammar school, the high road to university. In Victoria, secondary education was less harshly selective but in 1953 only about twenty per cent went to state high schools. A generation after my mother enrolled, Essendon High was still one of only a handful of high schools in metropolitan Melbourne, and it only began to teach students through to matriculation in 1953.

Like our suburb, Essendon High was socially mixed: it taught the children of both middle-class and working-class families and inspired a local pride captured in the lyrics of its school song:

> High school, my school,
> School where I'm proud to be;
> Second to none is Essendon,
> Kindly Mother to me.

Class and geography still shaped children's educational destiny. Three-quarters of the boys who enrolled in technical schools were from working-class families but only half of those who enrolled in high school had a similar background. My friend Roy Dunn, the son of a local bus driver, was a better than average student, but a family friend persuaded his parents that high schools were not practical enough. They sent him to Essendon Tech, where he consistently topped his class before leaving after four years to train as a telephone linesman, a decision he now regrets.

Education for girls was still largely governed by the assumption that they would work for only a few years, preferably in an occupation that prepared them well for what everyone expected to be their main vocation in life: full-time wives and mothers. That was probably my parents' attitude too. My sisters Helen and Janet would also become Essendon High School students. Helen had always wanted to be an infant teacher and departed for Melbourne Teachers' College two years after I arrived at university, while Janet followed a similar course to my mother, leaving after Form Five for a secretarial course at RMIT. In middle life she returned to study, completed an accounting degree and, before her premature death, became a director of the Victorian Auditor-General's Department.

As my first day at Essendon High approached, I was kitted out with a new grey serge suit, with short pants, school tie and jumper. At high school, Mum explained, my day would be divided into forty-minute periods and I would have to change classrooms and teachers at the sound of an electric bell. Dad asked one of our neighbours, an instrument maker, to recondition an old wristwatch so I was prepared for the new regime. While the watch kept good time, I didn't. My habitual lateness often landed me in detention, a punishment supposed to teach me the value of time by confiscating some of my own.

On Monday mornings we assembled in the school's quadrangle, a hollow square of red-brick classrooms around an asphalt yard, boys on one side and girls on the other. The national flag was broken from the mast and we boys saluted while the girls put their hands on their hearts to recite an oath of loyalty to the new Queen Elizabeth. 'I love God and my country, I honour the Queen,' we chanted, 'and [holding our breath] cheerfully obey my parents, teachers and the laws.' Victoria was alone among the states in obliging us to promise obedience, as well as love and respect, to our betters.

Our headmaster Les Garson—Gus as we called him—ran his school on traditional lines, with an emphasis on academic and sporting success, school spirit, Australian patriotism and social responsibility. As a young man, he had served in the Australian Flying Corps during World War I. Considering the mortality rate among pilots of that conflict, he was lucky to escape with nothing more than partial deafness, brought on, I suppose, by the thundering noise of the plane's engine. His disability, the price of service to his country, entitled him to our sympathy; but we gave him none, and happily exploited his hardness of hearing.

With his heavy jowls and hangdog expression, Gus resembled an amiable bloodhound. He was a Presbyterian elder and modelled the Protestant virtues of punctuality, industry and honesty. As exams approached, he urged us to burn the midnight oil, quoting the American poet Henry Wadsworth Longfellow:

> The heights by great men reached and kept
> Were not attained by sudden flight
> But they, while their companions slept,
> Were toiling upwards in the night.

Yet, while encouraging academic ambition—at least for the boys who would become 'great men'—Gus was wary of the materialism that too often inspired it. 'Social security based upon monetary rewards is often taken as signifying a successful climax to the preparation spent in the schoolroom,' he observed. 'But this is placing the earning of a competence above the wider, more embracing idea of living in the fullest sense.'

Essendon High was nominally co-educational, although boys and girls were usually taught in separate classes at least until Form Five. Even outside the classroom there was little mixing of the sexes: boys and girls were even supposed to walk home on opposite sides of Buckley Street. While sex was on everyone's minds and furtive glances and written intimations of passion passed across the gender gap, the level of sexual activity among my own friends was pitifully small, at least until the last year or so of school. I did not have a regular girlfriend myself until after I left.

My fellow student, the future philosophy professor Lauchlan Chipman, remembered Essendon High as 'a poor school' and our teachers as 'not highly qualified'. By current standards its physical facilities were certainly poor. The classrooms around the quadrangle had not changed since my mother's days. We had no decent library, only rudimentary science laboratories and no sporting facilities to speak of. Most of the staff, however, had at least a bachelor's degree, some a master's and one or two PhDs. Some were past their best and others, it must be admitted, were sadistic and even abusive. But it takes only a few inspirational teachers to make a difference.

Ken McGregor was a traditionalist. He parted his hair down the middle in the old-fashioned way and wore a tartan tie. He stood for everything that is now unfashionable in English teaching: Shakespeare and Milton, rote learning of poetry, formal grammar and stern classroom discipline. But he was a born actor who turned every lesson into a memorable performance. Each year he invited the Melbourne theatrical stalwart J Beresford Fowler and a band of wandering players to present a Shakespeare play on the stage of our school hall, with dustbin lids for shields and scenery drawn on large sheets of brown paper by Mr Clemson's art students. As background to our study of *Julius Caesar*, he sent me off to the Public Library, as we called it then, to research an essay on 'Roman Religion', opening a vista onto the world of learning as expansive as Keats's first dip into Chapman's Homer. Most of my school history teachers, I confess, were less inspiring. Alf House, then nearing retirement, had studied history thirty years earlier under Professor Ernest Scott. His professor's *Short History of Australia* remained our main textbook forty years after its publication. By matric I realised I had to forage for myself.

If I developed any historical imagination in my teens, it came mostly from outside the classroom. My grandfather Vic Hewett loved the city and pointed out buildings he associated with its history. Noting my boyhood interest in all things aeronautical, he shrewdly directed it towards the history of the pioneering flights of Kingsford Smith, Bert Hinkler and Amy Johnson. His Christmas presents were always grown-up books carefully chosen to capture my interest, such as Frank Clune's *The Overland Telegraph* or Arthur C Clarke's *The Exploration of Space*. He was a member of the Bread and Cheese Club and the Henry Lawson Society, and his Christmas and birthday gifts also included collections of Lawson's and Paterson's poetry, which he apparently rated above their prose.

Lauchlan Chipman believed his career as a philosopher began as a high school debater. Lauchlan and I, together with the future European operatic diva Stella Axarlis, made up the Hill House debating team in 1957. The topic was that old chestnut, capital punishment, and we drew the easier side in arguing for its abolition. I visited the Public Library to read the 1949–53 British Royal Commission Report, carefully noting down its key finding. Nowhere, the commission found, had the abolition of the death penalty caused homicides to increase, nor its reintroduction caused them to fall. This became the knockout punch in my speech. With Lauchlan's deadly logic and Stella's faultless elocution, we made a winning combination. When I got to university and joined student protests against the Victorian Government's decision to hang the murderer Ronald Ryan, I knew we had history, as well as logic and morality, on our side.

Of the 200 boys and girls who started at Essendon High with me in 1953, 167 made it to Form Four, ninety-nine to Form Five and just fifty-one—thirty-three boys and eighteen girls—to Form Six. Most girls had departed, usually for office jobs, after Form Four. Of the thirty-eight students in my matric class whose parents' occupations I could trace, twenty-two were working class, including several labourers, process workers and the like; nine were lower middle class, such as clerks; and only eight were middle class. They included two doctors, a schoolteacher and an accountant. Ten were children of recent migrants, mostly from northern or eastern Europe. A couple of Chinese Malayan students, the first of what would become a large influx, joined us in matric. Most of us went on to university, where four became doctors.

In my final years I became a prefect, garbed with a ribboned blazer and the authority to enforce school discipline by reprimanding boys walking down the girls' side of Buckley Street or not wearing their school caps. Our most sacred responsibility was care of the national flag we kept in the Prefects Room, ready to be saluted in the quadrangle on Monday mornings. But after six years of relatively good behaviour I left Essendon High under a cloud. Then, as now, the last day of school was an occasion for high jinks. We planned a prank at the expense of one of our favourite teachers, Jack Grenfell, reputedly an ex-World War II commando and a square-jawed he-man we admired and feared. Someone found a long, coffin-shaped box and scrawled in chalk along the side 'He talked back to Jack'. Thoughtlessly, I offered the national flag to be draped over it. When our new headmaster Mr Thompson heard of it, I was summoned to his office and dressed down. My offence, of course, was not discourtesy to a teacher but desecration of the national flag.

My mild gesture of rebellion pales beside the radical convulsions of the 1970s. The demands for student democracy that swept across university campuses during the Vietnam War soon reached the quadrangle of Essendon High. Prefects—'puppets dancing to the tune of the school hierarchy' as one rebel called them—were replaced by a popularly elected student representative council. A ballot of students and parents voted overwhelmingly to make uniforms optional. The name 'high school' was jettisoned for the more inclusive 'college'. Lauchlan Chipman deplored the 'crude imposition' of newly fashionable 'anti-elitist educational ideologies'. Many of his contemporaries, who remembered the Essendon High School of the 1950s and 1960s as a gateway to their own success, probably agreed.

As I approached the end of my secondary education, an old question returned. What should I be? My parents made an appointment with the Education Department's Vocational Guidance

Branch, where aptitude tests confirmed what I already knew: that people and words, not things and numbers, were my strongest suit. I returned with a list of possible jobs. Journalism looked attractive but the irregular hours were discouraging. Law was another possibility. The prospect of being exposed to what my mother called 'the seamy side of life' was exciting, but even with a Commonwealth scholarship, my parents would have had to fund my living expenses.

Meanwhile, the crowded classrooms of my own school pointed to an obvious avenue of opportunity. I graduated in 1958, the year before the baby boom peaked in the high schools and when I would enter university. Along with 648 others I was awarded a secondary teaching studentship that paid all my fees and a stipend of seven pounds a week. In return, I promised to serve the Education Department for three years after I graduated. We called this agreement 'the bond', although it is hard to think of a less oppressive form of industrial slavery. Its generosity was a measure of the state's teacher deficit.

Teaching was a vocation ready-made for swotty lower middle-class children, idealistic and eager to rise above our parents, but not too far. Teachers then enjoyed better pay and conditions and a higher status than they do today. They dressed in jackets and ties, skirts and dresses. They were called Mr and Miss by parents as well as students. My sister Helen would become a primary teacher and half of my Davison cousins would also join the profession. If my father had been a lawyer or businessman, I may have taken up the Commonwealth scholarship I had also been offered. But teaching was something I thought I could do, and the student stipend meant that my parents, who had two daughters still to educate, would no longer have to support me. Out of my seven pounds a week, I paid my mother two pounds a week board. My father signed me up with the Rechabites, a teetotal friendly society, and persuaded me to take out a life-insurance policy with Prudential, as he and his father had done before me. I still have that policy; it will pay about enough to bury me.

Room at the Top

Looking back, I realise that we were beneficiaries of a unique time. A hole in the fence of privilege had suddenly opened up and we snuck through, hoping to enlarge it so that others might follow. We were confident that an expanding modern society would provide ample places for educated people like us. 'There's always room at the top,' the American lexicographer Daniel Webster famously remarked. My Fourth Grade primary teacher Mr Cecil passed Webster's saying on to us, along with his copperplate handwriting and Victorian verse.

For a while, it seemed as though more room really was opening up at the top. An increasing proportion of school leavers went on to university and, as the tertiary sector of the economy expanded, more jobs opened up in well-paid white-collar occupations. Through the 1950s and 1960s, the hole in the fence got larger with a gradual reduction in income inequality and increased social mobility. The peak came in the early 1970s when the Whitlam government abolished university fees. Many of my students then were mature-aged women who had left school early, like so many of my own classmates, and were getting a second chance at higher education.

But in the 1980s the engine began to stall. The room at the top—the share of wealth and power enjoyed by those who began outside the room—shrank. Rampant credentialism required those who got access to higher education to keep upgrading their qualifications. The rich, and those who could afford the fees, closed the hole in the fence by sending their children to private schools dedicated to securing government-subsidised university places. The state high schools which once rivalled them in reputation and performance won a smaller share of funds and prestige. While private schools built larger and more opulent swimming pools, gymnasiums, libraries, performing arts complexes and wellness centres, the red-brick quadrangle at Essendon High stayed much as it had been in 1912.

I now look back a little ruefully at the educational revolution that produced us, and that we helped to grow. We were members of what the British socialist Michael Young dubbed 'the meritocracy', a class based on educational attainment or merit. In his 1958 book *The Rise of the Meritocracy*, Young warned of the dangers of replacing the old hierarchies of birth and seniority with a new system of educational merit. Since then the meritocracy has grown exponentially. The American philosopher Michael Sandel now deplores what he sees as 'the tyranny of merit'. 'In an unequal society,' he explains, 'those who land on the top want to believe their success is morally justified. In a meritocratic society, this means the winners must believe they deserve their success through their own talent and hard work.' The consequence is that the losers are also made to feel they deserve to lose.

I read Young's book in 1963 when I was studying for a Diploma of Education and discussed it with my fellow students. What was so wrong with meritocracy, we wondered. We considered that our success was deserved, a just reward for our talent and hard work. Being young at a time when the world really did seem to be opening up, we can perhaps be excused our conceit. Yes, we did work hard, and maybe we had some talent too. But compared with our parents and children, we had to press only lightly on the door of opportunity for it to open. We took too little account of the circumstances that prevented many of our contemporaries from even getting near that door.

There is really no such thing as a self-made man or woman. All of us are creatures of our times and of ancestral influences we may be reluctant to acknowledge, at least until age and curiosity make us ponder them. I now look back with new appreciation at the struggles of my parents and grandparents, who had to contend with tougher times than we did. The golden age—the unique period between the end of World War II and the 1970s that made my own generation—did not extend to our children and grandchildren. 'What would happen when the golden age came to end?' a British historian asks. 'What if there was no more room at the top, and not everyone could reasonably aspire to a better life?' Is that where we are now? At the dawn of the golden age, my old headmaster Les Garson condemned the belief that 'social security based upon monetary rewards' should be the first objective of education. Seventy years after he wrote these words, we are better able to appreciate where that heresy has landed us.

England-bound Australian students (philosopher Robin Haack, engineer Val Karpowski, historian Graeme Davison and literary critic Geoffrey Hiller) on a shore excursion to the Pyramids from RMS *Orcades*, September 1964.

CHAPTER 12

Towards England

FROM THE MOMENT I arrived, I knew that university was for me. I had ventured onto the campus only once during my schooldays, for a Shakespeare Society examination, so everything about it was new and wonderful. The idea of a place devoted to the pursuit of knowledge and the exchange of ideas thrilled me, as it still does. I drank it all up like a thirsty camel arriving at an oasis.

People still called the University of Melbourne 'The Shop', a title redolent of the proprietary outlook of its main clients, Melbourne's upper middle class. It was 'part of the private language of confident people', as its historian Richard Selleck shrewdly observed. About two-thirds of my fellow students came from the twenty per cent of families with fathers in professional or managerial jobs. I was part of the one-sixth who came from the forty per cent of families whose fathers were in manual jobs. Only one-third of my fellow students were women, although in Arts the proportion was about half and rising rapidly.

An aura of middle-class privilege still lingered around the sandstone Old Arts Building with its crenellated clock tower. Lecturers wore gowns, young men wore slacks and jackets, and women wore skirts, twin-sets and sometimes pearls. Our teachers addressed us as Mr and Miss. The blue jeans and first-name informality of 'The Uni' were a decade away. Our university was still an intimate, antipodean version of John Henry Newman's ideal, 'an alma mater knowing her children one by one, not a foundry, or a mint or a treadmill'. I was among about 400 full-time first-year Arts students, but thanks to the last-minute suggestion of a family friend, I enrolled in English and History Honours, immediately joining the smaller cohort of bright students who would accompany me through the next four years.

Honours tutorials were small, no more than eight to ten students. 'Do you like it, Mr Davison?' my English tutor, the formidable Miss Gay Tennant, asks from her wheelchair. The subject is the border ballad 'Lord Randal'. I do like it—love it, in fact—but I stumble to explain why. My female classmates, future literary luminaries Hilary McPhee and Penny Curtis, are more fluent and assured. More emotionally mature, too, probably. Literary criticism seems to follow methods and canons of taste I have yet to comprehend.

From the outset I am more at home in history. My tutor, Professor Kathleen Fitzpatrick, is the legendary lecturer in charge of our course on Tudor and Stuart history. Her lectures—elegant, even majestic—live brightly in my memory. She reads a passage from *Areopagitica*, John Milton's famous defence of intellectual freedom. 'I cannot praise a fugitive and cloistered virtue, unexercised and unbreathed, that never sallies out and sees her adversary'—as she reads, Milton's words resonate with her liberalism, catch my sympathies and lodge in my memory.

We read the debates between the officers of Cromwell's New Model Army assembled in the church at Putney in the autumn of 1647. They are thrashing out what to do with King Charles when they capture his capital. I feel as though I am in the room with them. They belong to another time yet, as they debate the proportions of liberty, authority and equality in their new government, they are my contemporaries. History, I begin to see, is not the cold retrieval of dry facts but a lively, open-ended conversation with the people of the past. Towards the end of term I knock on my professor's office door. I have come to collect my first essay on the agrarian problem of the sixteenth century. When 'Katie'—as we call her behind her back—returns my essay with encouraging handwritten comments and a first-class mark, I glimpse a possible path ahead. Could I become a historian?

As well as lectures and tutorials, I thrived on the lunchtime talks, campaigns and conferences that were then an integral part of campus life. I got at least half my education from them. The religious and anti-religious clubs and societies were then as popular as the political ones. In my mid-teens, the era of the Billy Graham crusade, I mixed with evangelicals but at university I gravitated to the more liberal Student Christian Movement. Looking back, I am struck by its chummy innocence, theological pretension and political naivety, yet SCM was a hospitable halfway house between my inherited faith and the secular world views I was encountering at university. It was at the forefront of the movements to abolish capital punishment and the White Australia Policy, educate Aboriginal people, oppose apartheid, ban nuclear armaments and promote ecumenism, causes inspired by a Christian ethic of nonviolent activism. Women were more prominent in its leadership than in many other university clubs and societies. I became co-secretary of its Melbourne University branch, attended conferences in Mittagong and Adelaide, and organised the first joint SCM–Newman Society conference. I joined the ALP Club, the campus home of the social-democratic left, and sympathised with the attempts of Gough Whitlam, who spoke at the Mittagong conference, to reform the hardline Victorian branch. The membership of SCM peaked in the early 1960s but declined in the more febrile atmosphere of the anti–Vietnam War and Women's Liberation movements. It was all but spent by the time I returned to Melbourne University as a lecturer in 1970. Yet in its fellowship of earnest truth-seekers I clarified my beliefs, made lifelong friends and met the love of my life.

I had hoped for more Australian literature and history than we were offered in our first two years. Just as I arrived at Melbourne University, one of our professors, John La Nauze, coolly surveyed Australian historical writing. Australia, he observed, was a 'derivative and dependent society'. Because it was derivative, we had to begin by studying its parent, nineteenth-century Britain. Only in my third year did I at last approach the history of my own country. I resisted La Nauze's view at first but came to recognise its merit. After all, my own family was as much British as Australian.

Our Australian history lecturer was a 35-year-old Sydney graduate, Allan Martin. He was as unassuming and modest as the elders of the department were imposing and remote. He turned our class into a group research project on the history of the Victorian gold rush, encouraging us to select our own topics, dig into the rich primary sources of the State Library, and present our conclusions in pre-circulated papers. We began to think of ourselves as apprentice historians, and to see writing and publishing as the natural way to do it. I toured the goldfields with fellow student John Ritchie, following an itinerary written on the back of an envelope by our guest lecturer, Geoffrey Blainey. I had saved enough from my stipend to spend my third year in Ormond College, sharing a study with fellow history student Garry Trompf. There, in discussion with Ritchie and Tony Ostor, we planned our own historical publication, *The Melbourne Historical Journal*. The first issue, cranked out on a cyclostyle machine, appeared in 1961. Copies were advertised as essential exam fodder and sold during lunch hour from little tables erected outside the Baillieu Library. In 1962 it went into print, from the same printer, Brown, Prior and Anderson, that also printed the History Department's more prestigious *Historical Studies*. It has now appeared, sometimes irregularly, for over fifty years.

Russel Ward's famous book *The Australian Legend* had recently appeared. The real Australia, according to Ward, was the bush. The folk traditions of the bush workers, popularised through Sydney's *Bulletin* magazine, were the foundation of Australia's national ethos.

Allan Martin encouraged us to dissect Ward's arguments. To me, the priority Ward gave to the bush was odd, for Australia was one of the most urbanised nations on earth. My grandfather Vic Hewett was a man of the suburbs, yet he was also a devotee of the bush poetry and short stories of Henry Lawson. My father and Hughie Maebus were mates as much as the shearers and stockmen of the outback. I began to wonder why our national myth was so disconnected from the places where most of us lived. I published a first critique of Ward's book in the second edition of *The Melbourne Historical Journal.*

The Australian Legend was an example of what Martin called 'The Whig View of Australian History'. This was the idea that history followed a 'line of progress'. The job of the historian was to discern and describe its unfolding, a process thought to be as inevitable as the passage of time itself. Most Australian historians, Martin noted, identified the rural working class and the Labor Party as the standard-bearers of progress, and relegated the middle class and the non-Labor parties and factions to subordinate roles. He questioned this view.

Melbourne University Historical Society Conference, Warburton, 1962.
The author, back row, fifth from left, among other future academics Bill Kent, Dale (Butler) Kent, John Ritchie, Cameron Hazlehurst, Axel Clark, John Lack and Jaynie Anderson.

How would Australian history look if we took a wider view—of the cities and suburbs, the middle class and lower middle class, non-Labor factions and parties, for example? He advanced his ideas tentatively but nudged us closer to the Australia I knew. We began to talk about the prospect of an Australian *urban* history.

I took a small step towards it in my honours dissertation. I decided to investigate the colonial class structure and politics of Richmond, the inner working-class suburb where the Labor Party first won representation. To capture the complexities of urban society, historians would need to experiment with new techniques, Martin believed. His wife Jean, a sociologist, guided me towards the writings of the Chicago School of urban sociologists. Sitting beside hobos seeking warmth in the Newspaper Reading Room of the State Library, I trawled through contemporary newspapers. In the Richmond Town Hall, I extracted occupational data from council rate books. To plot Richmond's social geography, I roamed the back streets looking at old houses and taking photographs. One afternoon as I walked down Docker Street, a pale blue Holden drew alongside. Two burly men jumped out, bundled me into the back seat and began to go through my carry bag. The Richmond CID was on the trail of a housebreaker and I was evidently a suspect. 'So what are you up to, son?' one detective inquired. 'Historical research, sir.' Policeman (incredulously): 'And how long have you been on this caper?' The truth was that I'd hardly begun. But now I knew: I was an urban historian.

Looking back, the biggest gap in our education was the history of the First Peoples of the land. 'Why weren't we told?' the historian Henry Reynolds would later ask. The answer was not that it was beyond recall, but that it was simply uncongenial to the 'line of progress' that had been pre-defined as our subject. Our undergraduate tutorials followed the topics in Manning Clark's two-volume *Select Documents in Australian History*. Its index contained more than 200 references to 'gold' but only six to Aboriginal people, including 'Aborigines, not a serious threat'. In his survey of Australian history, John La Nauze relegated the Aboriginal people to 'a melancholy anthropological footnote'. Only after I had completed the course did I begin to realise what our teachers hadn't told us.

In 1963, while I was studying for a Dip. Ed., I joined an expedition to Cape Barren Island in Bass Strait. Many Australians believed that the Indigenous people of Tasmania had died out with the death of Truganini, 'the Last Tasmanian'. But Cape Barren Island was home to a small community of about 100 people, descendants of black Tasmanian women brought there by European sealers in the early nineteenth century. Their abduction had saved them from the fate of the rest of their people, who perished during the Black Wars or on nearby Flinders Island.

The leader of our expedition was Jack Goodluck, a 35-year-old Methodist clergyman. He had recently worked among Aboriginal people in the Northern Territory. Reluctant to resume parish ministry and uncertain what to do next, he recruited a small party of younger Methodists, mostly student teachers like myself, for an exploratory visit to the island. They included Garry Trompf, who had already studied Aboriginal pre-history with one of our lecturers, John Mulvaney. Almost sixty years later, neither Garry nor I can recall exactly what Jack expected the expedition to achieve. But his invitation came at a moment when many of us were looking beyond the suburbs for adventure, friendship and perhaps a project or a cause. In 1964, my sister Helen, an infant teacher, spent a summer volunteering at Yirrkala, a Methodist mission in Arnhem Land. It was a significant time in the history of Aboriginal Australia, just months after Methodist missionaries had helped the Yolngu people write a bark petition asserting their rights to land against the incursion of bauxite miners, although Helen heard little of the matter during her visit. She would later make friends among Methodist indigenous communities in Fiji and Western Australia.

We flew to Flinders Island and boarded the weekly mail boat at Lady Barron. Then, rolling in a heavy swell, we sailed down the breathtaking Franklin Sound to the western tip of Cape Barren Island. At 'The Corner', as it was known, a jetty, a primary school, a cemetery and an Anzac memorial formed the nucleus of the settlement. We camped in the school ground with the permission of the teacher, explored the island, speared garfish and made tentative approaches to the locals. Over the course of the week, relations became friendlier. We talked about football—they were Collingwood supporters to a man—and sang country music. Many younger people had left or, as I discovered later, had been compulsorily removed for education or employment on the Tasmanian mainland. They included some who would later become leaders of the Tasmanian Aboriginal movement. But the older men and women still pursued the islanders' traditional way of life, killing and preserving the migratory mutton birds for their oily flesh and feathers. Like the shepherds and bandits of the Scottish Borders, they followed the rhythms of nature rather than the measured time of clock and calendar.

Before flying back to Melbourne, we visited Wybalenna on the west coast of Flinders Island. It was here in the 1830s that the Protector of Aborigines George Robinson presided over the forced removal of the Indigenous people of Tasmania. Robinson was a man of our religious tradition, a humanitarian with Methodist connections. He knew that the Aboriginal people had been robbed of their lands. He forcefully condemned the settlers who had hunted and murdered them. Yet he was vain, ambitious and eager to please his employers. He convinced himself that the traumatised and dispossessed black Tasmanians should be moved to Flinders Island 'for their own good'. Exiled from their country and exposed to strange food and a severe climate, all but a few of them perished. We knew only a fraction of what historians have since uncovered about what many now call a genocide, but enough to grasp its enormity.

All that remained of the Wybalenna settlement in 1963 were a few scattered graves and the carcass of Robinson's chapel, now a barn. Its brick walls had been broken open to ease the stowage of hay bales. Handmade bricks were strewn all over the surrounding area. It looked wrecked beyond recovery, although it was later restored and is now a hallowed place. Moved by the poignancy of the scene, I picked

Almost unrecognisable, the chapel of George Augustus Robinson's Aboriginal settlement at Wybalenna, Flinders Island in 1967. Courtesy Tasmanian State Archives.

up a brick, packed it in my haversack and took it back with me to Melbourne. I placed it on a bookshelf above my desk, a reminder of a colonial tragedy. After years of heritage advocacy, I hesitate to confess this act of vandalism; every modern conservation principle condemns it. Yet the antiquarian who collects relics of the past and the historian who writes about it are first cousins. That stolen brick imprinted the story of Wybalenna on my memory more indelibly than any book or document.

Essendon Man

During my five years at Melbourne University I remained an indentured servant of the Education Department, but my service lay so far in the future that I seldom thought about it. Once a term, however, we were required to attend an assembly at the Secondary Teachers' College. One day, I opened the envelope containing my pay cheque to find an invitation to see the college principal. This was usually a sign of trouble. I knocked on Mr McDonell's door and introduced myself. 'I suppose you will be leaving us then?' he said. What had I done? Unknown to me, the universities had persuaded the Education Department to release a small number of secondary teaching students to become university teachers. My results had evidently marked me out for academic conscription.

Nine of us, including my fellow history students Garry Trompf, John Ritchie and Roger Thompson, were offered tutorships at Melbourne or Monash. Our bond was transferred from the Education Department to the universities. In the meantime we were permitted to study overseas if an opportunity arose. Of the nine, all except one were men. I was not aware, during my undergraduate years, of being encouraged or rewarded at the expense of my female classmates. The expectation that men would have careers and women would have husbands and babies was then so prevalent, however, that I may have missed what was obvious from the other side of the gender divide.

Casting a wide net, I began to apply for scholarships to study in England. I was surprised, in view of my modest sporting credentials, to be shortlisted for the Rhodes Scholarship. As well as two interviews, candidates were invited to dine with the selection panel, a test of our table manners as well as our conversation. As I tackled the first course, I noticed that the candidates, and only the candidates, had a cherry in their fruit cocktail. Problem: what to do with the pit? Do you spit it out, delicately take it out with your fingers, or extract it with your spoon? Where do you put it afterwards: on your plate, in your pocket or back in the bowl? My life so far had not prepared me for this challenge. I felt sure that there was a correct answer but I didn't know it. So I simply swallowed the pit, hoping that no-one would notice.

There was a more serious problem. I had planned to study for a doctorate with the leading urban historian of that time, Asa Briggs. But Briggs had recently left Oxford, where the Rhodes was tenable, for the new University of Sussex. Should I withdraw my application and hope to find another way to Sussex? I consulted John La Nauze, one of my referees, and himself a former Rhodes Scholar. His response was emphatic: 'Anyone who has the chance to be a Rhodes Scholar should seize it.' So I sank my doubts and proceeded to the final interview.

'Essendon Man 1964 Rhodes Scholar' was the front-page headline in *The Age* the next morning. I wondered if the selection of a Brighton or Hawthorn man would have been considered newsworthy. I was pleased for my parents and suburb but could not adjust my sense of self to the expectations of the award. When I finally got to Oxford, I would be relieved to discover that many of the seventy new Rhodes Scholars were as bookish as I was. Only two of us, however, were tradesmen's sons.

Return Voyage

In September 1964, I said goodbye to my family and girlfriend and boarded the Peninsula and Orient liner *Orcades*. Barbara and I had met on the last day of an SCM conference in Adelaide and immediately fell in love. We were thrilled to have found each other but the timing was inconvenient, to say the least. Barbara was still halfway through her occupational therapy course and I was committed to Oxford. But we promised to write to each other, hoping that our relationship would survive the two years' separation.

I would retrace the same route my father and his family had followed just over fifty years earlier in another Orient liner, the *Orontes*. Like them, I was an assisted migrant, thanks to the free passage provided by the British Passenger Lines Conference to Australian students bound for British universities. I marvel now at the good fortune that enabled the grandson of a migrant who landed in Melbourne with twenty pounds to return to England's most famous university at England's expense, but I gave it no thought at the time. I was bound for Balliol College, following in the path of other Australian historians, including Manning Clark and Keith Hancock, and my professors Max Crawford and John La Nauze. We would be over a month at sea and our itinerary—from Melbourne via Adelaide and Fremantle, thence to Colombo, Bombay, Aden, Port Said, Suez, Naples and Gibraltar—connected the outposts of Empire. Our ship, recently converted into a one-class liner, reproduced an imperial racial hierarchy with its English upper deck, Indian and Chinese cabin crew, and Lascars toiling unseen in the engine rooms below.

My grandparents had emigrated at the high noon of empire but I was returning in its late afternoon. Arriving in Colombo, my first sight of an Asian city, I was struck by the 'ornamental architecture of the British Raj … built to last a thousand years but now grimy and sometimes disused'. Sri Lanka was in the midst of an election campaign. From the port, we drove through streets thronged with children and lined with flags, including the hammer and sickle of the local Communist Party, into the lush countryside where rice-growers stood in the paddy fields with garments hoisted up to their waists. In the historic hill town of Kandy we lunched in the faded splendour of the Queen's Hotel. I wrote portentously:

> Here amidst the last vestiges of British imperialism—the white columns and slatted window shades, the slowly revolving fans (like arms trying to grip each other), the slightly tarnished table silver, and the servile table waiters—we ate our curry and drank our tea, and put our sixpences under the plate.

In Bombay I glimpsed the imposing Gateway of India, erected to commemorate the 1911 visit of the Emperor of India George V. In Aden, a free-trade port with a line of tacky duty-free shops and a British military base, I watched British warplanes buzzing overhead. As we entered the Suez Canal, I joined fellow Australian students on a day-excursion to Cairo and the Pyramids. Colonel Nasser, President of Egypt, was hosting a conference of the Non-Aligned Nations.

Men in uniform were everywhere and warlike slogans with portraits of Nasser and other prominent leaders of the Non-Aligned Nations lined the streets. In Australia we had read distant reports of 'the winds of change' sweeping through the Third World, but by the end of my voyage I had gauged their impact for myself.

Term was about to begin in Oxford when the *Orcades* reached Naples. To make up time, I took the overland train and channel ferry to London, sitting up all night. When the boat train pulled into Victoria Station, I caught a cab and sped across the city to Paddington Station. Historic landmarks flitted by like shuffled postcards. It was on the Oxford train that my sleepless journey caught up with me. As we neared our destination, a fellow passenger, a kind middle-aged woman, woke me. As I gazed across the Meadows towards the dreaming spires of All Souls and Christchurch, I realised that she was watching me, enjoying the spectacle of the weary colonial's arrival in his mecca.

I arrived in Oxford on the eve of the British elections. On the night of the poll, I squatted on the floor of the crowded Balliol Junior Common Room amidst my new friends, gazing at a tiny black-and-white TV screen as the BBC's and Oxford's electoral expert David Butler declared victory for the Labour Party's and Oxford's Harold Wilson. Wilson, an avuncular, pipe-smoking Yorkshireman, was a scholarship boy and a graduate in Philosophy, Politics and Economics (PPE or 'Modern Greats'), the course I was to follow myself. I was excited by Labour's vision of a modern Britain forged 'in the white heat of a technological revolution', prepared to shed its imperial burdens and illusions, to look more towards its European neighbours, and to cast off the barriers of class, race and region that had fettered its progress. Over the next two years I would see those hopes fade as the Wilson government struggled to lift Britain's economic performance, lurched from one balance of payments crisis to the next, wound down its military commitments East of Suez, and applied to join the European Common Market only to be blocked by De Gaulle, the French president.

Balliol was the most meritocratic of Oxford's colleges. It was a byword for academic excellence, democratic access, internationalism and what one of its most famous alumni, British Prime Minister Herbert Asquith, called 'the tranquil art of effortless superiority'. Some of my fellow students were quite effortlessly brilliant, although many others achieved the effect by a swan-like combination of surface equanimity and furious underwater paddling. It was exhilarating to be part of an international community of bright students, many of them fellow Rhodes Scholars. Some were Australians, but my closest friendships were with Americans, Canadians, Scots and English grammar-school boys. One became a US senator and others became senior members of the Carter and Clinton administrations. I rowed in the Balliol Second Eight with a future New Zealand High Court judge, skied in Austria with a future Australian head of Foreign Affairs, travelled in Eastern Europe and the Soviet Union with the

Three Brits, three Americans, a New Zealander and an Australian rowed in Balliol College's Second Eight at the Torpids bumping race on the Isis, March 1965.

future head of the World Resources Institute, and walked in the Lake District and the Cairngorms with future Oxbridge and American philosophy professors.

Oxford prized quickness of mind and fluency of speech and writing, qualities honed by its famous tutorial system. Each week I wrote two essays and discussed them, one to one, with my tutors. I was a novice in both philosophy and economics, but I was thrown in the deep end with the philosophers Richard Hare and Anthony Kenny, economist Paul Streeten and social theorist Steven Lukes. However, while I enjoyed the zestful, combative style of Oxford academic life, I began to feel dissatisfied with the speed-dance of the PPE curriculum. While it was well suited to the needs of future administrators and politicians, who must get to the essentials of complex issues very quickly, it was less suited to the instincts of a scholar wanting to investigate them thoroughly. My closest friendships were with philosophy students, and the dominant 'ordinary language' style of Oxford philosophy seemed to come easily to me, but left me feeling that something important had been left out. Social theory studied in isolation from its application to real-world problems was similarly dissatisfying.

Living in England was a homecoming of sorts, for I had grown up at a time when England, or a sentimental version of it, still permeated the lives of most Australians. My mother, in particular, loved the England of thatched cottages, hawthorn hedges, country lanes and church steeples, although, of course, she had never seen it. She read us the stories of Peter Rabbit and Winnie the Pooh, and we read the stories of Enid Blyton and WE Johns for ourselves. We listened on the radio to the music of King's College Chapel and the Royal Philharmonic. At school we studied Shakespeare, Milton and Keats. The humour of Flanders and Swann, the Goons and *Beyond the Fringe*, although un-Australian, was congenial to us. Even at university I had studied more English history and literature than Australian.

In Oxford the second-hand England of colonial memory was suddenly visible everywhere. From my room in Balliol I looked down onto the Broad where a Gothic memorial marked the spot where the Protestant martyrs Cranmer, Latimer and Ridley were burned at the stake in 1555. Nearby, along the Turl, was Lincoln College where Methodism's founder John Wesley had been a fellow. Every day, as I entered Balliol's Dining Hall, I saw portraits of prime ministers Asquith and Macmillan and the imperial viceroys, Curzon and Milner. Having grown up in a land supposedly bereft of history, I sometimes felt that I was in one with too much. It was like 'being in a book', as one Australian visitor acutely remarked.

Australia Calls

My benefactor Cecil Rhodes created his scholarships to produce a new kind of imperial leader, white men of strong intellect and character imbued with English values and loyalty to the British throne. I was happy enough to accept his benevolence but I rejected his imperialism. By the 1960s, the alignment of Australian and British interests was no longer to be taken for granted. In his famous book *Australia* (1930), a previous Victorian Rhodes Scholar, the historian Keith Hancock, praised the ideal of 'the independent Australian Briton'. It was 'not impossible', he declared, in a much-quoted passage, 'for Australians, nourished by a glorious literature and haunted by old memories, to be in love with two soils'. After Oxford, he spent half his life in England and became the foremost imperial historian of his time.

While nourished by English history and literature, and attracted to many features of English academic and public life, I did not feel the divided loyalties—to country and calling—that Hancock strove to reconcile. I always knew that my future was in Australia, not England, and although I would teach and research British history, and often return to the United Kingdom over the years, it has never felt like my home. A recent study suggests that when Britain joined the European Common Market, Australians felt like 'abandoned Britons'. I was there at the time and experienced nothing of the kind.

I was not a Briton, independent or abandoned. To me, it was as natural for a post-imperial Britain to seek its destiny in Europe as it was for a post-colonial Australia to find its destiny in Asia. (That Britain, having entered Europe, might one day leave under the leadership of a Balliol man, Boris Johnson, would have been inconceivable to me.) I was British Australian, perhaps, in the sense that others would later call themselves Irish Australian, Italian Australian or Chinese Australian, but the joining denoted family and cultural origins, not a competing loyalty.

The England I encountered, after all, was nothing like the England my grandparents had left. The difference was not just chronological. Oxford was not Birmingham and the Broad was not Moseley Road. When I arrived I knew little about my English relatives, and almost nothing of the story I have told here. I was clearly in no hurry to reconnect with them for it was not until March 1966 that I made an attempt. My cousin Tom was also living in Oxford and working as a production engineer at the Morris plant in Cowley; his father Frank had been the last of the Australian Davisons to visit Birmingham, in 1929. One Sunday, Tom and I met another of my Davison cousins, Joan Horsburgh, who was working as a supply teacher in London, and we drove together to Birmingham, stopping off along the way to take in the sights of Stratford, Warwick and Coventry.

By 1966 most of John and Ada's siblings had passed on. Edith Harding, who had shared the Davisons' crowded house in Ascot Vale after her husband was killed on the Western Front, had died in 1950. Her married daughter Margaret, however, was still alive and expecting to meet us. At the last moment, however, there was a hitch. Tom received a message that there was an illness in the family and no-one would be able to see us. Afterwards we learned that it was our great-aunt, 69-year-old Lillian Cardall, Ada's youngest sister, who was ailing.

After Shakespeare's Stratford, Warwick Castle and Coventry Cathedral, Birmingham was a disappointment. The Bull Ring, the heart of the city, had been blitzed to make way for a tangle of highways and ugly modern buildings. 'Huge, sprawling and uninspiring,' I wrote to my parents. A St Patrick's Day procession straggled through the half empty streets. Even the marchers looked 'pretty ground down'. 'Emigrating to Australia was probably a good move,' I concluded. Only later did we discover that our great-aunt had passed away that very afternoon.

I'm sorry now that we didn't attempt another visit. Perhaps Margaret would then have passed on her childhood recollections of Australia. She may have introduced us to our surviving great-aunt Nellie—the sister Ada so envied when she married Rowland Scurrah and went to live in the big house in Streetly. They could have pointed out the hardware shop on Moseley Road where my father was born and the Islington Wesleyan Church where my grandparents met. Together we could have visited our great-grandfather Thomas Davison's grave in the Erdington churchyard.

A few years later, my sister Helen came on a working holiday to London. Like so many Australian visitors, she was thrilled to be experiencing things she had only imagined from afar. 'I have picked my first wild primroses and forget-me-nots, heard the first cuckoo, eaten roast beef and Yorkshire pudding, played darts in a little pub,' she reported excitedly to her family back home. 'I would love you all to be here to see how "Englishy" England is.' Soon she was going out with Barry, a fellow teacher from Bristol, and the following year they were engaged. After their marriage, they spent two years in Australia before returning to England to live. It was then that my father and mother made their one trip to England to visit their daughter and son-in-law and were reunited with Dad's long-lost cousin Margaret.

Legacies

'Listen, our ancestors!' ninety-year-old Thomas had exhorted my Uncle Frank when he visited in 1929. In 1966 I knew nothing of his clock or of the five generations of Davison households for whom it had kept time. Thomas was indulging a fantasy: that the clock had absorbed some of the lives of its previous owners. In listening to its voice, he thought we might hear an echo of their voices too. I sometimes wonder whether we humans are not the same—inheritors, not just of our forebears' genes, but also of characteristics they acquired by habit or intent and passed, by some mysterious Lamarckian mechanism, to us.

Knowing more of the Davisons' history, I detect continuities and affinities invisible to me as I grew up. For more than 200 years, they were skilled manual workers. Both my father and my uncle Frank inherited a love of solid geometry and of shaping things from metal—Dad as a plumber and Frank as a hot-metal printer. William, Richard and Thomas were all pieceworkers rather than wage earners, while Dad was a self-employed tradesman, a status that arguably reinforced an ethic of self-regulation more than time-service. A household clock was probably more important to a worker who had to monitor his personal efficiency than to a wage earner who had his time measured for him.

By and large, the Davisons have followed Richard and Thomas's moderate Labour or centrist politics: 'Mr Davison was a model foreman and manager.' 'True to his employer, true and just to the men.' I am struck now by how many of my forebears occupied similar middling positions in the class structure. Even back in the Borders, the Davison were sidekicks and subalterns rather than leaders or followers. Were we lackeys of our employers? Or were we constructive intermediaries? As an academic middle manager in troubled times, I sometimes asked that question myself.

My father and grandfather, both Methodists, followed their ancestor Richard Davison in taking the pledge. Self-restraint, whether it was from drink, gambling, sex or war, was an essential part of their outlook. I didn't remain a teetotaller for long but I'm glad Richard took his stand: we might all be back in Caldewgate if he hadn't. Perhaps the self-discipline required to get us free of poverty became redundant once modest prosperity was achieved. The habit was so well learned, however, that it was only slowly discarded. The liberationist movements of the 1970s and 1980s, and the educational ideals that grew out of them, challenged the old Protestant ethic of intense self-regulation. I was born too soon to experience their full effects. Some correction was in order, but I wonder if the pendulum—an appropriate horological metaphor?—swung too far.

Such reflections, however, were far from my mind in 1966 as I shook the dust of Birmingham from my feet and headed back to Oxford. My final examinations were approaching and I was looking forward to going home. John La Nauze was right: Oxford had been an enriching experience. But I knew now that Australian history was my calling. I would move forward by going home and looking back. I planned to write a PhD thesis on the history of nineteenth-century Melbourne and had secured a scholarship at the Australian National University. In the time we had been apart, Barbara and I had written to each other almost weekly, but had only one conversation—an awkward semi-public telephone call from the porter's lodge at Balliol. We had both seen other people, but nothing serious, and were eager to know if we had a future together. After my exams, I hitchhiked in Wales, Germany, Denmark and Italy before flying home in October. The BOAC 707 was rescheduled but my message conveying the news reached Melbourne only after Barbara and my parents had left for Essendon Airport. It was almost two days before I turned up, late as usual.

My bungled reunion, I am glad to relate, had a happy sequel. After two years, Barbara and I were still in love and soon decided to marry. She had now completed her course and we would spend the first years of our marriage in Canberra. During the round of family introductions we paid a visit to Aunty Cissie, the great-aunt with whose story this book began. We called at her little flat at the back of 49 Washington Street and she led us into the sitting room where her father's long case clock resided among the other impedimenta of her fractured life. Nothing was said at the time but we later learned that she had taken to Barbara and blessed our union. Since she was not easily pleased, and approval was almost the only thing—apart from her clock of course—that she had left to give, this was something to treasure. But, as far as I recall, she was not among our wedding guests, and I don't remember visiting her again before she died, aged ninety, in June 1968. Soon afterwards the house was sold and her father's clock passed to my father.

The clock remained in my parents' lounge room, unwound and unloved, for almost forty years. Only after my mother died in 2004, and the house at 16 Banchory Street was sold and the contents were distributed, did the clock at last come to our house. By then its movement had seized up. It had stopped short, as the song goes, perhaps never to go again. However, I found an expert horologist and after a few weeks he brought it back, restored to life if not to faultless punctuality. For the first time in decades it resumed its steady rocking gait and its cheerful metallic ring.

I had been waiting for its return to perform a little ceremony. One day when some of our grandchildren called, I ushered them into our living room, and as the clock struck the hour, I raised my finger and said, 'Listen, our ancestors!' They are kind children and put it down, I'm sure, to an old man's eccentricity. But if ever they should have a wish to know about their Davison ancestors, all they need do is listen to the clock and read this book.

Acknowledgements

EVERY FAMILY HISTORY is but a phase in the long conversation we have with our forebears and descendants, and I could not have written this book without the many family members, friends and colleagues who have shared it with me. I mention especially my sister Helen Hobbs, the only living witness to the story I tell in the concluding chapters of the book, and my cousin Tom Davison, whose father Frank Davison, older brother of my father George, was the most devoted keeper of the Davison family's memories. Without the records now in Tom's keeping, including Frank's journal record of his remarkable interview with our great-grandfather Thomas Davison, this book could not have been written. Almost every Thursday afternoon for the past two or three years, Tom and I have walked our neighbourhood, and he has tolerantly listened to my questions, discoveries and conjectures, quietly nudging me in the right direction. Our cousin the late John Porter was the first to attempt a genealogy of the family and I have drawn on some of his research. My other cousins, Bev Brooks, Joan Welch and Helen Spring, have supplemented the record in various ways. So have my boyhood friends Jim Coomes and Roy Dunn, who remember our Essendon childhood and my parents so vividly, and my fellow student Garry Trompf who shared memories of our 1963 expedition to Cape Barren Island. I also acknowledge Earlene Giglierano whose email contact initiated the detour into DNA genealogy described in Chapter Three. This book is dedicated to my own children and grandchildren but it is meant for all the Davison descendants.

In following the Davisons into 'deep time', I have travelled back into their ancestral homelands in Carlisle, Annan, the Scottish Borders and the English Midlands. I acknowledge the assistance of archivists, genealogists and librarians at the Cumbria Archives, the Carlisle Library, the Tullie House Museum, Dumfries and Galloway Family History Centre, the Birmingham Library and the University of Warwick's Modern Records Centre. Nike Hide, Secretary of the Davidson Clan Association, and Alan James, curator of the remarkable archive at the Stead McAlpin works in Cummersdale, have provided helpful advice and vital information. I continue, in all my work, to rely on the wonderful support of staff at the Monash University Library, the State Library Victoria and the Public Record Office of Victoria. I also acknowledge the assistance of the Uniting Church Archives, Scout Heritage Victoria, the Essendon Historical Society and the Essendon High School Ex-Students' Association.

Since I began, thirty years ago, to explore the territory between academic and family history, the traffic across the border has steadily increased. Much of this book was written during the long Melbourne lockdown when I was reliant on the rapidly burgeoning electronic archive of online databases. I first presented some of my conclusions to the conference 'Related Histories: Studying the Family' in Canberra in 2017 and I have been encouraged by the interest of other members of that community, especially Malcolm Allbrook, Tanya Evans, Stephen Foster and Sophie Scott-Brown. I have presented papers on various aspects of the book to my colleagues in the School of Philosophical, Historical and International Studies and to the 'Research Connections' seminar I convene with David Chandler.

David and Marian Quartly read the chapters as they appeared, made incisive comments and provided loyal support. Many years ago, Tony Dingle and Seamus O'Hanlon interviewed my father for another project; I am grateful to have had access to their transcript. Tanja Luckins read Chapter Seven and offered valuable advice on repatriation records, discussions with Carolyn Rasmussen clarified aspects of anti-war movements in the 1930s, and Peter Gronn made incisive comments on the educational issues discussed in Chapter Eleven. Tom Griffiths and Janet McCalman, dear friends and admired colleagues, gave invaluable advice and made supportive comments on the completed manuscript. My wife Barbara enters the story briefly at the beginning and end of the book. Everything I know about family is enriched by her love and the life we have shared with our parents, children and grandchildren.

I am grateful to Nathan Hollier, Louise Stirling and the team at Melbourne University Publishing, and to editor Paul Smitz, proofreader Eugenie Baulch, illustrator Guy Holt and typesetter Patrick Cannon for their astute contributions to the editing and production of this book.

Notes

I have made extensive use of the standard genealogical sources, such as parish registers, official registrations of births, marriages and deaths, probate records, city directories and British census records, often accessing them through Ancestry, Find My Past, Family Search, Scotland's People and other online databases. These are too many to cite individually except where critical judgement was required.

Introduction

My book on time-telling in Australia: *The Unforgiving Minute: How Australia Learned to Tell the Time*, Oxford University Press, Melbourne, 1994; also see my 'The Secret Life of the Strasburg Clock' in Graeme Davison and Kimberley Webber (eds), *Yesterday's Tomorrows: The Powerhouse Museum and Its Precursors 1880–2005*, Powerhouse and UNSW Press, Sydney, 2005, pp. 148–59. Fernand Braudel's remark is in his *On History*, Chicago University Press, Chicago, 1980, p. 47. Charles Taylor's discussion of identity is in his 'The Politics of Recognition' in David Theo Goldberg (ed.), *Multiculturalism: A Critical Reader*,

Blackwell, Oxford, 1992, p. 79. My previous essays on family history: 'Ancestors: The Broken Lineage of Family History' in my *The Use and Abuse of Australian History*, Allen & Unwin, Sydney, 2000, pp. 80–100; 'Speed Relating: Family History in a Digital Age', *History Australia*, vol. 6, no. 2, 2009, pp. 43.1–43.10; and Foreword to Malcolm Allbrook and Sophie Scott-Brown (eds), *Family History and Historians in Australia and New Zealand: Related Histories*, Routledge, London, 2021, pp. ix–xv. On heirlooms and heritage: 'Heritage: From Patrimony to Pastiche' in *The Use and Abuse of Australian History*, pp. 110–30, and 'My Heritage Trail' in Anna Clark and Paul Ashton (eds), *Australian History Now*, NewSouth, Sydney, 2013, pp. 181–97.

1 Listen, Our Ancestors!

History of my mother's family: *Lost Relations: Fortunes of My Family in Australia's Golden Age*, Allen & Unwin, Sydney, 2015. Cissie described her voyage in Elizabeth Davison, Part of a Letter Sent to a Friend Kate Describing Voyage to Australia [1934], in possession of Tom Davison. The exemplary heirloom histories are Edmund de Waal, *The Hare with Amber Eyes: A Hidden Inheritance*, Vintage Books, London, 2010, and Tim Bonyhady, *Good Living Street: The Fortunes of My Viennese Family*, Allen & Unwin, Sydney, 2011. David Lowenthal's discussion of heirlooms is in his *Possessed by the Past: The Heritage Crusade and the Spoils of History*, The Free Press, New York, 1996, pp. 62–3. The lawyer's perspective is in Patricia Davidson, 'Heirs and Heirlooms Can Create Hurdles in Estate Administration', *Estate Planning*, vol. 41, no. 8, August 2014, pp. 25–9. Robert Hodgson's business in Annan is listed in John Smith, *Old Scottish Clockmakers from 1453 to 1850*, Oliver and Boyd, Edinburgh, 1921, p. 191, and the style of the clock's dial in Gavin Lucas, 'The Changing Face of Time: English Domestic Clocks from the Seventeenth to Nineteenth Century', *Journal of Design History*, vol. 8, no. 1, 1995, pp. 1–9; also Brian Loomes, *Country Clocks and Their London Origins*, David and Charles, Newton Abbot, 1976, pp. 101–6, 121. An experienced clock repairer, Greg Gabel, who examined the clock, also gave a date of c.1780. David Landes's account of the pendulum clock is in his *Revolution in Time Clocks and the Making of the Modern World*, Belknap

Press, Harvard, Cambridge, MA, 1983, pp. 114–24; Davidsons and Hodgson in Annan: see *Early Annan Census 1801 1811 1821*, Dumfries and Galloway Family History Society, April 2009, pp. 2, 6. On the price of long case clocks see EP Thompson, 'Time, Work and Industrial Capitalism', *Past and Present*, no. 38, 1967, p. 67; and Alun C Davies, 'Rural Clockmaking in Eighteenth-Century Wales: Samuel Roberts of Llanfair Caereinion, 1755–1774', *Business History Review*, vol. 59, spring 1985, p. 60. Compare the similar estimates of American historians, based on inventories from contemporary wills: Carlene Stephens, *On Time: How America Has Learned to Live by the Clock*, Smithsonian Institution, Washington, 2002, pp. 47–51; and Mark M Smith, 'Counting Clocks, Owning Time: Detailing and Interpreting Clock and Watch Ownership in the American South, 1739–1865', *Time and Society*, vol. 4, no. 3, 1994, pp. 321–39. Frank Davison recounts his grandfather Thomas's remark in his Travel Diary, August 1929 (in possession of Tom Davison). Cumberland custom is recalled in James Walter Brown, *Round Carlisle Cross*, Cumberland News, Carlisle, 1951, pp. 130–1. Queen Victoria and Albert are in Julia Baird, *Victoria: The Queen*, Random House, New York, 2016, pp. 320, 323. Thomas Hardy's 'Old Furniture' is in his *Moments of Vision and Miscellaneous Verses*, Macmillan, London, 1917. I am grateful to my cousin Helen Spring for bringing this lovely poem to my attention.

2 Before the Clock

When I refer to the region, I write Borders and Borderers, but in speaking of the dividing line between the kingdoms I use the lower-case border. On fathers beating knowledge into sons, see MJH Robson, History and Traditions of Sheep-farming in the Scottish Border Hills, PhD, University of Edinburgh, 1977, p. 41. The classic statement on the value of oral traditions in African history is Jan Vansina, *Oral Tradition: A Study in Historical Methodology*, Routledge, London, 1965; for Australia see Paul Behrendt, 'The Importance of Oral History to Aboriginal Society', *Oral History Association of Australia Journal*, no. 16, 1994, pp. 2–5. Geoffrey Blainey's contention is in his *Before I Forget: An Early Memoir*, Hamish Hamilton, Sydney, 2019, p. 197. Robert Fenwick, Locating Scotland's Ordinary Folk, among the Lesser Known Sources for Social and Family History Research, c.1630–c.1790, PhD thesis, University of Edinburgh, 2006, pp. 11–15 discusses the attrition of early Scottish parish registers. My estimate of the prevalence of the Davison name in Dumfries and Roxburgh is based on Old Parish birth registers in the database Scotland's People at https://www.scotlandspeople.gov.uk. The psychologists of memory are Hilde Ostby and Ylva Ostby, *Adventures in Memory: The Science and Secrets of Remembering and Forgetting*, Greystone Books, Vancouver and Berkeley, 2018, p. 109. Hilary Mantel's remark is in her *The Mirror and the Light*, 4th Estate, London, 2020, p. 220. Mark McKenna reflects on the *Return to Uluru*, Black Inc., Carlton, 2021, pp. 177–88. For 'roots tourism' in Scotland see Kalyan Bhanari, 'Imagining the Scottish Nation: Tourism and Homeland Nationalism in Scotland', *Current Issues in Tourism,* vol. 19, no. 9, 2016, pp. 913–29; and Tawny Paul, 'Encountering the Imaginary Heritage: Roots Tourism and the Scottish Diaspora', in Angela McCarthy and John M Mackenzie (eds), *Global Migrations: The Scottish Diaspora since 1600*, Edinburgh University Press, Edinburgh, 2016, pp. 199–219. Hugh Trevor-Roper discusses 'The Invention of Tradition: The Highland Tradition of Scotland' in Eric Hobsbawm and Terence Ranger (eds), *The Invention of Tradition*, Cambridge University Press, Cambridge, 1983, pp. 15–42. Walter Scott on the Borderers is in *The Poetical Works of Sir Walter Scott*, Griffith, Farran Oakden and Welsh, London and Sydney [1907], p. 1. For published work on the Davidson clan or surname, see: Archie McKerracher, *Davidson: The Origins of the Clan Davidson and Their Place in History*, LangSyne Publishing, Newtongrange, 2018; and Flora Davidson, 'Davidson Borderers' in *The Davidsons: The Clan, Its History and Its People*, The Clan Davidson Association, Dingwell Ross-shire, n.d., pp. 21–9. I am grateful to Nick Hide, secretary of the association, who kindly made available typescript notes from original sources compiled by Ms Davidson and referred me to articles in the association's journal *The Phaeon*. The main authorities on the history of the Border reivers, such as George MacDonald Fraser's excellent *The Steel Bonnets: The Story of the Anglo-Scottish Border Reivers*, HarperCollins, London, 1986, focus on the most powerful surnames and on the conflicts in the Western Marches, seldom mentioning lesser families like the Davisons. Jon Tait's lively *Dick the Devil's Bairns: Breaking the Border*

Mafia, Tradition Gmbh, 2019, pp. 165–70, gives more attention to the East Teviotdale surnames, including the Davisons. Unfortunately, none of these books and chapters is footnoted. On the origin of the Davidson name: J Stuart et al. (eds), *The Exchequer Rolls of Scotland*, Edinburgh, vol. 4, 1878–1908, p. x. On the significance of surnames, see: TI Rae, *The Administration of the Scottish Frontier, 1513–1603*, Edinburgh University Press, Edinburgh, p. 5; and Anna Groundwater, *The Scottish Middle March 1573–1625 Power, Kinship, Allegiance*, Royal Historical Society, Woodbridge, Suffolk, 2010, pp. 52–3. Carey's observation: Sir R Carey to Burghley, 17 September 1596, *Calendar of Border Papers*, Joseph Bain (ed.), vol. 2, HM Register House, 1896, p. 189. On Pont's cartography see Jane A Dawson, *Scotland Re-Formed 1488–1587*, Edinburgh University Press, Edinburgh, 2007, pp. 326–8. The study of Border gentry is Maureen M Meikle, *A British Frontier? Lairds and Gentleman in the Eastern Borders 1540–1603*, Tuckwell Press, East Lothian, 2004, pp. 13–16; on 'gentlemen' see Howard Pease, *The Lord Wardens of the Marches of England and Scotland*, Constable, London, 1912, p. 175. On 'kindly tenants': TC Smout, *A History of the Scottish People 1560–1830*, Fontana Collins, Glasgow, 1979, pp. 135–6; Groundwater, *The Scottish Middle March*, pp. 35–6; and Robson, History and Traditions of Sheep-farming, pp. 49–50. Contemporary view of 'heritours': *Geographical Collections Relating to Scotland Made By Walter Macfarlane*, Edinburgh University Press, Edinburgh, vol. 3, 1908, p. 160. The housing of Border families is based on Andrew Borde, *The First Book of the Introduction of Knowledge* (1551), Early English Text Society, 1870, p. 136; Robson, History and Traditions of Sheep-farming, pp. 233–4; and HG Ramm, RW McDowall and Eric Mercer, *Shielings and Bastles*, Royal Commission on Historical Monuments (England), HMSO, London, 1970. *The Statistical Account of Roxburghshire,* Blackwood, Edinburgh, 1841, pp. 464–5 notes that whereas in the 1790s houses in the region of Morebattle were still mostly of one storey and thatched, they were now mostly of stone and slated. Meikle, *A British Frontier?*, p. 3 discusses limitations of the wardens' dispatches. Alison A Chapman, 'Marking Time: Astrology, Almanacs and English Protestantism', *Renaissance Quarterly*, vol. 60, 2007, pp. 1257–90, and Alexandra Walsham, *The Reformation of the Landscape: Religion, Identity, and Memory in Early*

Modern Britain and Ireland, Oxford University Press, Oxford, 2011, ch. 1, discuss the value of almanacs. Quotations come from *Caledonia's Everlasting Almanac*, [Edinburgh] 1702. 'The Battle of Otterbourne' is from *Border Ballads*, selected and edited by William Beattie, Penguin, Harmondsworth, 1952, p. 34. List of Scottish raids in Forster to Burghley, 30 June 1590, *Border Papers*, vol. 2, pp. 360–5. Fraser on the motivation for raids in his *The Steel Bonnets*, p. 107. Jenny Wormald's analysis of blood feuds is in 'Bloodfeud, Kindred and Government in Early Modern Scotland', *Past and Present*, no. 87, May 1980, p. 57. The raid on Haltwistle is described in Northumberland to Henry VIII, 23 August 1532, *State Papers Published under the Authority of His Majesty's Commission: King Henry the Eighth, 1830–1852*, vol. 4: Part IV: Correspondence relative to Scotland and the Borders, 1513–1534, London, 1836, pp. 611–14; also Northumberland to Henry VIII, 23 August 1532, J Gairdner (ed.), *Letters and Papers, Foreign and Domestic, of the Reign of Henry VIII*, vol. 5: 1531–32, Longman & Co., London, 1880, p. 540. Rae, *The Administration*, pp. 147–52 notes the coincidence of many raids with the full moon, an observation confirmed in the case of the Haltwhistle raid by the perpetual lunar calendar. The size of Teviotdale force: see *Border Papers*, vol. 2, p. 106. Prominence of Davisons in murders on border is shown in Sir William Eure to the Privy Council, 31 December 1541, Joseph Bain (ed.), *The Hamilton Papers: Letters and Papers Illustrating the Political Relations of England and Scotland*, vol. 1, [Edinburgh] 1890, pp. 141–2. Compare Eure to Lisle, 6 December 1542, ibid., vol. 3, p. 319. Lisle, Tunstall and Uvedale to Privy Council, 8 December 1542, ibid., p. 313. Battle of Hadden Rig: George Bowes and Brian Layton to Rutland, 24 August 1542, Angus and Sir George Douglas to Privy Council, 25 August, *Letters and Papers, Foreign and Domestic*, vol. 17, 1542, pp. 371, 377–8. The Tryst: Ordnance Survey Name Books, 1858–60, Roxburghshire, vol. 25, OS1/29/25/2. Stephen Davison's escapade: Lisle to the Council, 13 December 1542, *Letters and Papers, Foreign and Domestic*, vol. 17, 1542, p. 661. George Davison's boast and bargain: Lisle to Tunstall, 5 January 1543, *Hamilton Papers*, vol. 4, p. 359, and Suffolk and Tunstall to Privy Council, 12 June 1543, ibid., vol. 6, pp. 541–2. Henry VIII upbraids the Davisons: Henry VIII to Suffolk, 22 June 1543, Lord Parr to Duke of Suffolk,

17 July 1543, Henry VIII to Sadler, 22 July 1543, ibid., vol. 6, pp. 547, 573–5, 587. On his 'rough wooing', see Marcus Merriman, *The Rough Wooings: Mary Queen of Scots, 1542–1551*, Tuckwell Press, East Linton, 2000, pp. 152–6; and Merriman, 'The Assured Scots: Scottish Collaborators with England during the Rough Wooing', *Scottish Historical Review*, vol. 47, no. 143, Pt 1, April 1968, pp. 10–34. Objectives of 'assured Scots', Scheme for Conquest of Scotland, February 1544, *The Hamilton Papers*, vol. 8, pp. 287–8; and Merriman, 'The Assured Scots', pp. 10, 23–5. Battle of Ancrum is described by Fraser, *The Steel Bonnets*, pp. 260–1. English commander on 'treason' of 'assured Scots': Shrewsbury to Henry VIII, 2 March 1545, *Hamilton Papers*, vol. 11, pp. 564–6. Walter Scott castigates 'renegades' in his *Tales of Grandfather*, Robert Cadell & Houston, Edinburgh, vol. 1, 1843, pp. 224–5; Robert Borland, *Border Raids and Reivers*, Thomas Fraser, Dalbeattie, 1898, p. 200 defends them. Scars on countryside: Joseph Yair, 'The Parish of Eckford' in William Blackwood, *The Statistical Account of Roxburghshire,* Edinburgh 1841, pp. 223–4; also see George Chalmers, *Caledonia or, An Account Historical and Topographic of North Britain*, London, 1810, p. 95. Reprisals against Davisons are described in *Register of the Privy Seal*, vol. 4, pp. 111, 181. George as hostage: *Acts of the Lords of Council in Public Affairs 1501–1554*, Her Majesty's General Register House, Edinburgh, 1932, p. 636; and Mary, Queen Dowager, to John Wemyss, 20 July 1555, Sir William Fraser (ed.), *Memorials of the Family of Wemyss of Wemyss*, Edinburgh, 1888, pp. 9–10. Evidence of Davisons' links with Cessford Kers: *Calendar of Scottish Papers*, vol. 10, p. 195; and Eure to Burghley, 5 May 1596, *Calendar of Border Papers*, vol. 2, p. 129. Davisons at 1645 Land Tax Rolls available at https://scotlandsplaces.gov.uk/search/place/Roxburghshire?id=27. On Birnyrig branch: *Register of the Privy Council of Scotland*, vol. 2, pp. 475, 686–7. John Knox's declaration quoted in Meikle, *A British Frontier*, pp. 210–13. On the decline of feuding, see Keith M Brown, *Bloodfeud in Scotland 1573–1625: Violence, Justice and Politics in Early Modern Society*, John Donald, Edinburgh, 1986, p. 276; Rae, *The Administration of the Scottish Frontier*, p. 260; and Groundwater, *The Scottish Middle March*, p. 135. James I's objective is quoted in ibid., p. 188. TM Devine on the decline of the tenantry: *The Lowland Clearances: A History of the Dispossessed*, Allen Lane, London, 2018,

pp. 83–6. Banishment of John Davidsoune: *Records of the Privy Council of Scotland*, vol. 14, p. 689. Hearth Tax Rolls at https://scotlandsplaces.gov.uk/digital-volumes/historical-tax-rolls/hearth-tax-records-1691-1695. The battle against old church festivals: Nigel Yates, *Preaching, Word and Sacrament: Scottish Church Interiors 1560–1860*, Bloomsbury, London, 2009, p. 12; and new church calendar: *A Collection of the Laws in Favour of the Reformation in Scotland, in Three Parts*, Edinburgh, 1749, p. 33 and Act XII Discharging the Yule Vacance, *Acts of the Scottish Parliament*, 1640/6/22; and Smout, *A History of the Scottish People*, pp. 78–9. George Davidson's infringement: James Fleming Leishman, 'The Lairds of Cockburn', *History of the Berwickshire Naturalists' Club*, vol. 26, 1926, 1927, 1928, Neill and Co., Edinburgh, 1929, p. 74, and new almanacs: Alexandra Walsham, 'The Reformation and "The Disenchantment of the World" Reassessed', *Historical Journal*, vol. 52, no. 2, 2008, pp. 497–528. On Covenanters in general see Smout, *A History of the Scottish People*, pp. 161–6 and in Teviotdale John Smith and Duncan Stewart, *The Covenanters of Teviotdale and Neighbouring Districts,* Walker and Son, Galashiels, 1908, p. 58. Offences by Davidsons in *Register of the Privy Council*, Series 3, vol. 9, p. 200, ibid., vol. 10, pp. 515, 542, 577. Description of John Blackader's discourses quoted from Smith and Stewart, *The Covenanters of Teviotdale,* p. 95. Covenanter preachers Smith and Stewart, *The Covenanters of Teviotdale,* pp. 95, 186–9. For John Wilson's biography see https://www.mustrad.org.uk/articles/j_wilson.htm.

3 The Peasant in the Town

The Lowland Clearances: Thomas Devine, *The Scottish Clearances: A History of the Dispossessed*, Allen Lane, London, 2018, pp. 83–5; and Peter Aitchison and Andrew Cassell, *The Lowland Clearances: Scotland's Silent Revolution,* Tuckwell, East Linton, 2003. Reports of depopulation in Hownam in Sir John Sinclair, *Statistical Account of Scotland*, Edinburgh 1791–1799, vol. 1, pp. 51–2; and compare also vol. 21, Appendix 4, pp. 15–16. Also in *Statistical Account*, vol. 3, p. 121 (Linton), vol. 3, p. 263 (Makerston), vol. 11, pp. 320–1 (Oxnam), vol. 1, pp. 6–7 (Jedburgh), vol. 10, p. 587 (Kelso), vol. 19, p. 611 (Yetholm). Robert Davidson recalls his life in 'Autobiography' in his *Leaves from a Peasant's Cottage Drawer* (1848), Matador, Leicester, 2008, pp. 1–5. William Riddell Carre mentions Davidson's occasional resort to poor relief in his *Border Memories or Sketches of Prominent Men and Women of the Border*, James Thin, Edinburgh, 1876, p. 269. Scott's raid is described in Lucy MacRae, Walter Scott's *The Minstrelsy of the Scottish Border*: The Dynamics of Cultural Memory, PhD thesis, University of Edinburgh, 2014, pp. 128 ff; and John Sutherland, *The Life of Walter Scott: A Critical Biography*, Blackwell, Oxford, 1995, pp. 43–7, 75–7. Walter Scott on ballads as relics: Scott to Washington Irving, 1817, quoted in WFH Nicholaisen, 'Scott and the Folk Tradition' in Alan Bold (ed.), *Sir Walter Scott: The Long Forgotten Melody*, Vision and Barnes and Noble, London, 1983, p. 130. Davidson's lament: 'Sim and Sandy', *Leaves from a Peasant's Cottage Drawer*, pp. 22–3. Clergyman's opinion of the border: *Statistical Account of Scotland*, vol. 3, p. 491, as quoted by Linda Colley, *Britons Forging the Nation 1707–1837*, Yale University Press, New Haven, 2005, p. 16. Canonbie and the Debatable Lands: Graham Robb, *The Debatable Land: The Lost World between Scotland and England*, Picador, London, 2018, pp. 19–20. Rory Stewart, *The Marches: Border Walks with My Father*, Vintage, London, 2016, pp. 192–6. Davidsons in Canonbie: Walter F Davidson and Nick Hide, 'The Davidson Families from Canonbie, Dumfries-shire', *The Phaeon Clan Davidson Association*, 2016, 2017. Allen family in Eden Valley: *Westmorland Hearth Tax Michaelmas 1670 & Surveys 1674–75*, eds Colin Phillips, Catherine Ferguson and Andrew Wareham, British Record Society, vol. 124; and *The Parish Registers of Bolton, 1647–1812*, transcribed and indexed by Col. Francis Haswell, Cumberland and Westmorland Antiquarian Society, Penrith, 1944. Ancient monuments in Crosby Ravensworth: Rev. GF Weston, 'Crosby Ravensworth', *Transactions of the Cumberland and Westmorland Antiquarian Society* (*Trans C&WAAS*), vol. 2, 1876, pp. 205–24. Battle of Clifton Moor: Jacqueline Riding, *Jacobites: A New History of the '45 Rebellion*, Bloomsbury, London, 2016, pp. 321–4. Local fears of Border invasions in Joseph Nicholson and Richard Burn, *The History and Antiquities of the Counties of Westmorland and Cumberland*, W Strahan and T Cadell, London, 1777, pp. 10–11. Boys' games described in Adam Fox, 'Vernacular Culture and Popular Customs in Early Modern

England: Evidence from Thomas Machel's Westmorland', *Cultural and Social History*, vol. 9, no. 3, 2012, pp. 338–41. Movement of cattle from Scotland in ARB Haldane, *The Drove Roads of Scotland* (1952), Edinburgh University Press, Edinburgh, 1971, pp. 177–9; JD Marshall, 'The Rise and Transformation of the Cumbrian Market Town', *Northern History*, vol. 19, no. 1, 1983, pp. 151–2; and Peter Roebuck, 'Cattle-Droving through Cumbria after the Union: the Stances on the Mulgrave Estate, 1707–12', *Trans C&WAAS*, vol. 12, 2012, pp. 147–8. Local pasturing of cattle: Andrew Pringle, *General View of the Agriculture of the County of Westmorland*, Chapman and Company, Edinburgh, 1794, pp. 23–4; and Roebuck, 'Cattle-Droving', pp. 148–9, 151–2. Occupational structure of villages from Lorraine Ashcroft (ed.), *Vital Statistics: The Westmorland 'Census' of 1787*, Curwen Archive Texts, Berwick, 1992, pp. 173–80. Itinerant tailors in *The Manners and Customs of Westmorland … in the Former Part of the Eighteenth Century*, Hudson and Nicholson, Kendal, 1827, pp. 6–7. Moral policing in Rebecca Probert, *The Changing Legal Regulation of Cohabitation: From Fornicators to Family 1600–2010*, Cambridge University Press, Cambridge, 2012, pp. 24–51. Rising illegitimacy debated by Belinda Meteyard, 'Illegitimacy and Marriage in Eighteenth-Century England', *Journal of Interdisciplinary History*, vol. 10, no. 3, winter 1980, pp. 479–89; and Laurence Stone, 'Illegitimacy in Eighteenth-Century England: Again', ibid., vol. 11, no. 3, winter 1981, pp. 507–9. High marriage rate in Westmorland villages in Rebecca Probert and Liam D'Arcy Brown, 'Westmorland Weddings: A Study of the 1787 Census', *Family and Community History*, vol. 16, no. 1, 2013, pp. 32–44; and Rebecca Probert, *Marriage Law and Practice in the Long Eighteenth Century*, Cambridge University Press, Cambridge, 2009. Population of Annan: Sinclair, *Statistical Account*, vol. 19, pp. 447–52, vol. 20, p. 599. Defoe's opinion of Westmorland in his *A Tour through the Whole Island of Great Britain* (1769), London, 1978, p. 550. Remnants of feudalism: CE Searle, 'Custom, Class Conflict and Agrarian Capitalism: The Cumbrian Customary Economy in the Eighteenth Century', *Past & Present*, no. 110, February 1986, pp. 106–33. Hold of customary tenants: Nicholson and Burn, *The History and Antiquities*, p. 501; and JV Beckett, 'Inheritance and Fortune in the Eighteenth Century: The Rise of Sir James Lowther', *Trans C&WAAS*,

vol. 87, no. 2, 1987, pp. 171–8. Impact of enclosure: CE Searle, 'Cumbria's Parliamentary Enclosure Movement: A Comparative Case Study in Rural Quiescence', *Trans C&WAAS*, vol. 95, no. 2, 1995, pp. 247–69; idem, 'Customary Tenants and the Enclosure of the Cumbrian Commons', *Northern History*, vol. 29, no. 6, 1993, pp. 126–53; Ian Whyte, '"Wild, Barren and Frightful"—Parliamentary Enclosure in an Upland County: Westmorland 1767–1890', *Rural History*, vol. 14, no. 1, 2003, pp. 21–38; Ian D Whyte, 'Patterns of Parliamentary Enclosure of Waste in Cumbria: A Case Study from North Westmorland', *Landscape History*, vol. 22, no. 1, 2000, pp. 77–89; and Ian Whyte, 'Parliamentary Enclosure and Changes in Landownership in an Upland Environment: Westmorland, c.1770–1860', *Agricultural History Review*, vol. 54, no. 2, 2006, pp. 240–56. Enclosure and supply of pasture: Pringle, *General View of the Agriculture … of Westmorland*, pp. 23–4. Enclosure acts in Searle, 'Cumbria's Parliamentary Enclosure Movement', pp. 263–6. Place of Annan in droving routes: John A Thomson, *History of Annan and District*, vol. 2, the author, Annan, 1991, pp. 107–14. Jacobites' march north: Riding, *Jacobites*, pp. 325–33. Breeches as Lowland dress: 'Glengarry vs The Celtic Society', *Blackwood's Magazine*, vol. 12, 1820, p. 360. Scott's opinion: Scott to Sir Thomas Lauder, as quoted in Rosemary Hill, *Time's Witness: History in the Age of Romanticism*, Allen Lane, London, 2021, p. 207. Cotton mill in Annan: Thomson, *History of Annan and District*, p. 126. 'Modern: up with the times': CA Bayly, *The Birth of the Modern World 1780–1914*, Blackwell, Oxford, 2004, p. 10.

4 The Sad Sound of the Factory Bell

Carlisle and attacks from north: Daniel Lysons and Samuel Lysons, 'The City of Carlisle' in *Magna Britannia: Volume 4, Cumberland* (London, 1816), pp. 56–81. Abolition of taxes on Scots: George Topping, *Memories of Old Carlisle,* Steel Brothers, Carlisle, 1922, pp. 91–3. Friction between Scots and English schoolboys recalled by James Walter Brown, *Round Carlisle Cross*, Cumberland News, Carlisle, 1951, p. 123. Carlisle's plebeian subculture in Susan L Cooper, Traditional Forms of Entertainment in Nineteenth-Century Carlisle, PhD thesis, University of Indiana, 1980, pp. 104–53; Topping, *Memories of Old Carlisle,* pp. 113–14; *Carlisle Patriot*, 29 June 1861; *Carlisle Journal*, 1 May 1863; and *Paisley Herald*, 14 May 1870. Mortality in Carlisle: WA Armstrong, 'The Trend of Mortality in Carlisle between the 1780s and the 1840s: A Demographic Contribution to the Standard of Living Debate', *Economic History Review,* vol. 34, no. 1, February 1981, p. 97. EP Thompson's 'Time, Work-Discipline and Industrial Capitalism': *Past and Present*, no. 38, 1967, pp. 56–97. Design of dial: Gavin Lucas, 'The Changing Face of Time: English Domestic Clocks from the Seventeenth to Nineteenth Century', *Journal of Design History*, vol. 8, no. 1, 1995, p. 7. Carlisle clockmakers' boast: *House of Commons Journals*, vol. 51, p. 251, as quoted in Thompson, p. 65. Accounts of time management and work discipline in mechanised factories: Harry Braverman, *Labor and Monopoly Capital: The Degradation of Work in the Twentieth Century,* Monthly Review Press, New York, 1974, pp. 139–53; and Sidney Pollard, *The Genesis of Modern Management: A Study of the Industrial Revolution in Great Britain*, Penguin, Harmondsworth, 1965, pp. 213–36. Persistence of handwork: Raphael Samuel, 'Workshop of the World: Steam Power and Hand Technology in Mid-Victorian Britain', *History Workshop*, no. 3, spring 1977, pp. 6–72. Critiques of Thompson: Richard Whipp, '"A Time to Every Purpose": An Essay on Time and Work' in Patrick Joyce (ed.), *The Historical Meanings of Work,* Cambridge University Press, Cambridge, 1987, pp. 210–36; Barbara Adam, *Time and Social Theory*, Temple University Press, Philadelphia, 1990, pp. 104–26; and Paul Glennie and Nigel Thrift, 'Reworking E.P. Thompson's "Time, Work-Discipline and Industrial Capitalism"', *Time and Society,* vol. 5, no. 3, 1996, pp. 275–99. William Davidson the convict: *Carlisle Journal*, 25 September 1819; *Carlisle Patriot*, 4, 11 March 1820; *Carlisle Patriot*, 4 March 1820; and New South Wales Certificate of Freedom, 19 December 1828. McAlpin and Stead: EA Rose and CGE Bunt, *Two Centuries of Chintz, 1750–1950, as Exemplified by the Productions of Stead, McAlpin & Co*, F. Lewis, Leigh on Sea, 1957, pp. 20–2; and Wages Book in Stead McAlpin Company Archives, Cummersdale. Origins of workforce in Wigton: 1851, 1861 census. Operations in Cummersdale: *Carlisle Patriot*, 5 March 1836; William Whelan, *A History and Topography of the Counties of Cumberland and Westmoreland*, 1860; and SD Chapman, 'Quantity Versus Quality in the British Industrial

Revolution: The Case of Printed Textiles', *Northern History*, vol. 21, 1985, pp. 175–92. Techniques of block printing: Andrew Ure, *A Dictionary of Arts, Manufactures and Mines*, vol. 1, Longmans, London, 1853, pp. 310–11; 'Flowers, Dust Sheets and Carlisle Gaol', *The Gazette*, 20 August 1977; and Rose and Bunt, *Two Centuries of Chintz*, p. 22. William's wages: Stead McAlpin Wage Books, Company Archives, Cummersdale; and John Burnett, *A History of the Cost of Living*, Penguin, Harmondsworth, 1969, pp. 247–52. A Mary Anne Davidson died in Wigton in 1843 but I cannot confirm that she was William and Mary's daughter. A James Davidson also died in Wigton in 1850. Neither shows up in the 1851 census. What became of the third daughter, Jane, is equally mysterious, but three women of that name died and were buried at St Mary's Carlisle in 1821, 1829 and 1837. 'The situation is healthy': *Carlisle Patriot*, 5 March 1836. William's potatoes: *Carlisle Journal*, 6 June 1846. His grandsons' employment: Certificate for a Child to Be Employed, no. 788, 1865, Stead McAlpin Company Archives; and Alan James Personal Communication, 28 June 2018. Clock an indication of prosperity: GR Porter, *The Progress of the Nation*, John Murray, London, 1847, p. 533. Arrival of railway: *Carlisle Journal*, 6 May 1843. Heine as quoted in Wolfgang Schivelbush, *The Railway Journey: Trains and Travel in the 19th Century*, Blackwell, Oxford, p. 44. Row houses and tenements: Michael Daunton, 'Public Space and Private Space: The Victorian City and the Working Class Household' in Derek Fraser and Anthony Sutcliffe (eds), *The Pursuit of Urban History*, Edward Arnold, London, 1983, pp. 212–33; compare Alan Harris, 'Denton Holme, Carlisle: Part 2, The Growth of a Suburb', *Trans C&WAAS*, vol. 67, 1967, pp. 206–28. Handloom weavers: Duncan Bythell, *The Handloom Weavers: A Study of the English Cotton Industry in the Industrial Revolution*, Cambridge University Press, Cambridge, 1969, pp. 66–93; compare EP Thompson, *The Making of the English Working Class* (1963), Pelican Books, London, 1968, pp. 297–346. Weavers as clock owners: W Radcliffe, *The Origin of Power Loom Weaving*, Stockport, 1828, as quoted in Thompson, 'Time, Work Discipline', p. 70. Muggeridge and Dixon: *Carlisle Journal*, 23 June 1838. These estimates were confirmed by independent investigations by the Poor Law Commissioners; see Royal Commission of Inquiry into Administration and Practical Operation of Poor Laws, Appendix B2

Answers to Town Queries, *Commons Sessional Papers*, 1838, Part 1, p. 26. Robert Rawlinson's report in his *Report to the General Board of Health on a Preliminary Inquiry into the Sewerage, Drainage and Supply of Water, and the Sanitary Condition of the City of Carlisle, 1850*, p. 50. Death rates in Armstrong, 'The Trend of Mortality', pp. 94–114; and report about Caldewgate and Botchergate: Royal Commission into the State of Large Towns and Populous Districts, Second Report and Minutes of Evidence, Sessional Papers, vol. XVIII, 1845, pp. 209–12. For character of houses, see 1841 and 1851 census, advertisement for Dwellings in Byron Street, Caldewgate, *Carlisle Journal*, 8 April 1853; Jeremy Godwin, 'Duke Street, Carlisle, a Street of Handloom Weavers', *Trans C&WAAS*, vol. 88, no. 2, 1988, pp. 225–38; Hannah Barker and Jane Hamlett, 'Living above the Shop: Home, Business and Family in the English "Industrial Revolution"', *Journal of Family History*, vol. 35, no. 4, 2011, pp. 311–28; and Catherine Hall, 'The Butcher, the Baker, the Candlestick-maker: The Shop and the Family in the Industrial Revolution' in her *White, Male and Middle Class: Explorations of Feminism and History*, Polity Press, London, 1992, pp. 94–107. Desire for domestic privacy: Leonore Davidoff and Catherine Hall, *Family Fortunes: Men and Women of the English Middle Class 1780–1850*, Hutchinson, London, 1987, pp. 383–8. Sir James Graham: *Carlisle Journal*, 23 March 1839; and criticism of his sale of land at Netherby: ibid., 24 January 1851. Political ferment in Caldewgate: June Barnes, 'Liberty or Death', *Trans C&WAAS*, vol. 84, no. 2, 1984, pp. 205–13; idem, 'The Trade Union and Radical Activities of the Carlisle Handloom Weavers', *Trans C&WAAS*, vol. 78, no. 2, 1978, pp. 149–61; *Leeds Intelligencer*, 11 November 1830; Katrina Navickas, 'Captain Swing in the North: The Carlisle Riots of 1830', *History Workshop Journal*, no. 71, spring 2011, pp. 5–28; and *Northern Star*, 22 December 1838, 4 September 1841. Shoemakers and radicalism: EJ Hobsbawm and Joan Wallach Scott, 'Political Shoemakers', *Past and Present*, no. 89, November 1980, pp. 86–114; and Mayhew's opinion: *The Unknown Mayhew*, eds EP Thompson and Eileen Yeo, Penguin, London, 1971, p. 279. Chartists' databank: http://www.chartistancestors.co.uk/chartist-ancestors-databank/ (accessed 31 December 2017). Joseph Hume: *Carlisle Journal*, 26 May 1852; see also 19 December 1851. Richard Davison to Temperance Soirée: *Carlisle Journal*, 3 January 1851.

Drinking usages: JFC Harrison, *The Early Victorians 1832–51*, Weidenfeld and Nicolson, London, 1971, p. 72. Apprentices and drinking customs: Topping, *Memories of Old Carlisle*, p. 236. 'Who wouldn't be a teetotaler?': Brian Harrison, *Drink and the Victorians: The Temperance Question in England 1815–1872*, Faber and Faber, London, 1971, pp. 128–32. Temperance Hall: Margaret Forster, *Rich Deserts and Captain's Thin: A Family and Their Times 1831–1931*, Chatto and Windus, London, 1997, pp. 43, 104–7. Thomas as chorister: 'Thomas Davison' in Birmingham Operative Tin–plate, Sheet Metal and Braziers' Society Fifty-Eighth *Annual Report and Balance Sheet* for the year ended 31 December 1917, p. 3; and Advertisement for Choristers, *Carlisle Patriot*, 3 May 1856. Carlisle Cathedral clock: David WV Weston, *Carlisle Cathedral History*, Bookcase, Carlisle, 2000, p. 85. Set to London time: *Carlisle Patriot*, 10 December 1841. Choristers' regime: 'Thomas Davison', Brown, *Round Carlisle Cross*, p. 73. John's misbehaviour and precentor's tardiness: Records of the Cathedral Choir and Grammar School, Cumbria County Record Office. Thomas's golden handshake: 'Thomas Davison', p. 3. Dean Tait and the labouring classes: *Carlisle Journal*, 3 November 1854; Edith Davidson to Thomas Davison, 23 November 1929, letter in possession of Tom Davison; and Peter Marsh, 'Tait, Archibald Campbell', *Oxford Dictionary of National Biography*, 'Thomas Davison', p. 3. Tinplate: JH Jones, *The Tinplate Industry*, P.S. King & Son, Westminster, 1914, p. xviii; and WJ Reader, *The Metal Box: A History*, Heinemann, London, 1976, pp. 7–8.

5 The Workshop of the World

On the pattern of cityward migration, see DB Grigg, 'E. G. Ravenstein and the "Laws of Migration"', *Journal of Historical Geography,* vol. 3, no. 1, 1977, pp. 41–54. Union provisions for migrating workers in EJ Hobsbawm, 'The Tramping Artisan' in his *Labouring Men: Studies in the History of Labour,* Weidenfeld and Nicolson, London, 1964, pp. 34–63; and Ted Brake, *Men of Good Character: A History of the National Union of Sheet Metal Workers, Coppersmiths, Heating and Domestic Engineers*, Lawrence and Wishart, London, 1985, pp. 54–9. The distinctive class character of Birmingham is the subject of Asa Briggs,

Victorian Cities, Odhams Press, Watford, 1963, pp. 187–9; idem, *History of Birmingham*, vol. 2, Oxford University Press, Oxford, 1952, pp. 28–66; and Jane Jacobs, *The Economy of Cities*, Penguin, Harmondsworth, 1972, pp. 87–94. GM Young's observation is in his *Victorian England Portrait of an Age*, second edn, Oxford University Press, London, 1957, p. 124. For a critique of the consensus view of Birmingham politics, see Clive Behagg, 'Myths of Cohesion: Capital and Compromise in the Historiography of Nineteenth-Century Birmingham', *Social History*, vol. 11, no. 3, October 1986, pp. 375–84. JH Hopkins is described in 'John Satchell Hopkins, Obituary in the Institution of Engineers Obituaries, 1898', as quoted in *Grace's Guide to British Industrial History*, https://www.gracesguide.co.uk/John_Satchell_Hopkins. The origins of the tinplate workers' union are mentioned in Briggs, *Birmingham*, p. 63. Participants in the 1866 Reform demonstration are listed in *Birmingham Journal*, 1 September 1866, and the 1867 event in *Birmingham Journal*, 27 April 1867 (supplement). Local conditions for compounding rents are described in *Aris's Birmingham Gazette*, 27 July 1867, and the increase of the borough franchise in John Davis and Duncan Tanner, 'The Borough Franchise after 1867', *Historical Research*, October 1996, pp. 318–19. Estimate of voters in Thomas Davison's ward from 1871 Census of Population and Houses and *Birmingham Daily Post*, 18 November 1868. Thomas's speech at the Temperance Hall is quoted in 'Thomas Davison', p. 5. Also see Minutes of the Birmingham Operative Tin–Plate Workers' Society [1868], Modern Records Centre, 992/5/1 University of Warwick. Trygve Tholfsen on the respectable workingman in his 'The Origins of the Birmingham Caucus', *The Historical Journal*, vol. 2, no. 2, 1959, p. 176. The union's expectations of members are defined in *Rules of the Birmingham Operative Tin-Plate Workers' Society* [1891], Modern Records Centre, University of Warwick. Edgbaston as the factory owners' suburb: David Cannadine, *Lords and Landlords: The Aristocracy and the Towns, 1774–1967*, Leicester University Press, Leicester, 1980, pp. 94–123. Alfred Hopkins on unions: *Birmingham Daily Post*, 7 December 1889. Thomas's negotiations with his employer: 'Thomas Davison', p. 5; and Brake, *Men of Good Character*, pp. 163–6. Memories and photographs of Old Ladywood are collected at the website http://www.oldladywood.co.uk. Thomas as manager: 'Thomas

Davison', pp. 3–6. Thomas at Conservative Working Men's Association: *Birmingham Daily Post*, 31 January 1893. Death of Satchell Hopkins and demise of firm: Mr Satchell Hopkins (obituary), *Times*, 12 February 1898. American competition and decline of tinplate industry: Jones, *The Tinplate Industry*, p. 274. Demise of JH Hopkins: *London Gazette*, 18 October 1898, p. 6081; and *Birmingham Daily Post*, 1 September 1900. Satchell Hopkins estate: *Birmingham Daily Post*, 15 April 1898.

6 Towards Australia

Cardalls as 'pride of Islington in the old days': *Islington (St Martin's Street) Wesleyan Sunday School Old Scholars' and Teachers' Magazine*, May 1938, Islington Wesleyan Chapel Records, MC 88, Heritage Collections, Library of Birmingham (hereafter *Islington Old Scholars' Magazine*). Descriptions of the Islington church: *Birmingham Daily Post*, 29 April 1889; and Robert Currie, *Methodism Divided: A Study in the Sociology of Ecumenicalism*, Faber and Faber, London, 1968, pp. 103–7. At the 1851 religious census, only about 4 per cent of Birmingham's population attended a Methodist religious service compared with 28 per cent of Cornwall's and 14 per cent of the West Riding of Yorkshire. Barnes: 'Our Second President', *Islington Old Scholars' Magazine*, no. 2, 1914, pp. 2–3. Forward Movement: KS Inglis, *Churches and the Working Classes in Victorian England*, Routledge and Kegan Paul, London, 1963, pp. 78–80. Drunkard not to enter: *Birmingham Daily Post*, 30 October 1863. Extensions to chapel: *Birmingham Daily Post*, 21 August 1884, 29 April 1889. Millennial Methodists: Kenneth Newport, 'Methodists and the Millennium Eschatological Expectation and the Interpretation of Biblical Prophecy in Early British Methodism', *Bulletin of the John Rylands Library*, vol. 78, no. 1, 1996, pp. 103–22. And for Wesley on time: John Wesley, 'Sermon 93 On Redeeming the Time' (1782), The Sermons of John Wesley, http://wesley.nnu.edu/john–wesley/the–sermons–of–john–wesley–1872–edition/sermon–93–on–redeeming–the–time/ (accessed 26 January 2021); and John Wesley, 'Sermon 50 On the Use of Money', *Sermons on Several Occasions*, First Series, Methodist Publishing House, London, n.d., pp. 696–708. Debates among historians: Max Weber, *The Protestant Ethic and the Spirit of Capitalism* [1904–05],

Scribner, New York, 1958, p. 175; also compare EP Thompson, *The Making of the English Working Class*, Pelican edn, London, 1968, pp. 395–403, and Bernard Semmel, *The Methodist Revolution*, Heinemann, London, 1973, pp. 71–9. Time-thrifty local preachers: WB Carter, 'The Local Preacher: No. 5', *The Local Preacher's Magazine and Christian Family Record*, vol. 15, 1865, p. 131; and Rev. Richard Smetham, 'The Eternally Permanent and the Constantly Fluctuating; or, a New Testament Echo to an Old Testament Oracle', *Wesleyan Methodist Magazine*, January 1878, p. 7. Methodism becoming lower middle class: Harold Perkin, *The Origins of Modern English Society 1780–1880*, Routledge, London, 1969, p. 356. John Davison's Deed of Gift of Furniture in Contemplation of Marriage, December 1899, in possession of Tom Davison. Victorian ideal of marriage: Leonore Davidoff and Catherine Hall, *Family Fortunes: Men and Women of the English Middle Class*, Hutchinson, London, 1987, pp. 247–71. Frank and Phyllis's memories of shop in Moseley Road: Memories of Frank Davison—Eldest Son of John Potter Davison—Grandson of Thomas Davison—Great Grandson of Richard Davison, 8 August 1974, handwritten notes in possession of Tom Davison; and undated letter of Phyllis Davison to Helen Hobbs, email from Joan Welsh to Graeme Davison, 3 January 2018. Migration and decline of Methodism: Robert Wearmouth, *The Social and Political Influence of Methodism in the Twentieth Century*, Epworth Press, London, 1957, pp. 46–7; and *The Times*, 5 August 1912. Imprint on Chartism: Harold Perkin, *The Origins of Modern English Society 1780–1880*, Routledge, London, 1969, pp. 356–64; and dominance of libertarianism: Bernard Semmel, *The Methodist Revolution*, Heinemann, London, 1977, pp. 3, 146–69. Methodism as imperial: *The Methodist*, 25 November 1899, as quoted in Troy Duncan, 'Methodism and Empire' in Glen O'Brien and Hilary M Carey (eds), *Methodism in Australia: A History*, Ashgate, Abingdon, 2015, p. 117. Bazaar: Grand Imperial Bazaar Brochure, M7/11, Islington Wesleyan Church Records, Library of Birmingham. Perks' Brotherhood: 'Mr Perks's Scheme', *Cornishman*, 25 July 1907; 'Great Methodist Scheme', *Hull Daily Mail*, 10 May 1907; and *Daily News*, 14 August 1907. Victorian scheme: 'Assisting Immigrants', *Argus*, 24 July 1909. Taverner: 'Settlement for Emigrants', *Birmingham Gazette and Express*, 7 June 1910. Flow to Australia:

Geoffrey Sherington, *Australia's Immigrants 1788–1978*, Allen & Unwin, Sydney, 1980, pp. 92–3; 'Emigration within the Empire', *Times*, 24 May 1912; and Richard Broome, *Arriving*, Fairfax, Syme and Weldon, Sydney, 1984, pp. 136–8. Chamberlain's opinion: *Times*, 1 February 1909. Coal strike: ibid., 7, 10 March 1912. Political unrest: Henry Pelling, 'The Labour Unrest, 1911–1914' in his *Popular Politics and Society in Late-Victorian Britain*, Macmillan, London, 1968, pp. 147–64; and Standish Meacham, '"The Sense of an Impending Clash": English Working Class Unrest before the First World War', *American Historical Review*, vol. 77, no. 5, December 1972, pp. 1343–64. Assisted immigration scheme: *Weekly Times*, 24 August 1912. How much assistance did John receive? The authorities kept making small adjustments to the fares; this is my estimate based on information in the *Victorian Yearbook*, 1911–12, p. 262 and 1912–13, p. 188.

7 Voyage and Landfall

Account of the voyage based on Harold Harding, 'Diary of Voyage Tilbury to Melbourne Australia, Nov 8th 1912', copy of typescript in possession of the author; also his 'Greetings from Australia, 28 January 1913', *Islington Old Scholars' Magazine*, 1913, pp. 8–9. Details of the ship's company: *Age*, 16 December 1912. Victorian-born fitter than immigrant: *Weekly Times*, 19 October 1912. George Davison's 'recollection' of landfall: 'Memoirs of an Essendonian', handwritten notes in the possession of the author. Employment conditions: *Labor Call*, 10 April 1913, p. 2. Temperance Township: Michael Cannon, *The Land Boomers*, Melbourne University Press, Carlton, 1966, pp. 117–18; Graeme Davison, *The Rise and Fall of Marvellous Melbourne*, Melbourne University Press, Carlton, 1978, pp. 212–30; and Geoffrey Curr, 'Liberalism, Localism and Suburban Development in Melbourne 1870–1900', *Historical Studies*, vol. 19, no. 74, April 1980, pp. 41–58. Its respectability: *Age*, 31 July 1890. Harold Harding's impressions of Melbourne: 'Greetings from "Down Under"', *Islington Old Scholars' Magazine*, 1914, pp. 8–9. 'Rattery': *Essendon Gazette*, 12 March 1914; and Fred Todd: ibid., 1 June 1974, 21 May 1977. Churches and migration: James Jupp, 'Religion, Immigration and Refugees' in Jupp (ed.), *The Encyclopedia of Religion in Australia*,

Cambridge University Press, Melbourne, 2009, p. 645. Louie to Ada, postcard in possession of the author. News of Nellie's engagement: Ada Davison to Nellie Scurrah, 9 July 1914, letter in possession of Tom Davison. I wondered how this poignant letter had made its way back to Australia—Nellie may have shown it to Frank, Ada's son, when he stayed with the Scurrahs in 1928 and he probably brought it back for her. Call of Empire to Methodists: *Methodist Spectator*, 6 August 1915, p. 1145. Ages of recruits: LL Robson, 'The Origin and Character of the First A.I.F. 1914–18: Some Statistical Evidence', *Australian Historical Studies*, vol. 15, no. 61, 1973, pp. 737–49. Physical requirements: Enlistment papers of Harold Harding, Reg. no. 4723, NAA B2455; Lloyd Robson, *The First AIF: A Study of Its Recruitment*, Melbourne University Press, Parkville, 1970, p. 23; and Peter Cochrane, *Simpson and the Donkey: The Making of a Legend*, Melbourne University Press, Parkville, 1992. Dials on public clocks: Robson, *The First AIF*, p. 47. Godless Hun and change on height requirements: Michael McKernan, *The Australian People and the Great War*, Collins, London, 1980, pp. 14–42, 46. History of 21st Battalion: Neil C Smith, *The Red and Black Diamond: The History of the 21st Battalion 1915–1918*, Mostly Unsung Military History, Gardenvale, 1997, p. 2. Australians and the Somme: Joan Beaumont, *Broken Nation: Australians in the Great War*, Allen & Unwin, Sydney, 2013, p. 184. Hine's description in Smith, *The Red and Black Diamond*, pp. 44–5. Harold's will is in Harold Harding Probate, 1916, VPRS 7591/150/945. Bean's opinion: CEW Bean, *The Australian Imperial Force in France*, 1916, 12th edn, Australian War Memorial Canberra, 1941, p. 918; and 21st Battalion at Buire: 21st Battalion War Diary, 13 October, 3–6 November 1916, AWM4 23/38/15. Widows: Peggy Bette, 'Widows', *The International Encyclopedia of the First World War*, https://encyclopedia.1914–1918–online.net/article/war_widows (accessed 11 April 2021). Religion and sacrifice: Ken Inglis, 'The Anzac Tradition', *Meanjin*, vo. 24, no. 1, 1965, pp. 25–44; idem, *Sacred Places: War Memorials in the National Landscape*, Miegunyah Press, Melbourne, 1998, pp. 2, 471–4; Pat Jalland, *Australian Ways of Death: A Social and Cultural History 1840–1918*, Oxford University Press, Oxford, 2002; and Stuart Piggin and Robert D Linder, *Attending to the National Soul: Evangelical Christians in Australian History 1914–2014*,

Monash University Publishing, Clayton, 2020, pp. 84–9. Harold's fob watch being stolen mentioned in his 'Diary of Voyage Tilbury to Melbourne, 26 November'. Wristwatches and battle: Graeme Davison, *The Unforgiving Minute: How Australia Learned to Tell the Time*, Oxford University Press, Melbourne, 1994, pp. 107–8; and Carlene Stephens, *On Time: How America Has Learned to Live by the Clock*, Smithsonian, Washington, 2002, pp. 134–5. Edith's circumstances after Harold's death: Harold Harding Enlistment Papers, NAA B2455, p. 53; and Harold Harding Probate, 1916, VPRS 7591/150/945. Under the War Pensions Act, no. 34 1914, the amount of the pensions paid to war widows was graduated according the husband's rank; as a private, Harold was entitled only to the basic £52 per annum. Edith Harding, Application for Assistance 18 December 1918 and Recommendation of Essendon Committee, Harold Harding Repatriation File B73 R41583, NAA. Increase in pension: *Argus*, 9 December 1918. Mrs Ward: *Camperdown Chronicle*, 10 October 1918. Methodists and conscription: Stuart Piggin and Robert D Linder, *Attending to the National Soul: Evangelical Christians in Australian History 1914–2014*, Monash University Publishing, Clayton, 2020, pp. 29–59; Don Wright and Eric Clancy, *The Methodists: A History of Methodism in NSW*, Allen & Unwin, Sydney, 1993, pp. 129–36. Woodfull on Mannix: *Age*, 3 September 1917. Thanksgiving Service: *Flemington Spectator*, 21 November 1918.

8 The Years between

The demographer RT Appleyard, *British Emigration to Australia*, ANU Press, Canberra, 1964, p. 165, interviewed British migrants on the boat, while the historians James Hammerton and Alistair Thomson, *Ten Pound Poms: Australia's Invisible Migrants*, Manchester University Press, Manchester 2005, p. 65, interviewed British immigrants many years later in Australia. Australia's poor economic performance in the inter-war period is described by Ian W McLean, *Why Australia Prospered: The Shifting Sources of Economic Growth*, Princeton University Press, Princeton, NJ, 2013, pp. 174–5. For the debate about the outlook of the Depression generation, see Don Aitkin, Michael Kahan and Sue Barnes, 'What Happened to the Depression Generation?' in Robert

Cooksey (ed.), *The Great Depression in Australia*, *Labour History*, no. 17, 1970, pp. 174–81; Dan Potts, *The Myth of the Great Depression*, Scribe Publications, Carlton, 2006, pp. 331–41; and Joan Beaumont, *Australia's Great Depression*, Allen & Unwin, Crow's Nest, 2022, pp. 211–24. George Davison recorded his childhood experiences in his 'Memoirs of an Essendonian', manuscript in possession of the author. On the perils of the 'dead-end job', *Weekly Times*, 15 August 1925; and the decay of the apprenticeship system: Ann Larson, *Growing up in Melbourne: Family Life in the Late Nineteenth Century*, Demography Department, Australian National University, 1994, pp. 127–8. Phyllis Davison's apprenticeship: Phyllis Davison to Chas. Lane and Co. Pty Ltd, Apprentice Indenture, in possession of her daughter Bev Brooks. The judge who declared that women would grow up to marry was Charles Heydon (1918) as quoted in Edna Ryan and Anne Conlon, *Gentle Invaders: Australian Women at Work 1788–1974*, Nelson, Melbourne, 1975, p. 83. For Higgins's judgment, see Federated Clothing Trades of the Commonwealth of Australia and J.A. Archer and Orrs no. 66 1918, 13, *Commonwealth Arbitration Repor*ts, 1919, pp. 647ff; and on his masculinist assumptions: Mark Hearn, 'Securing the Man: Narratives of Gender and Nation in the Verdicts of Henry Bournes Higgins', *Australian Historical Studies*, vol. 37, no. 127, 2006, pp. 1–24. Frank Davison extracted details of his employment history from a diary he later destroyed in a summary in the possession of his son Tom Davison. Conference on printing apprenticeship reported in *Argus*, *Ballarat Star*, 19 October 1921, and *Argus*, 17 March 1922. Recent historians of adolescence have questioned the weight that Hall gave to the supposed frustrations of dependence among the young and given greater weight to the shifting values of their elders: see Joseph F Kett, 'Reflections on the History of Adolescence in America', *The History of the Family*, vol. 8, 2003, pp. 355–73. *Age* editorial opinion on 'The Australian Adolescent': 2 September 1929. The early history of Scouting in Victoria: Graeme Davison, *City Dreamers: The Urban Imagination in Australia*, NewSouth, Sydney, 2016, pp. 132–4; and AR Milne and CB Heward, *Those Boy Scouts: A Story of Scouting in Victoria*, Victorian Scout Archives, Hawthorn [1987], p. 20. On Baden-Powell as misogynist and latent homosexual: Tim Jeal, *Baden-Powell*, Hutchison, London, 1989, pp. 74–109. Obituary and memorial for

Cecil Stevens: *Essendon Gazette*, 30 April, 15 October 1942; and Lindsay White, Unpublished History of the First Moonee Ponds Scout Group Based on Parents' Committee Minutes (First Moonee Ponds History). Stevens on 'The Spiritual Basis of Scouting' in *Australian Scouting*, 1 May 1927. Lord Foster's opinion on Scouting's civic aim: *Age*, 14 January 1924, *Australian Scouting*, vol. 2, no. 3, 1924. Some historians insist that, despite the leaders' protestations, the movement aimed to prepare young people for military service: see John Springhall, 'Baden Powell and the Scout Movement before 1920: Citizen Training or Soldiers of the Future?', *English Historical Review*, vol. 102, October 1987, pp. 934–42. Frank Davison's recollection of the early days of Scouting in '21 Years' in *50 Years of Scouting 1916–1965, 1st Moonee Ponds Group Boy Scouts* [1965], p. [7]. The Eltham camps are described in White, First Moonee Ponds History. The Boronia accident is reported in *Argus*, 27 April 1926; *Australian Scouting*, June 1926, p. 2; *Wellington Times*, 24 May 1926; and White, First Moonee Ponds History. The Royal Park experiment is described in White, First Moonee Ponds History, and Stevens's own account in *Australian Scouting*, October 1926, p. 2. Frank Davison's address at Wesley College: *Age*, 21 September 1927. The class composition of Scouts in Britain: JO Springhall, 'The Boy Scouts, Class and Militarism in Relation to British Youth Movements 1908–1930', *International Review of Social History*, vol. 16, no. 2, 1971, pp. 125–58; in the Empire: Robert H MacDonald, *Sons of Empire: The Frontier and the Boy Scout Movement 1890–1918*, University of Toronto Press, 1993, p. 11. In his *The Road to Gundagai*, Hamish Hamilton, London, 1965, p. 155, Graham McInnes observed that his fellow Scouts in Toorak were mostly the sons of railwaymen, fitters, carpenters and automobile station owners; my analysis of the social background of First Moonee Ponds Scouts, based on the occupations of members of the parents' committee, may overstate the white-collar component. The Australian Scout not a snob: *The Australian Scout's First Book*, Deaton and Spencer, Sydney, 1931, reprinted 1936, p. 7. The 'anxious class' in Stuart Macintyre, *The Oxford History of Australia, vol. 4, 1902–1942: The Succeeding Age*, Oxford University Press, Melbourne, 1986, pp. 145–6. Frank's account of the Arrowe Park Jamboree in White, First Moonee Ponds History, and his 1929 Travel Diary, in possession of Tom Davison.

9 A Tale of Two Houses

On immigrant aspirations to home-ownership see Graeme Davison, 'Colonial Origins of the Australian Home' in Patrick Troy (ed.), *A History of European Housing in Australia*, Cambridge University Press, Melbourne, 2000, pp. 254–68; Blair Badcock, 'Home Ownership and the Illusion of Egalitarianism' in ibid., pp. 254–68; and A James Hammerton and Alistair Thomson, *Ten Pound Poms: Australia's Invisible Immigrants*, Manchester University Press, Manchester, 2005, pp. 218–47. John Davison's purchase of land at Glenroy is documented by receipts from Sully and Harwood, Estate Agents for 1 May 1920 for Land at Lot 116 Section B Glenroy Heights Estate, in possession of Tom Davison, advertisement in *Portland Guardian*, 5 May 1927; and the background in Andrew Lemon, *Broadmeadows: A Forgotten History*, City of Broadmeadows/Hargreen, Melbourne, 1982, p. 145. Purchase of 49 Washington Street in Contract of Sale, Tadgell Brothers as Agent for Winifred Olley, 25 March 1930, papers in possession of the author. George's recollections are in his 'Memoirs of an Essendonian'. Will of John P Davison, September 1933, VPRS 28/P0004/497/707. Position of mortgage-holders during the Depression is outlined in Joan Beaumont, *Australia's Great Depression*, Allen & Unwin, Sydney, 2022, pp. 242–3; and David Potts, *The Myth of the Great Depression*, Scribe, Melbourne, 2006, pp. 107, 151. Grace (Davison) Horsburgh recalled the circumstances of her father's death to her daughters, Joan Welsh and Helen Spring. The National Bank's policy on marriage of employees is described in *Launceston Examiner*, 2 April 1938; and *Age* and *Argus*, 25 May 1938. Frank's employment record comes from the previously described summary from his diaries. Plumbers' unemployment rates come from 1933 Commonwealth Census. George recounted his Depression experiences in an interview with Tony Dingle and Seamus O'Hanlon, 13 July 1994. The origins and early history of the North Essendon Methodist Church are outlined in *Essendon North Methodist Church Eightieth Anniversary 1888–1968*. Cyril Walklate's biography comes from Janet McCalman, *Vandemonians: The Repressed History of Colonial Victoria*, Miegunyah Press, Melbourne, 2021, pp. 306–7; *Mercury*, 2 May 1936; and *Gippsland Standard*, 12, 19 December 1917. His vision of the New Christian Social

Order comes from *Age*, 9 March 1934, p. 8. Walklate's activity and views on Anti-Sweating League: *Argus*, 21 October 1932, 24 June 1933; and *Age*, 31 January 1935. Melbourne's quiet Sunday was praised by Rev. AA Lee in FB Smith, 'Sunday Matters' in Bill Gammage and Peter Spearritt (eds), *Australians 1938*, Fairfax, Syme and Weldon, Sydney, 1987, p. 393. Walklate's views on employment condition in *Argus*, 10 February 1934; *Age*, 6 August 1934; and *Mercury*, 14 December 1935; and his letter to the prime minister in *Worker*, 14 June 1933. Vic Hewett's address on 'The Challenge of the Church to the New Age' is summarised in Essendon North Methodist Men's Society Minutes, 5 April 1939, MEL 02186829, Victorian Uniting Church Archives. For the history of Victorian state high schools, see A Max Badcock, 'The Secondary Division' in LJ Blake (ed.), *Vision and Realisation: A Centenary History of State Education in Victoria*, Education Department, Melbourne, 1973, pp. 45–55, 482–4; and Richard Teese, *For the Common Weal: The Public High School in Victoria 1910–2010*, Australian Scholarly Publishing, North Melbourne, 2014, pp. 9–28. Headmaster James King outlined his ideals in *Essendon High School Magazine*, December 1925, pp. 1–2. The mediocre retention and examination performance of the private schools is described by Janet McCalman, *Journeyings: The Biography of a Middle-Class Generation 1920–1990*, Melbourne University Press, Carlton, 1993, pp. 121–7, 305–10. Headmaster James Hill advanced his views in *Essendon High School Magazine*, June 1928, p. 1, December 1929, p. 1; and *Argus*, 21 December 1931. King's reference for my mother: Emma May Hewett, Reference from J. King Headmaster Essendon High School 15 December 1925, in author's possession. W Neill Eagle Star Insurance Company to Miss EM Hewett 30 August 1926, in possession of the author. Jessie Ackerman on the Australian business girl in her *Australia from a Woman's Point of View*, Cassell and Co., London, 1913, Cassell Australia, North Ryde, 1981, p. 236. The typist is viewed as the type of a 'modern girl' in Liz Conor, *The Spectacular Modern Woman: Feminine Visibility in the 1920s*, Indiana University Press, Bloomington, 2004, pp. 39–76. Preference for women typists over male clerks is discussed in *Sunday Mail*, 8 December 1935; and 'Do Girls Prefer to Work in Offices?', *Daily News*, 6 June 1935; and whether plain ones were preferable to pretty ones in *Sun* (Sydney), 20 January 1929; and

Daily Telegraph, 17 January 1938. The activities of the Essendon North Methodist Men's Society Meeting come from their minutes, 1937–39. Oswald Barnett's pacifism is outlined in his *The New Testament Basis of Pacifism*, Christian Pacifist Movement, August 1940, p. 26. General Conference statement on Peace and War is reported in *Methodist*, 25 June 1938, p. 6, and North Essendon men's response in Men's Society Meeting Minutes, 3 May 1939. Christopher Waters, *Australia and Appeasement: Imperial Foreign Policy and the Origins of World War II*, I.B. Taurus and Co., New York, 2016, pp. 260–6, is a judicious summary of contemporary opinion. Builder Matt Atkinson writes to purchaser George Davison, 23 August 1939, letter among other contents of a file in author's possession. I interviewed my parents for an earlier account of my parents' house, 'The Family Bungalow: 16 Banchory Street' in Susan Marsden, *Our House: Histories of Australian Homes*, Australian Heritage Commission, 2001, https://vgls.sdp.sirsidynix.net.au/client/search/asset/1262118. The puzzle of working-class home finance is discussed in my *The Rise and Fall of Marvellous Melbourne*, Melbourne University Press, second edn, 2004, pp. 350–1; see also David Merrett, 'Paying for It All' in Patrick Troy (ed.), *A History of European Housing in Australia*, Cambridge University Press, Melbourne, 2000, p. 248. Ada Davison's disappointment about loss of her rooms and fears of approaching war in Ada Davison to Frank and Betty Davison, Thursday [April 1940?], letter in possession of Tom Davison.

10 Revving up

Historians who confirmed Australia's boom performance are Michael Keating, 'The Evolution of Australian Macroeconomic Strategy since World War 2' in Simon Ville and Glenn Withers (eds), *The Cambridge Economic History of Australia*, CUP, Port Melbourne, 2015, p. 441; and McLean, *Why Australia Prospered*, pp. 176–83. Tony Judt reflects on the restraint of the immediate postwar years in his *Postwar: A History of Europe from 1945*, Vintage Books, London, 2010, p. 226. Statistics of men in uniform and reserved occupations in SJ Butlin, *War Economy 1939–1942*, Australian War Memorial, Canberra, 1955, p. 491. Noel McLachlan argued that Anzac marginalised the non-enlisted men in his 'Nationalism and the Divisive Digger: Three Comments', *Meanjin*, vol. 27, no. 3, September 1968, pp. 302–8. The vilification of British men in reserved occupations is described by Juliette Pattinson, '"Shirkers", "Scrimjacks" and "Scrimshanks"?: British Civilian Masculinity and Reserved Occupations, 1914–1945', *Gender and History*, vol. 28, no. 3, November 2016, pp. 709–27. Plumbers listed among reserved occupations in *Argus*, 28 September 1939, and *Sun* (Sydney), 13 March 1942. Getting around reserved occupations listing to enlist in armed forces in Mark Johnston, 'The Civilians Who Joined up', *Journal of the Australian War Memorial*, issue 29, n.d., https://www.awm.gov.au/articles/journal/j29/civils. George Davison's transactions with the Manpower authorities in his personal file, in author's possession, and records of fellow members of the Wanderers' quartet are from their enlistment and service records in National Archives of Australia and North Essendon Methodist wartime newsletters in Uniting Church Archives. George and May Davison's transactions with the mortgage on 16 Banchory Street are in correspondence with McNab and McNab, Solicitors, 25 March 1944, in author's possession. Value of the house estimated from sales of similar houses in Essendon as given in contemporary newspapers. Opening of new Essendon Baby Health Centre: *Age*, 17 January 1939. On the influence of Dr Truby King: Kerreen Reiger, *The Disenchantment of the Home: Modernizing the Australian Family 1880–1940*, Oxford University Press, Melbourne, 1985, pp. 128–52. My feeding and care regime is contained in blue Health Centre Booklet, in author's possession. On Spock's influence in Australia, see 'At Home with Margaret Sydney', *Australian Women's Weekly*, 23 October 1968. George Davison's musings on home in interview with Tony Dingle and Seamus O'Hanlon. Robert Menzies speeches to 'The Forgotten People' discussed in Judith Brett, *Robert Menzies' Forgotten People*, Macmillan, Melbourne, 1992, pp. 5–27; and Peter Mares, *No Place Like Home: Repairing Australia's Housing Crisis*, Text Publishing, Melbourne, 2018, pp. 166–8. Display gardens in postwar period are described by Peter Timms, *Australia's Quarter Acre: The Story of the Ordinary Suburban Garden*, Miegunyah Press, Melbourne, 2006, pp. 148–69. Erving Goffman distinguished between front-stage and back-stage performances in his *The Presentation of Self in Everyday Life*, Pelican, Harmondsworth, 1961, pp. 32–40. The piano and the lower middle class: see Humphrey McQueen in *A New Britannia*, Penguin, Ringwood, 1970, pp. 117–19. Many Airspy photographs are now digitised and searchable through the State Library Victoria catalogue. Max Weber defines the traditionalist in *The Protestant Ethic and the Spirit of Capitalism*, Scribner, New York, 1958, pp. 59–65.

11 Taking off

Carla Pascoe, *Spaces Imagined, Places Remembered: Childhood in 1950s Australia*, Cambridge Scholars Publishing, Cambridge, 2011, p. 18, comments on the confusion of personal and collective memories. For a cautionary approach, see Mark Peel, 'Between the Houses: Neighbouring and Privacy' in Patrick Troy, *A History of European Housing in Australia*, Cambridge University Press, Melbourne, 2000, pp. 269–86. While I already knew the names of the occupations of our Banchory Street neighbours, I was able to confirm them from a list compiled by my old neighbor Jim Coomes from directories and I checked the occupations against electoral rolls. On the life of Lorimer Fison see WEH Stanner, 'Lorimer Fison', *Australian Dictionary of Biography*, vol. 4, pp. 175–6; JG Fraser, 'Howitt and Fison', *Folklore*, vol. 20, no. 2, 30 June 1909, pp. 144–80; and Helen Gardner and Patrick McConvell, *Southern Anthropology: A History of Howitt's and Fison's Kamilroi and Kurnai*, Palgrave Studies in Pacific History, Basingstoke, Hampshire, 2015. Memories of the Aboriginal presence in Essendon are from 'Memoirs of George Gregor Bishop 1908', as quoted by Fred Cahir, 'Finding Indigenous History in the RHSV Collections', *Victorian Historical Journal*, vol. 85, no. 1, June 2014, p. 23. The copy of this 'Memoir' cited by Cahir is currently missing from the RHSV Collection but it is reproduced in the typescript 'History of Essendon' by James McJunkin, pp. 96 ff. in the Moonee Ponds Regional Library. Fire at Aberfeldie State School in Robert W Chalmers, *From Counting Frames to Computers: The History of the Aberfeldie Primary School No. 4220* [1995], pp. 43–5. My Sixth Grade essay in exercise book in author's possession. Details of proportions of children progressing to secondary school in England and Victoria from Peter Mandler, *The Crisis of the Meritocracy: Britain's Transition to Mass Higher Education since the Second World War*, Oxford

University Press, Oxford, 2020, pp. 39–49; and Richard Teese, *For the Common Weal: The Public High School in Victoria 1910–2010*, ASP, Melbourne, 2014, pp. 50–75; also see WC Radford, *School Leavers in Australia 1959–60*, ACER, Melbourne, 1962. Headmaster Les Garson's view of the objectives of high school education in *Essendon High School Magazine*, 1950, p. 3. Lauchlan Chipman recalled his time at Essendon High in *The University in Regional Australia*, Inaugural Professorial Lecture, Monash University Gippsland Campus, 26 May 1995, pp. 5–6. Statistics of enrolments in successive classes came from class lists in Essendon High School magazines, 1953–59; and my analysis of the occupational background of students in my matriculation class was compiled by matching class lists with local electoral rolls. For changes in the 1970s, see *Essendon High School Magazine*, 1976, p. 9; and memoirs in *Essendon High School 75th Anniversary 1913–1988*. Michael Sandel's critique of meritocracy appeared in his *The Tyranny of Merit: What's Become of the Common Good?*, Allen Lane, London, 2020, p. 13; and Young's in Michael Young, *The Rise of the Meritocracy*, Thames and Hudson, London, 1958, reprinted Transaction Publishers, New Brunswick, New Jersey, 1994. Mandler ponders the end of the 'golden age' in his *The Crisis of the Meritocracy*, p. 195.

12 Towards England

I have recalled my apprenticeship as a historian in a valedictory lecture, *History as a Vocation*, Monash University, 2005; and Tom Griffiths has written a perceptive account in Chapter 11, 'Walking the City: Graeme Davison' in his *The Art of Time Travel: Historians and Their Craft*, Black Inc., Melbourne, 2016, pp. 220–46. Richard Selleck discusses the term 'The Shop' in his *The Shop: The University of Melbourne 1850–1939*, Melbourne University Press, Carlton, 2003, p. 146. DS Anderson and AE Vervoorn, *Access to Privilege: Patterns of Participation in Australian Post-Secondary Education*, Australian National University Press, Canberra, 1983, pp. 128–34, provide a statistical profile of Melbourne University entrants around 1960. John Henry Newman on the university as an 'alma mater' in his *The Idea of a University* (1852), Doubleday, New York, 1959, p. 165. Statistics of the student body in 1959 come from

University of Melbourne Calendar, 1960, pp. 663–4. Judged by parental background, the honours school was no more socially exclusive than the general student population: see Anderson and Vervoorn, *Access to Privilege*, p. 130. Kathleen Fitzpatrick wrote about her academic life in 'A Cloistered Life' in Patricia Grimshaw and Lynne Strahan (eds), *The Half-Open Door*, Hale and Iremonger, Sydney, 1982, pp. 118–33. The passage from Milton that moved me is John Milton, *Areopagitica* (1644) in *Milton's Prose*, Oxford University Press, London, 1949, p. 290. Renate Howe, *A Century of Influence: The Australian Student Christian Movement 1896–1996*, UNSW Press, Sydney, 2009, captures the changing character of the movement. JA La Nauze's survey is 'The Study of Australian History, 1929–1959', *Historical Studies*, vol. 9, no. 33, pp. 9–33. I recall the origins of the *Melbourne Historical Journal* in 'Beginnings' in Keith Wotherspoon and Erik Ropers (eds), *Written into History: Celebrating Fifty Years of the Melbourne Historical Journal 1961–2011*, Melbourne, 2012, Melbourne Historical Journal Collective, pp. 33–8. The urban origins of Australia's bush legend became the subject of my 'Sydney and the Bush: An Urban Context for the Australian Legend', *Historical Studies*, vol. 18, no. 71, October 1978, pp. 191–209; and 'Rethinking the Australian Legend', ibid., no. 43, no. 3, September 2012, pp. 429–51. AW Martin, 'The Whig View of Australian History', was originally given as a paper to Section E of the 1962 ANZAAS conference. It circulated widely in cyclostyled form but was not formally published until 1982 when it appeared in *Teaching History*, vol. 16, no. 3, pp. 7–25, and later in AW Martin, *The Whig View of History and Other Essays*, John Nethercote (ed.), Melbourne University Press, Carlton, 2007, pp. 1–27. I did not read it until many years later but I heard its arguments in the concluding lecture of our course in Australian history towards the end of 1961, when Martin was probably writing it. Henry Reynolds's account of his historical education at the University of Tasmania in his *Why Weren't We Told? A Personal Search for the Truth about Our History*, Penguin, Melbourne, 2000, pp. 12–16, is similar to my own. Among the recent studies of the 'Black War' and Robinson's settlement on Flinders Island are: James Boyce, *Van Diemen's Land*, Black Inc., Melbourne, 2008, pp. 261–317; Lyndall Ryan, *Tasmanian Aborigines: A History since 1803*, Allen & Unwin, Sydney, 2012, pp. 219–52; Cassandra Pybus,

Truganini: Journey through the Apocalypse, Allen & Unwin, Sydney, 2020; and for a more nuanced reading, compare Inga Clendinnen, 'Reading Mr Robinson' (1995) in *Inga Clendinnen: Selected Writings*, James Boyce (ed.), La Trobe University Press/Black Inc., Melbourne, 2021, pp. 59–78. On the kinship between historians and antiquarians, see Tom Griffiths, *Hunters and Collectors: The Antiquarian Imagination in Australia*, Cambridge University Press, Melbourne, 1996. My selection as Rhodes scholar was reported in *Age*, 22 November 1964. The occupational background of my cohort of Rhodes Scholars is drawn from Ralph Evans (ed.), *Register of Rhodes Scholars 1903–1995*, Rhodes Trust, Oxford, 1996. My views on the fading Empire in Ceylon (Sri Lanka) come from letters to my parents, in author's possession. The phrase 'being in a book' is from Alison Griffiths, quoted in Graeme Davison, 'Tourists, Expats and Invisible Immigrants: Being Australian in England in the 1960s and 70s', in Carl Bridge, Robert Crawford and David Dunstan (eds), *Australians in Britain: The Twentieth Century Experience*, Monash University ePress, Clayton, 2009, p. 14:3. Cecil Rhodes's aspirations for the scholarships are covered in Philip Ziegler, *Legacy: Cecil Rhodes, the Rhodes Trust and Rhodes Scholarships*, Yale University Press, New Haven, 2008; and George Walker, '"So Much to Do": Oxford and the Wills of Cecil Rhodes', *Journal of Imperial and Commonwealth History*, vol. 44, no. 4, August 2016, pp. 697–716. 'Independent Australian Briton' is in WK Hancock, *Australia,* London, 1930, Jacaranda Press, Brisbane, 1961, p. 51. See also his autobiography *Country and Calling*, Faber, London, 1954. Jim Davidson describes Hancock's student experience in Oxford in '"Home" Becomes Away: Melburnians in Oxford in the 1920s' in Bridge et al., *Australians in Britain*, pp. 9:1–3. 'Abandoned Britons' in James Curran and Stuart Ward, *The Unknown Nation: Australia after Empire*, Melbourne University Press, Carlton, 2010, pp. 26–57. My account of life in England draws on my letters to my parents and Barbara Grant. My reaction to Birmingham is in Graeme Davison to George and May Davison, 13 March 1966, letter in author's possession. I gave a fuller account of my sister Helen's experience in 'Tourists, Expats and Invisible Immigrants', pp. 14:8–12.

Index

Abbotsford (Scott's house) 35–6
Aberfeldie State School 224–5
Aboriginal Australians 6, 224, 241, 244–7
activism 241
adolescence 159–60
aerodromes and aircraft 220–2
agricultural practices
  agricultural cycle in Border region 32–4
  cattle droving 62
  changes in 44, 52–3, 66
Allan, Mary *see* Davidson, Mary (nee Allan)
ancestral lands 28–31, 48
  return to 5–6, 24–6
  see also Borders (England/Scotland); Dumfriesshire; family histories; memory; Roxburghshire; Teviotdale
Annan, Dumfriesshire 14, 16, 58, 59, 65, 66–7, 68–9
Anti-Sweating League 176–7
Armstrong, Lang Sandy 27–8
Ascot Vale, Melbourne 131–5
Asquith, Herbert 252
'assured Scots' 39–40, 56, 58
Australia
  British Australians (concept) 254–5
  importance of religion in immigration 135
  migrants' complaints 132–4
  national ethos 242–4
  way of life, post-World War I 148–9
  way of life post-World War II 147, 191–3, 199–213, 215, 236–7
Australian Imperial Force 136–40
The Australian Legend (Ward) 242–4
Axarlis, Stella 232

the backyard 209–13, 217
Baden-Powell, Robert 160; *see also* Scout movement
Balliol College, Oxford 249, 251, 252–4
Balsall Heath
  Moseley Road 116–19
Barnes, Jabez 111, 114–15
Barnett, Oswald 176, 185

bastles (bastilles, fortified farmhouses) 31
Birmingham 49, 97–108, 255–6
 culture 98
 economic conditions 97–8, 106–7, 148
 Edgbaston 104, 116
 family visits to 16–17, 18, 22, 148, 165–6, 255–6
 industrial relations 98, 102–4, 105, 107, 122
 Ladywood 96, 101, 104–5, 110–12, 118
 Methodism 110, 111–15, 121
 Moseley Road, Balsall Heath 116–19
 politics 106, 107
 residential manhood suffrage campaign 98–101
 see also metal trades
Birmingham Operative Tin Plate Workers' Society 98–9, 102–4, 107
birth, marriage and death records (Scotland) 22–3
Blainey, Geoffrey 22, 242
Borde, Andrew 32
Borders (England/Scotland) xii, 5, 26–7, 29–32
 border ballads 5–6, 23–4
 Clearances 51–4
 conflicts *see* conflicts between England and Scotland
 peace 44
 political border unimportance 56–7
 reivers 23–4, 25, 27–8, 30, 31, 34–6, 42–4, 48, 53, 73
 surnames and kinship 28–31, 55
 way of life 31–5, 42, 44–5
Bowes, Robert 36–8
Braudel, Fernand 2
Briggs, Asa 248–9
Bright, John 98, 100, 101
'British Australians' concept 254–5
British Empire 102–3, 107, 121, 122, 128–9
 leadership 254; *see also* Scout movement
 migrant loyalty in wartime 136–8, 144–5
 outposts and decline 250–1
British migrants *see* migration; migration to Australia
Buck, Bob 168
bushrangers 35–6

Caldewgate 82–90
Cape Barren Island 245
Cardall, Ada *see* Davison, Ada (nee Cardall)
Cardall, Edith (later Harding) 125, 132, 137, 140–3
Cardall, Nellie 136, 256
Cardall family 110–11, 120, 123, 125, 143, 256
Carey, Robert 29
Carlisle 70, 71–7, 84
 Caldewgate 82–90
 Cummersdale 77–81
 living conditions 84, 85–6, 93
 political discontent 86–7
 temperance movement 87–90
Carlisle Cathedral 90–4
cars 222
cattle thieves *see* reivers
cattle trade 62, 66
Cessford Castle 40–2
Chamberlain, Austen 122
Chamberlain, Joseph 106, 121
Chapman, SD 78
Charles Edward Stuart ('Bonnie Prince Charlie') *see* Jacobite rebellion

Chartism 86–7, 101
Chipman, Lauchlan 231, 232, 233
Christianity *see* Methodism; religion; the Reformation
cities *see* towns and cities
Clark, Manning 244, 250
Clarke, Ron 218
class cooperation *see* social contract between masters and workers
class divide *see* social class
Clearances 51–4
'clock babies' 198
clocks 17–19, 75–6
  author's fascination with 2
  Carlisle Cathedral clock 91
  grandfather clocks 14–19; *see also* grandfather's clock
  JP Davison's clock 116
  pendulum clocks 14–15
  production of 75
  social status symbol 81, 83, 107
  stopping after death 17–18
clothing, Scottish 67
clothing industry 63–4, 68, 69, 154–5; *see also* textiles
conflicts between England and Scotland 36–44, 56
  Jacobite rebellion 61, 66–7, 73
  see also war
cotton mills *see* textiles
Covenanters 46–8, 53, 55
crofters, eviction of 51–4
Cummersdale 77–81
Curtis, Penny 240

Dale, RW 100
Davidson, John (c.1745–1817) xiii, 16, 22, 23, 55, 57–60
  family 67–9
  move to Annan 59, 63–6
Davidson, John (born c.1827) 79–81
Davidson, Mary (nee Allan) xiii, 57, 59–60, 69
Davidson, Mary (nee Dixon) xiii, 76–7, 79–80
Davidson, Robert (the 'peasant poet') 52–4, 70
Davidson, Robert and family (of Marchcleugh) 30, 31, 40, 42, 45, 47
Davidson, Walter 58–9
Davidson, William Allan xiii, 22, 58, 68, 69–70, 76–81, 257
Davidson family
  ancestral homelands 28
  name (spellings) 28–9, 94
  see also Davison family
Davidson/Davison, Elizabeth (nee Downie) xiii, 82, 84–5
Davidson/Davison, Richard Allan xiii, 22, 77, 79, 82, 84–91, 94, 257
Davison (Thomas) and Son 110
Davison, Ada (nee Cardall) xiii, 10, 11, 12, 123, 124–5, 171, 172–3, 188
  emigration to Australia 109, 119–20, 124–30, 147–8
  life in Melbourne 130–6, 147–53, 169–72, 185
  marriage and family 110, 111, 115–18, 123, 147, 151; *see also* Davison, Frank; Davison, George Henry; Davison, Phyllis
  Methodism 110, 111–15
  see also Davison, John Potter
Davison, Barbara (nee Grant) xiii, 26, 28, 35, 249, 258–9; *see also* Davison, Graeme John
Davison, Elizabeth Ann ('Cissie') 2, 9–10, 11–14, 110, 117, 124, 125, 171, 172, 258–9
  clock *see* grandfather's clock

Davison, Frank 12, 24, 25, 49, 116, 147, 151, 168, 188
on emigration to Australia 119, 125, 127–8, 131, 134
home 170, 188, 196
marriage and family 158
memories of Moseley Street 117, 118
Scout 160–4, 166–7, 173
trade 156, 165–6, 173, 257
visit to Birmingham 16–17, 18, 22, 148, 165–6, 255
Davison, George (of Frogden) 37–8, 41–2, 43
Davison, George Henry xiii, 10, 12–13, 123, 147, 151, 168, 178, 183–9, 259
early life 150–3, 183–5
education 152–4, 157–8
home ownership 187–8, 196, 199–200
life at Banchory Street 199–213, 215–24
marriage and family 188–9, 196–8; *see also* Davison, Graeme John; Davison, Helen (later Hobbs); Davison, Janet; Davison, May (nee Hewett)
music-making 162, 183–5
Scout 160–3, 164
working life 134, 173–5, 193–4, 210–13, 226–7, 257
in World War II 193–6
Davison, Grace 12, 147, 151, 152, 171, 172, 181
Davison, Graeme John xiii, 194, 238
early life 196–224
education 224–34, 238, 239–42, 258
at Oxford 248–54, 258
see also Davison, Barbara (nee Grant)
Davison, Helen (later Hobbs) 194, 215, 218, 229, 234, 245, 256
Davison, James ('Jim') 105, 117, 123–4, 134–5
Davison, Janet 194, 229
Davison, John Potter xiii, 10, 11, 12, 49, 105, 109–25
appearance 109, 168
emigration to Australia 109, 119–20, 124–30, 147–8
family business 110, 115, 116, 124
life in Melbourne 130–6, 147–53, 169–72, 185
marriage and family 110, 111, 115–18, 123, 147, 151; *see also* Davison, Ada (nee Cardall); Davison, Frank; Davison, George Henry; Davison, Phyllis
Methodism 110, 111–15
working life in Australia 131
working life in Birmingham 110, 116–17
Davison, Mary (nee Shepherd) xiii, 101
Davison, May (nee Hewett) xiii, 178, 253, 259
early life 179–89
home ownership 187–8, 196, 199–200
life at Banchory Street 199–213, 215–24
marriage and family 188–9, 196–8; *see also* Davison, George Henry; Davison, Graeme John; Davison, Helen (later Hobbs); Davison, Janet
Davison, Phyllis 14, 116, 118, 134, 147, 151, 152, 154–5, 171, 172
Davison, Richard Allan *see* Davidson/Davison, Richard Allan
Davison, Rosemary 24

Davison, Thomas xiii, 11, 17, 22, 122, 257
 clock 13–14, 17, 18; *see also* grandfather's clock
 early life 84, 90–5
 family 101, 105, 115, 123, 124; *see also* Davison, Elizabeth Ann ('Cissie'); Davison, James ('Jim'); Davison, John Potter
 family business 110, 115, 116, 124
 political allegiances 105–6
 portrait of 9–10, 12, 107
 working life in Birmingham 97–107, 110
Davison, Tom 13, 24, 58, 255
Davison family 3, 4–5, 10–11, 23–32, 54–5, 257–8
 ancestral homelands 28–31, 48
 Baptism places 55–6
 as 'kindly tenants' 31–2
 mobility *see* migration; migration to Australia
 name (spellings) 28–9, 56, 94
 pattern of residence 42, 44
 reivers 23–4, 30, 31, 34–6, 42–3, 48
 in Scotland/England conflicts 36–43, 56
 strongholds 30, 40, 56
 way of life 31–5, 42, 44–5, 48–9
Davysoun, Stephen 37–8, 43
the depression *see* Great Depression
Dixon, George 83, 100, 101
Dixon, Mary *see* Davidson, Mary (nee Dixon)
Dixon Brothers' cotton mill 82, 83
DNA testing 58–9
Downie, Elizabeth *see* Davidson/Davison, Elizabeth (nee Downie)
Dumfriesshire 23, 56, 57, 67
 Annan 14, 16, 58, 59, 65, 66–7, 68–9
Eagle Star Insurance Company 181, 183
East Teviotdale xii, 20, 29–31, 36
 Covenanters, 47–8
 destruction of communities by English army 40–1
 see also Borders (England/Scotland)
economic conditions *see* way of life
Eden Valley, Westmorland 59–66
Edgbaston, Birmingham 104, 116
education 180–1, 185
 Carlisle Cathedral Grammar School 91–3
 at Oxford 248–54
 schools 153, 180–1, 224–34, 235
 secondary education 228–34
 technical education 153–8, 227, 228
 tertiary education 234–6, 239–48
 of women 232, 239
Elizabeth II, Queen, visit to Australia (1954) 213, 220
employment *see* work
England as 'Home' 135, 253
England/Scotland conflicts 36–44, 56
 Jacobite rebellion 61, 66–7, 73
 see also reivers
English migrants *see* migration; migration to Australia
Essendon, Melbourne 146, 170, 173–4, 190
 16 Banchory Street 187–8, 190, 199–213, 215–18, 259
 49 Washington Street 12, 152, 168, 170–2, 174, 188, 258
 Baby Health Centre 197–8
 description of 215–24
 Methodist Church 175–9, 186
 photographs of 208–9, 217
Essendon Aerodrome 220–2

Essendon Football Club 219
Essendon High School 180–1, 228–34

family histories 3–5
 surnames and kinship 28–31, 55
 see also ancestral lands; Davidson family; Davison family; memory
family structure 69
feudalism 31, 44, 65–6
First Peoples *see* Aboriginal Australians
Fitzpatrick, Kathleen 240–1
Flemington Training School 225–6
Flinders Island 245–6
folk heroes *see* bushrangers; reivers
football 219
Forrest, Richard 16
Forster, John 35
Forster, Thomas 37
Fraser, George MacDonald 35

garment-making 63–4, 68, 69, 154–6
garments, Scottish 67
Garson, Les 229–30, 237
Gellner, Ernest 26
genealogical research 5
 genetics in 58–9
 see also family histories
Glenroy, Melbourne 169–70
Goffman, Erving 202
'golden age' 191–3, 206–8, 236–7
Goodluck, Jack 245
Graham, James 85–6
grandfather clock song xi, 17
grandfather clocks 14–19
 price (18th century) 16
 Thomas's clock *see* grandfather's clock
 timekeeping 14–15
grandfather's clock 13–17, 18, 71, 81, 258–9
Grant, Barbara (later Davison) xiii, 26, 28, 35, 249, 258–9
Great Depression 149, 167, 170, 172, 173–5, 183

Hall, G Stanley 159
Hancock, Keith 250, 254
Hanna, Jack 183–4, 195
Harding, Edith (nee Cardall) 125, 132, 137, 140–3, 150, 152, 255
Harding, Harold
 emigration to Australia 125, 127–34
 military service and death 136–42
 wife and family 137, 138, 140–3, 150, 152, 255, 256
Harding, Margaret 137, 138, 140–1, 143, 150, 152, 255, 256
hardship *see* way of life
Hardy, Thomas
 'Old Furniture' 18
Harrison, John 88
Harvester Judgment (1907) 155–6
heirlooms 1, 2, 13
heritage, modern ideas of 2, 247
Hewett, Emma 175, 178, 179
Hewett, Joyce 180–1, 182
Hewett, May *see* Davison, May (nee Hewett)
Hewett, Vic 11, 109, 175, 177, 178–9, 231–2
Hewett family 5, 10–11
Higgins, HB 155–6
Highlander culture, suppression of 67
Hill, James 180–1
Hindley, Henry 91
history, study of 240–7, 253, 258
Hobbs, Helen *see* Davison, Helen (later Hobbs)

Hodgson, John 14
Hodgson, Robert 14, 16, 68, 71
'Home' (England) 135, 253–4
home at Blanchory Street
  backyard 209–13, 217
  description of 199–213
home ownership 169–70, 187–8, 196, 199–200
Hopkins (J.H.) and Sons 98, 99, 105–7
Hopkins family 104, 106, 115–16
Horsburgh, Bert 172
Hurst, Harriet 80
Huygens, Christiaan 14

identity 2, 3, 55; *see also* family histories; surnames and kinship
industrial relations 122
  in Birmingham 98, 102–4, 105, 107
  in England 122
industrial revolution 69–71, 74–6, 81–6, 97–8
  and Protestant husbandry of time and money 113–14
Islington Wesleyan Chapel, Ladywood 110, 111, 112, 114–15, 121, 124–5

Jacobite rebellion 61, 66–7, 73
James, Alan 78–9
Jedburgh, Scotland 28, 31, 40, 56
Judt, Tony 192

Ker family 28, 30, 31, 38, 39, 41–3, 44
King, James 180, 181
King, Truby 197, 198
kinship *see* family histories; surnames and kinship
Knox, John 43, 45–8

La Nauze, John 242, 244–5, 249, 250, 258
Ladywood, Birmingham 96, 101, 104–5, 110–12, 118
lairds' power and wealth 43–5; *see also* Ker family
Lammastide 34–5, 46
land of our ancestors *see* ancestral lands
Landes, David 15
Lawson, Henry 185, 232, 243
leisure pursuits 217–18, 219, 220–2, 224
Leslie, Rupert 183, 195
living conditions *see* way of life
Lloyd, George 121, 130, 140
long case clocks *see* grandfather clocks
Lowenthal, David 13
Lowland Clearances 51–4
Lowther, James 65–6
Luddism 83

McAlpin, Stead & Co 77–80, 81
McGregor, Ken 231
Macintyre, Stuart 165
McPhee, Hilary 240
Maebus, Hughie ('Yick') 211–12, 243
Manchester 97–8
Mannix, Daniel 144
Mansfield, Walter 124, 125
Mansfield, Walter (jnr) and Elizabeth 130–1, 134
Mantel, Hilary 25
marriage 64–5, 158–9
  Victorian ideal of 115–16
marriage records (Scotland) 22–3
Martin, Allan 242–4
Marx, Karl 165
Maxwell, Ian 23–4
Mayhew, Henry 87

Melbourne 130
  Ascot Vale 131–5
  Essendon *see* Essendon, Melbourne
  Glenroy 169–70
  photographs of 208–9, 217
  Sabbath observance 177
  'Temperance Township' 132
The Melbourne Historical Journal 242, 243
memory 21–2, 24
  keepers of memories 4–5
  see also ancestral lands; family histories
Menzies, Robert 200
Menzies government 186–7
meritocracy 236
metal trades 97, 98–100, 105, 110–11
  tinplate and tinplate workers 94–5, 98–100, 102–4, 106–7
Methodism 5, 11, 12, 25, 110, 111–15, 134, 165, 175–9, 222–3
  attitude to war and conscription 144, 176, 185–6
  ideas of time and work 113–14, 177–8
  loyalty to Empire 136, 138, 144–5
  migrants 120–2, 124–5
  missionaries 245
  Sabbath observance 177
  self-discipline 257–8
  social reform ideals 176–8
Methodist Men's Society 183–6
migration 54, 120
  within Borderlands 56, 57–62, 70
  Methodists 120–2, 124–5
  motives 119–20, 147–8
  to towns and cities 51–4, 70–1, 97–8
migration to Australia 54
  'British Australians' concept 254–5
  Davison family 10, 109, 119–20, 124–36, 147, 148; *see also* Davison, Ada (nee Cardall); Davison, John Potter
  England as 'Home' 135, 253–4
  migrant loyalty to Britain in wartime 136–8, 144–5
  migrants' complaints about Australia 132–4
modernisation 71; *see also* way of life
Moseley Road, Balsall Heath 116–19
Mulvaney, John 245
music-making 162, 183–5, 203

names *see* surnames and kinship
neighbourhoods 216–19

oral traditions 21–2
Orcades (ship) 249–51
Orontes (ship) 126, 127–30
Oxford University 248–54, 258

pacifism 176, 185–6
pagan traditions 33–4, 46
parenting regimes 197–8
Paterson, Banjo 6
pele towers 31
Perks, Robert 121
Phillips, H Palmer 176, 185
photography 208–10, 217
plumbing trade 134, 157–8, 173, 194
poets *see* Davidson, Robert (the 'peasant poet'); Scott, Walter
politics
  Carlisle 86–7
  Davison family 257
  Methodists 165
  see also conflicts between England and Scotland; war

Pont, Timothy 20, 29
Porter, Alan 13–14, 172
Porter, Grace (nee Davison) *see* Davison, Grace
Pratt, Charles 208–9, 217
Presbyterianism *see* Covenanters; Protestant ethic; the Reformation
primary school *see* education
Pringle family 30, 36, 38, 45
printed cotton 77–9
printing trade 156, 165–6, 178–9
prosperity 191–3, 206–8; *see also* way of life
Protestant ethic 113–14, 176–8, 212–13, 230, 258; *see also* Methodism; the Reformation
Protestant Federation 144

radio 200, 204, 205–6
railways 81–2, 91
the Reformation 45–8, 55
reivers 23–4, 27–8, 30, 31, 34–6, 42–4, 48, 53, 73
religion
  absence of religious symbolism in war commemorations 141–2
  Christian beliefs and festivals 33–4, 45–6
  importance in Australian immigration 135
  Protestant/Catholic divide 218–19
  the Reformation 45–8, 55
  Student Christian Movement 241
  see also Methodism
respectability 102–7, 164–5
return to one's roots *see* ancestral lands; family histories
Reynolds, Henry 244
Rhodes Scholarship 248–54
Ritchie, John 242, 243, 248
Robinson, George Augustus 246–7
'roots tourism' 26; *see also* ancestral lands
Roxburghshire 23, 44, 45, 55–8
rural population decline 51–4; *see also* migration: to towns and cities; way of life
Rutherford family 28, 30, 38, 45

Sandbrooks' Ironmongery 116–19
Sandel, Michael 236
schools *see* education
Scotland
  'assured Scots' 39–40, 56, 58
  birth, marriage and death records 22–3
  conflicts with England 36–44, 56
  Highlander culture suppressed 67
  Jacobite rebellion 61, 66–7, 73
  lairds' power and wealth 43–5; *see also* Ker family
  names 28–9
  traditions and symbols 26–8
  see also Borders (England/Scotland); reivers
Scott, Walter 26–7, 35, 40, 43, 53
  border ballads 5–6, 23–4, 27, 53
  promotion of Scottish national costume 67
Scout movement 160–5, 166
Scurrah, Rowland 136
secondary education *see* education
Selleck, Richard 239
sexual behaviour 64–5, 230
Shepherd, Mary *see* Davison, Mary (nee Shepherd)
Shurey, Harry 183, 195
Sinclair, John, *Statistical Account of Scotland* 51–2
Smetham, Richard 114

social class 44–5, 164–5, 232–3, 239, 243–4, 249, 257
  meritocracy 236
  respectability 102–7, 164–5
  social mobility 235
social contract between masters and workers 102–4, 105, 107, 122
Spock, Benjamin 198
Statistical Account of Scotland (Sinclair) 51–2
Stead McAlpin 77–80, 81
steam power 81–2, 98
Stevens, Cecil 160–1, 162, 164, 173
Stuart, Charles Edward ('Bonnie Prince Charlie') *see* Jacobite rebellion
Student Christian Movement 241
suffrage 98–101
surnames and kinship 28–31, 55

tailors 63–4
Tait, Archibald 92–4
Tales of the Borders (Wilson) 24, 49
Tasmanian Aboriginal people 245–7
Taverner, John 121–2
Taylor, Charles 3
teaching as a career 234
television 207–8
temperance movement 87–90, 132
Tennant, Gay 240
Teviotdale xii, 20, 29–36
  Covenanters, 47–8
  destruction of communities by English army 40–1
  see also Borders (England/ Scotland)
Teviotia Vulgo Tivedale 20, 29
textiles
  printing 77–9
  production 82–3, 84–5
  see also clothing industry
Tholfsen, Trygve 103
Thompson, Edward 75–6
Thompson, Roger 248
time 2, 18–19
  Borderers' sense of time and space 33–4
  Methodist ideas of 113–14, 177–8
  rhythms of nature 32–4, 246
  standards 91
  time-consciousness 75–6, 82
  timekeeping 14–15, 75, 142, 152, 257
  see also clocks; watches
tinplate and tinplate workers 94–5, 98–100, 102–4, 106–7
Todd, Fred 134–5, 142
towns and cities
  disease and mortality 84
  migration to 51–4, 70–1, 97–8
  urban society, study of 243–4
  see also way of life
trades societies *see* unions
Trompf, Garry 242, 245, 248
typists 181–3

unions 98–100, 102–4, 105, 107, 194
university education 234–6, 239–54
University of Melbourne 239–42
University of Oxford 248–54, 258
urban society, study of 243–4; *see also* towns and cities

Victoria, Australia
  assisted immigration 121–2, 130
  employment conditions 131
  Scout movement 160–5
  see also Melbourne

Walklate, Cyril 175–8, 185
'The Wanderers' quartet 183–4, 195

war
  conscription issue 144, 176
  public commemorations of 141–2
  World War I 136–45, 149, 176
  World War II 186–7, 189, 192, 193–6, 210
  see also conflicts between England and Scotland
Ward, Russel
  The Australian Legend 242–4
Ward, Wilhelmina 143
Warnock, William 185
watches 142, 218, 229
way of life
  Australia, post-World War I 148–9
  Australia, post-World War II 147, 191–3, 199–213, 215, 236–7
  Border region 31–5, 42, 44–5
  living conditions in Carlisle 84, 85–6, 93
  modernisation 71
  prosperity 191–3, 206–8
  traditional rhythms of nature 32–4, 246
weaving *see* textiles
Weber, Max 114, 212–13
Wesley, John 113–14, 115, 120, 134, 179, 213
Wesleyans *see* Methodism
Westmorland 59–63, 65
whistling 162
Whitlam, Gough 241
Whitlam government 235
Wilkinson, John 134, 142, 174
Wilson, John Mackay 49
  Tales of the Borders 24, 25, 49
Wilson government (Britain) 251
women
  education 232, 239
  employment 155–6, 181–3, 229
  equal pay advocacy 178
  in family histories 4
  keepers of memories 4–5
Woodfull, Thomas 136, 138, 144
work
  employment of women 155–6, 178, 181–3, 229
  Methodist ideas of 113–14, 176–8, 212–13
  social contract between masters and workers 102–4, 105, 107, 122
  see also clothing industry; garment-making; industrial relations; industrial revolution; metal trades; plumbing trade; printing trade
Work, Henry Clay
  grandfather clock song xi, 17
World War I 136–45, 149, 176
World War II 186–7, 189, 192, 193–6, 210
Wormald, Jenny 36
Wybalenna, Flinders Island 246–7

Young, GM 98
Young, Michael 236

THE MIEGUNYAH PRESS

This book was designed and
typeset by Cannon Typesetting
The text was set in 11½ pt Adobe Caslon Pro
with 15½ points of leading
The text was printed on 80gsm Woodfree
This book was edited by Paul Smitz

THE
MIEGUNYAH
PRESS

TEVIOTIA
Vulgo
TIVEDAIL
Part of Eusdail
DALIÆ PARS
Part of
Lidisdail
PARS
T V E E D
P A R T
T W E E D
L. of Lowis
Ettrick Riv.
Eltrick R.
Yarrow R.
Tweed Riv.
Castel of Newoork
Blakupphauch
Soundhoope
Newbrugh
Bellendenn
The Boggs
Pott Loch
Elmoore
Dodhead
Whytuphrse
North Sintoun
Sinntoun Mill
South Synntoun
Woodend
Shelfwood
Borthikbrae
Branxholme
Harwood
Crummhauch
Gaudylands
Hatck
Newbrug
Flecks
Kirktoun
Ormestoun
Colleforf hill
Eldenstoun
Newtown
Dodburne
Doddrigg
Langhburn
Robert hill
Marewood B.
Stobbycote
Dockeleuch
Langcleuch
Binks
Bowannhill
Carlanryik
Langhauch
Wyind
Drydenn
Glenkiry
Deepupp
Winterbrug
Woolhoop
Wardlarigg
Caerabanck
N. Dallorean
O. Dallorean
Kraig hill
Buckeleuch
Cleburne L.
Oldworck
Bowhill
Braidwood
Sel
Hartwoodmyirs
Clerkland
Grechlawes
Bewes Mill
Satchells
Horsleyhill
Midsheels
Bririyards
Burnfoot
Denmill
Wiltoun
Hummilknowes
Calmill
Orchart
Cruick
Stennaleuch
Hawa
Roull R.
Wachopp B.